P9-DDZ-825

AUSTRIAN ECONOMICS

CLASSICS
IN
AUSTRIAN ECONOMICS

A Sampling in the History of a Tradition

Edited by
ISRAEL M. KIRZNER

VOLUME III

THE AGE OF
MISES AND HAYEK

LONDON
WILLIAM PICKERING
1994

330.157
C614
vol. 3

Published by Pickering & Chatto (Publishers) Limited
17 Pall Mall, London, SW1Y 5NB

© Pickering & Chatto (Publishers) Limited
Introduction © Israel M. Kirzner

British Library Cataloguing in Publication Data
Classics in Austrian Economics: A Sampling
in the History of a Tradition. – Vol. III: The
Age of Mises and Hayek
I. Kirzner, Israel M.
330.9436
Set ISBN 1 85196 138 0
This volume ISBN 1 85196 157 7

Printed and bound in Great Britain by
Antony Rowe Limited
Chippenham

CONTENTS

University Libraries
Carnegie Mellon University
Pittsburgh, PA 15213-3890

INTRODUCTION

The ten papers collected in this volume are described as representing the 'Age of Mises and Hayek'. We shall indeed argue that the period from 1940 to 1970 does constitute such an 'age', an era in the history of the Austrian tradition with a character and an importance of its own. In this Introduction we will explore and defend this proposition, that this period has a character and an importance of its own for the long-run evolution of Austrian Economics. This discussion will thus set forth the general perspective from which these papers by Mises and by Hayek have been selected, and will place them, in particular, in the context of the 120-year-long history of the Austrian School.

We must, of course, acknowledge that several of the papers in this volume, both by Mises and by Hayek, belong chronologically to the interwar period, and might thus have been expected to have been included in Volume II of the present edition. Such an expectation, it should be added, might have appeared all the more plausible in the light of the circumstance (already pointed out in our Introduction to Volume II) that up until about 1940 the work of both Mises and Hayek hardly expressed with any clarity those important insights which their subsequent work would articulate (and upon which we base our identification of the post-1940 decades as making up the age of Mises and Hayek). Our justification for including these pre-1940 papers by Mises and by Hayek in the present volume is twofold. First, it seems convenient, simply on authorship grounds, to keep all the papers of these authors together. Second, there are grounds for maintaining that (although we have asserted that the age of Mises and Hayek did not properly begin before 1940, since their own work prior to 1940 did not yet articulate the key insights with which we shall identify the post-1940 decades), the post-1940 work of Mises and Hayek did not spring forth from a vacuum. There is in fact much in the formidable pre-1940 corpus of Mises's writings which foreshadowed, at least, the character of his later, more maturely subjectivist contributions.[1] And similarly for Hayek, there is sufficient continuity running through both his earlier work and his post-1940 writings to justify the inclusion of selected pieces of the former work together with those later papers which we see as belonging more unambiguously to the Age of Mises and Hayek.

The Character and Significance of the Age of Mises and Hayek

Briefly stated, our position will be that, in the decades between 1940 and 1970, Mises and Hayek were responsible, separately but in complementary fashion, for important extensions of the limited subjectivism which (as we have seen in the Introduction to Volume II) characterized the economics of interwar Vienna.[2] These extensions set post-1940 Austrian economics decisively apart from mainstream neoclassical micro-economics as it was developing during those same decades. The convergence towards the neoclassical mainstream which we saw as apparently characterizing interwar Austrian Economics (and as crystallized in the impact made, under Austrian influence, by Lionel Robbins's 1932 book) would, after 1940, *not* be a feature of the economics of Mises and of Hayek. Austrian economists, such as Machlup, who continued to maintain that what was important in the Austrian tradition had been successfully absorbed into the neoclassical mainstream, were evidently thinking of that tradition in its interwar manifestation, and were simply overlooking, or misreading, the post-1940 developments.

The post-1940 extension of subjectivism by Mises and by Hayek had a significance which went, we shall argue, beyond the substantive contributions of these two Austrian economists. The more radical subjectivism of their post-1940 work was to inspire the revival of interest in the Austrian tradition which has occurred subsequent to 1970 (the date which closes the period covered by the papers included in the present collection). From the perspective of the 120-year history of Austrian economics, therefore, the 1940–1970 period must appear as the era in which, while Austrian Economics was unquestionably in deep professional eclipse, there yet occurred profoundly important extensions of the subjectivist tradition, setting the stage for the late twentieth-century revival of professional interest in this tradition. In the course of this revival, the discovery of these contributions by Mises and by Hayek would stimulate explorations in the earlier history of the Austrian tradition which would lead back beyond the limited subjectivism of the interwar period, back beyond the foundational contributions of Böhm-Bawerk and Wieser (upon which so much of the interwar understanding was based), back to the original pioneering subjectivist insights of Carl Menger. The more radical subjectivism of Mises and of Hayek thus paved the way for a deepened appreciation, within the Austrian tradition, of what we have identified, in the Introduction to Volume I, as Menger's original vision. In this he saw how all economic phenomena and all human history are to be understood as the outcomes of human action, driven by the dreams and expectations, the desires and hopes, of human beings living in an open-ended world of radical uncertainty. We must now provide further details concerning the thesis which we have here outlined.

Mises, Hayek and the Extension of Austrian Subjectivism

In the Introduction to Volume II we have drawn attention to the limited character of interwar Austrian subjectivism. During that period the subjectivism of Austrian Economics consisted in its refusal to see economic phenomena as inexorably determined by physical constraints: it was subjective utility, tastes and preferences which must be invoked in order to account for the arrays of goods produced, methods of production employed, prices of consumer goods and of productive resources arrived at in markets. However, given the tastes and preferences of economizing agents, given the physical circumstances surrounding a known society, these arrays of economic outcomes are seen as emerging as if by themselves 'from the data'. Although, as we have seen, Hans Mayer expressed his discomfort at Pareto's assertion that economics has no need for individual decision-makers (only for the photographs of their indifference maps), the truth is that for interwar Austrians (as for most twentieth-century mainstream microeconomists) that assertion rather accurately captures their picture of the world.

What is often not noticed, however, is that, for this Paretian picture of the world to hold, it is necessary to confine analytical attention to states of affairs in which individual anticipations concerning the decisions being made by other market participants are in fact correct and mutually sustaining. (In other words, an analytical picture of the world in which the Paretian assertion holds true can never be more than the picture of a world *already* in equilibrium.) For if the prices or availabilities of goods expected by a market participant turn out not to occur, then his decision plan will have been frustrated and the actual outcome can no longer be held to have been implicit in the data (which were believed to define the framework for his decision-making). A more complete subjectivism will have to refer to a disequilibrium world, and will have to recognize that in such a world, in which mutual awareness among market participants must be seriously flawed and incomplete, actual outcomes must depend, not merely on the relevant physical constraints and on tastes and preferences (being expressed at the moment of choice), but, most decisively, also upon the beliefs and expectations of market participants, and upon the way in which these beliefs and expectations change as a result of disappointments suffered and surprises experienced.

A more radical subjectivism must, in this way, if it is to sustain the economists' appreciation for the systematic character of market processes, encompass far more than an understanding of the subjectivity of tastes. It must, in particular, also encompass two distinct further elements. First, it must embrace an understanding of the role of mutual *knowledge* and of the possible ways in which improved mutual knowledge may be *learned*. Second, it must, for its analytical building block, move beyond the notion of pure economizing, towards a more open-ended concept of decision-making (that is, it must focus on the individual decision-maker, not as confronted by correctly and certainly *known* sets of options, among which he simply selects that which ranks highest on his *given* scale of preferences, but rather as somehow encompassing within his decision the determination of which courses of action he may consider as available options, and also determination of the relative preferability to himself of the available alternatives). Our thesis here is that Mises supplied the second of these two elements necessary for a radical extension of Austrian subjectivism, while Hayek supplied the first. The new subjectivism achieved by focusing on open-ended decision-making (going beyond Robbins's *given ends* and *given* means); and on possible processes of systematically improving mutual awareness (going beyond a bland assumption of complete relevant mutual knowledge), offered for the first time the possibility of a meaningful theory of market equilibration. We see in these radical extensions of subjectivism by Mises and by Hayek two complementary advances in Austrian thought which together justify our identifying the 1940–1970 period as the Age of Mises and Hayek.

It was Mises, in his radical conception of the role of *human action*, with its inescapable element (in the world of uncertainty) of entrepreneurial discovery, who refused to confine economic analysis to equilibrium states of perfect mutual information. In so doing he explicitly and decisively rejected the idea that choices are made as if dictated by preference rankings somehow established prior to (or, at any rate, apart from) the acts of choice themselves.[3] In other words Misesian subjectivism, in understanding economic decisions, requires that we focus not on the 'state of affairs' (including given preferences) surrounding an act of choice (as if that state of affairs, in and of itself, determines choices made), but, most importantly, on the subjective *perception* by the agent of what the relevant state of affairs actually is. What drives market processes, Mises insisted, is the entrepreneurial function,[4] the drive for pure entrepreneurial profit; what makes the entrepreneurial function possible is the ability of some decision-makers more correctly than others *to anticipate* the course of events (and thus correctly to judge the relevant 'state of affairs').[5] It is the entrepreneurial process which enables the market, in an ever-changing world, continually to nudge production decisions towards the equilibrium pattern (that would be consistent with relevant consumer preferences).[6] Mises's view of the dynamic market process is represented in this volume by paper 26.

It was Hayek, in a series of papers beginning in 1937 (most of which are collected in his 1949 book, *Individualism and Economic Order*) who focused on the importance of individual knowledge of market conditions, of the learning process of which the market process consists, and on the market and economic consequences of dispersed information. (Much of this work is to be found in the present volume, particularly in papers 29, 30 and 31). By drawing attention, in this way, to the crucial role of mutual information, Hayek was able to see the competitive, equilibrating market process discussed by economic theorists as a process of systematic learning by market participants of their mutual attitudes. In so doing he was opening up a fresh dimension for subjectivism, viz. the manner in which individuals, through their interpretation of their experiences, arrive at what they believe about the world in which they must make their decisions.

What it is important to notice, in this extension by Mises and by Hayek of Austrian subjectivism, is that the new, more radical, subjectivism did not at all require the abandonment of the notion of systematic, equilibrating market processes (as did the radical subjectivism, for example, of Shackle or Lachmann). The notion of equilibration does not depend, for Mises or for Hayek, upon our freezing the subjective elements in the human agent into sets of given preferences and given perceived physical possibilities and constraints. On the contrary, it is precisely the extended scope for subjectivism (permitting our analytical recognition for the entrepreneurial element, and for learning processes inspired by disequilibrium market experiences) which makes possible, for the Mises-Hayek understanding of markets, those systematic processes of equilibration so central to economic theory. It is all this which supports our reading of the state of Austrian Economics from 1940 to 1970 (by which date virtually all the important contributions to economics by these two writers had been completed) as making up a distinctive and important new era in the history of the Austrian tradition.

Mises and Hayek Homogenized? A Digression

Our thesis, that the 1940–1970 period in the history of Austrian economics constitutes 'the age of Mises and Hayek' (and our identification of the unifying thread which joins together the work of these two Austrians, as consisting in their extensions of Austrian subjectivism) may not command the assent of all historians of economic thought, or even of all contemporary Austrian economists. In particular we wish to take note here of a recent paper by J. T. Salerno, in which he was explicitly concerned to deplore the tendency to 'homogenize' Mises and Hayek, and to argue, on the contrary, that Mises and Hayek were responsible for 'two very different paradigms,' a Hayekian paradigm deriving from Wieser, and a Misesian paradigm representing 'a development of Böhm-Bawerk's thought'.[7] In Salerno's view, present-day Austrians are, *whether they recognize it or not*, divided into two camps, a 'Misesian' camp and a 'Hayekian' camp, with each pursuing a wholly distinct path in the understanding of the nature and significance of market processes. Although Salerno does recognize a measure of what he terms 'the "Mengerian overlap" between the Misesian and Hayekian paradigms', he nonetheless insists on the need to rebut a common tendency among present-day Austrian economists 'to conflate the views of Mises and Hayek'.[9]

This is not the place to dissect Salerno's attempt at establishing the existence of two separate and conflicting 'paradigms' in present-day Austrian thought. Despite Salerno's careful scholarship and subtle textual analysis of both Mises's and Hayek's writings, he is by no means convincing in his assertion of a gulf separating their understandings of how the market works (nor, indeed, can this writer claim even to have grasped with clarity the precise basis upon which Salerno makes his assertion). After all, historians of ideas may legitimately differ on whether to regard the differences between figures in intellectual history, as grounds for treating them as contending figures, or whether to see them as offering jointly a single general position, based on the elements which these figures share. However we do feel compelled to insist here, at any rate, that our identification of the 1940–1970 period as constituting a joint 'age of Mises and Hayek,' based on their complementary extensions of Austrian subjectivism does *not* depend on any 'homogenization' of the ideas of Mises and Hayek.

We certainly do not need or wish to deny the existence of significant differences between Mises and Hayek in regard to fundamental methodological issues.[10] Although the economics profession has correctly viewed Hayek as supporting or extending the views of Mises on a number of key substantive issues (e.g. in the 'Austrian' malinvestment theory of the business cycle, and in the socialist economic calculation debate), it is certainly true that Hayek's understanding of economics is not based on Misesian epistemological foundations. For Mises economic understanding is grounded in a priori reasoning (on this see in this volume, papers 24, and 25); for Hayek this is, explicitly, not the case.[11] Nor is it our position that, throughout their respective careers (or in fact at any time or times during those careers) Mises and Hayek would each have been willing to accept the other's formulation of the manner in which markets work, without modification. What we do maintain, however, is that during the 1940s insights were (separately) articulated by Mises and by Hayek which, *taken together* must, from the long-run *dogmengeschichtliche* perspective, be seen as *mutually reinforcing* and as most significantly advancing Austrian understanding. To insist on the existence of conflicting Misesian and Hayekian 'paradigms' is – quite apart from its being unfortunate and confusing for Austrian research programmes of the 1990s – to divert attention from a highly significant episode in the history of the Austrian tradition. It is to this episode of subjectivist complementarity in the work of Mises and Hayek that we are here drawing attention.

The End of Convergence

We have cited, in the Introduction to Volume I, a statement by Mises from the early 1930s, to the effect that the various schools of economic theory active at that time were not substantially at odds with each other on the core propositions of the science. In the Introduction to Volume II we have further explored the convergence towards the British neoclassical mainstream which was indeed unmistakeably occurring in interwar Austrian Economics. The papers in the present Volume represent the age in which this convergent trend came to a somewhat abrupt halt.

By the end of World War II historians of economic thought were treating Austrian Economics as if it was no longer a live tradition. The eclipse of Austrian Economics which occurred during the late 1930s (and to which we devoted the final section of the Introduction to Volume II) seemed, from that post-war perspective, to be a permanent one. The histories of economic doctrines being written from that perspective tended to make references to Mises and to Hayek as surviving figures, relics of an earlier, but no longer vital, school of thought. What is of interest for our purposes is that such references tended (as we noted in the Introduction to Volume I) to emphasize the unfashionability, during this post-war period, of both the substance and the style of their work. To the extent that their work was identified as 'Austrian' (and it was so identified), the age of Austrian convergence towards the mainstream was over.

From the perspective we have set forth in this Introduction, this treatment of Mises and Hayek was (if not for the right reasons, then at least in substance) largely correct. Contemporary historians of economic thought seemed to have placed Mises and Hayek together as being unfashionable largely on such grounds as their shared critical position on the possibility of socialist economic calculation, or their common refusal to accept the validity of Keynesian doctrines. We would prefer to emphasize their distinctiveness from the contemporary Anglo-American mainstream by reference to the radical advances they were making, or enunciating, during the 1940s, in our understanding of the most basic propositions of economic science. What is beyond contention is the recognition that Mises and Hayek could not, by any stretch of imagination, be considered as part of the dominant mainstream of early post-war economics.

There is a certain drama, it seems to us, in the circumstance that the radical advances to which we have drawn attention were being (separately) made by these two Austrian economists, not on Austrian soil, at a time when it was the conventional wisdom in the economics profession that Austrian Economics was no longer alive. These advances were being made after most of the important figures in the 'interlocking circles' led in interwar Vienna by Mayer and by Mises had dispersed (for political or other reasons) and were to be found either in England or the United States. Precisely during the years when both the physical presence of an Austrian school and the doctrinal vitality of that school were seen as matters strictly for the history of economics, Mises and Hayek were developing and/or articulating insights which (*dogmengeschichtliche* hindsight now permits us to assert) were not only radically deepening Austrian economic understanding in a way which would stamp it as unmistakeably distinct from mainstream microeconomics, but which, decades later, would inspire a renaissance of interest in the Austrian tradition that would breathe new life into the Mengerian legacy. We can now see that the ideas which Mises and Hayek kept alive during the decades of Austrian eclipse were in fact ideas, adumbrated three-quarters of a century earlier by Carl Menger, which never were 'absorbed into the neoclassical mainstream'.[12]

The Socialist Calculation Debate: Its Relevance for the Age of Mises and Hayek

This volume contains two important papers published in the course of the celebrated interwar debate on the possibility of socialist economic calculation. The first of these papers is the original 1920 paper by Mises (here published as paper 22) in which he challenged the very possibility of central planning. The second of these papers (here paper 29) is Hayek's final (1940) critical assessment of the various attempts by socialist writers during the 1930s, to meet Mises's challenge. Following up on the ideas suggested in a section of the Introduction to Volume I, we wish to draw especial attention to these papers, and to the socialist calculation debate in general, in regard to what we have called the Age of Mises and Hayek.

The socialist calculation debate occurred during the interwar years. It would be possible for a historian of economic thought to treat the Austrian side of the debate (i.e. the side represented most prominently in the contributions of Mises and Hayek) as merely expressing the contemporary economics of interwar Vienna. While not categorically incorrect, such a judgment would, in our view, be misleading and overly narrow. The truth is that it was *in the course of* the socialist calculation debate that Mises and Hayek seem to have become alive to those fresh insights which they articulated only during the 1940s (after the debate had died down, and at a time when, in the contemporary mainstream view, the Austrian position in the debate had been definitively refuted in the work of Lange and of Lerner).[13] During this debate it appears that Mises and Hayek came to appreciate more deeply than before the extent to which their own position depended on understanding the market as an entrepreneurial process of mutual discovery. Our inclusion of these two papers in the present volume illustrates the point made early in this Introduction: with the benefit of hindsight, we can see how the pre-1940 work of these two writers anticipated, at least to some extent, their important post-1940 explicit advances in Austrian understanding. It is no accident that some of the most stimulating work in the late-twentieth-century renaissance of Austrian Economics has been in the revisionist history-of-ideas examination of the interwar debate on socialist economic calculation.[14]

An example of the manner in which the Austrians, in the calculation debate, were being impelled ahead of their fellow interwar Austrians (and without, it should be observed, themselves quite noticing that this was in fact occurring) is the clash between Schumpeter and Hayek (noticed briefly at the end of the Introduction to Volume II) on an aspect of this debate. Schumpeter (in his 1942 *Capitalism, Socialism and Democracy*, see p. 175 in the 3rd (1950) edition) had declared that there was in fact *no* problem for socialist economic calculation, because 'consumers in evaluating ("demanding") consumers' goods *ipso facto* also evaluate the means of production which enter into the production of these goods'. Hayek expressed his surprise that 'an economist of Professor Schumpeter's standing should thus have fallen into a trap which the ambiguity of the term "datum" sets to the unwary'.[15] The sense in which valuation of factors of production is implied in the valuation of consumers' goods is a *logical* one, Hayek pointed out; and such an implication can be asserted only with respect to a mind which knows simultaneously not only all valuations of consumers' goods but also all the conditions of the supply of the various factors of production. While valuations of consumers' goods and the conditions of factor supply may be the 'data', without a process through which knowledge of the data is arrived at, such data cannot be presumed immediately and automatically to generate values for the productive factors.

What is noteworthy here is: (a) that Hayek was articulating an insight concerning the role of knowledge and its discovery (in the market process through which factor prices are generated) that was, as far as mainstream microeconomics is concerned, ahead of its time; (b) that he was expressing surprise that an economist of Schumpeter's standing had overlooked this insight. It seems clear that, in enunciating this insight, Hayek did not believe himself to be making an analytical innovation (since, if that were the case, he could hardly have been surprised at Schumpeter's error). Yet, on the other hand, it seems clear that Hayek *had*, in this confrontation with Schumpeter, been impelled to articulate something new, since this insight had *not* been so stated (or at any rate, so clearly stated) before – and since in fact it *had* escaped Schumpeter (as well-trained as any interwar Austrian could have been!).

As Hayek pointed out in his criticism of Schumpeter, the error must be attributed to preoccupation with equilibrium theorizing (in which it is taken for granted that the objective facts embodied in relevant simultaneous equations are, in effect, fully known to market participants). Although the Austrian tradition had, of course, not employed Walrasian simultaneous equation analysis for the understanding of markets, there was little in interwar Austrian Economics apart from the Hans Mayer paper discussed in the Introduction to Volume II (where the paper is included as paper 16), that rendered interwar Austrian Economics inconsistent with equilibrium theory. (In his 1937 paper on 'Economics and Knowledge', in which Hayek had begun to develop his critique of equilibrium theory, he had cited Mayer's 1932 paper.)[16] It was the debate concerning socialist economic calculation which appears to have been the catalyst that influenced the Austrians in articulating their non-equilibrium understanding of the systematic character of market processes. And it was certainly blindness to this aspect of the Austrian side of that debate which for so many decades permitted the belief in mainstream economics that Mises's challenge to the possibility of socialist calculation had been successfully met by the work of Lange and Lerner.

Concluding Observations

Not all the papers in this volume can be linked directly to the fresh insights introduced by Mises and by Hayek during the 1940–1970 period, which as we have argued, justify our view of this period as a distinct era in the history of the Austrian tradition. We have also included several other classic papers by these writers, both for their intrinsic importance in the work of these economists, and for their general importance in any survey of Austrian work. Paper 23 provides a statement by Mises of what has come to be known as the Austrian (monetary, or malinvestment) theory of the business cycle. Paper 27 offers a classic work by Hayek concerning the intertemporal economy, which is often cited in advanced work on general equilibrium theory for its pioneering role in the development of that theory in its modern form. Finally, Paper 28 (1935) provides a well-known and important work by Hayek in which he explored some of the subtle problems in capital theory with which he would deal more extensively in his *Pure Theory of Capital* (1941).

Together with the remaining papers in this volume, these contributions offer, it is hoped, a useful introduction to the work of two major figures in the history of Austrian Economics. Taken altogether, the classic papers included in the entire three volumes of the present collection provide a sampling of the major economic contributions of the leading figures during the first century of an important school of modern economic thought. The importance of this school is certainly enhanced by the circumstance that it has, in the final decades of this century (i.e. in the decades immediately following the closing date for the present collection), enjoyed a significant revival within the profession. This development, which contemporary historians of economic thought have treated as rather remarkable, is both a tribute to and evidence of the continued vitality and fascinating quality of the ideas assembled in these volumes. This collection will therefore, it is hoped, contribute not only to a deeper understanding of a historic century in modern economic thought, but also to its continued refinement and progress during the century ahead.

NOTES

1. Besides a number of important passages in *The Theory of Money and Credit* [original German edition, 1912], (New Haven: Yale University Press, 1953), other relevant passages in this regard are to be found in the various papers collected in Mises's *Epistemological Problems of Economics* [original German edition, 1933], (New York: New York University Press, 1981).
2. We have argued this thesis in 'Ludwig von Mises and Friedrich von Hayek: The Modern Extension of Austrian Subjectivism', N. Leser,

ed., *Die Wiener Schule der Nationalökonomie* (Vienna: Böhlau, 1986), reprinted in Israel M. Kirzner, *The Meaning of Market Process: Essays in the Development of Modern Austrian Economics* (London: Routledge, 1992).

3. L. Mises, *Human Action* (New Haven: Yale University Press, 1949), pp. 102ff.
4. Mises, *Human Action*, op. cit. pp. 249, 297.
5. Mises, *Human Action*, op. cit. p. 288.
6. Mises, *Human Action*, op. cit., p. 335.
7. Joseph T. Salerno, 'Mises and Hayek Dehomogenized', *Review of Austrian Economics*, vol. 6, no. 2, pp. 114ff.
8. Salerno, op. cit. p. 145.
9. Salerno, op. cit. ibid.
10. For discussion of some of these differences see Kirzner, *The Meaning of Market Process*, op. cit., pp. 119ff.
11. See F. A. Hayek, 'Economics and Knowledge', originally published in *Economica*, February, 1937, reprinted in *Individualism and Economic Order* (London: Routledge and Kegan Paul, 1949); see also *Law, Legislation and Liberty*, vol. 3, *The Political Order of a Free People*, (Chicago: University of Chicago Press, 1979), p. 205, n. 51 for Hayek's observation on a basic philosophical disagreement which he has with Mises.
12. On this see further, E. Streissler, 'Menger, Böhm-Bawerk, and Wieser: The Origins of the Austrian School', K. Hennings and Warren J. Samuels, eds, *Neoclassical Economic Theory, 1870 to 1930*, pp. 178–81. On the part played by Schumpeter in keeping Mengerian ideas alive during this period, see Stephan Boehm, 'The Austrian Tradition: Schumpeter and Mises's, Hennings and Samuels, eds, op. cit., and I. M. Kirzner, 'Commentary' (to this paper by Boehm), especially p. 244.
13. The writer has elaborated this thesis in *The Meaning of Market Process*, op. cit., ch. 6.
14. See especially Don Lavoie, *Rivalry and Central Planning: Socialist Calculation Debate Reconsidered* (Cambridge: Cambridge University Press, 1985).
15. F. A Hayek, *Individualism and Economic Order*, op. cit., p. 91.
16. F. A. Hayek, 'Economics and Knowledge', *Economica* iv (new series, Feb. 1937), p. 34 fn. I am indebted to M. Rizzo for pointing out this footnote to me (and for noting the absence of this footnote from the version of the paper reprinted in *Individualism and Economic Order*, op. cit).

The Age of
Mises and Hayek

Ludwig von Mises, 'Economic Calculation in the Socialist Common-wealth' (1920), trans. Hayek (ed.), *Collectivist Economic Planning* (London, 1935), pp. 87–130.

Ludwig von Mises (1881–1973) wrote this famous paper under the title 'Die Wirtschaftsrechnung im sozialistischen Gemeinwesen' *Archiv für Sozial wissenschaften*, vol. 47 (1920). It ushered in the celebrated interwar debate on the possibility of rational economic calculation under a system of central planning. The present translation was made by S. Adler, and was included by Hayek in his edited collection of papers on this debate.

22

Economic Calculation in the Socialist Commonwealth[1]

LUDWIG von MISES

Introduction

There are many socialists who have never come to grips in any way with the problems of economics, and who have made no attempt at all to form for themselves any clear conception of the conditions which determine the character of human society. There are others, who have, probed deeply into the economic history of the past and present, and striven, on this basis, to construct a theory of economics of the 'bourgeois' society. They have criticized freely enough the economic structure of 'free' society, but have consistently neglected to apply to the economics of the disputed socialist state the same caustic acumen, which they have revealed elsewhere, not always with success. Economics, as such, figures all too sparsely in the glamorous pictures painted by the Utopians. They invariably explain how, in the cloud-cuckoo lands of their fancy, roast pigeons will in some way fly into the mouths of the comrades, but they omit to show how this miracle is to take place. Wherever they do in fact commence to be more explicit in the domain of economics, they soon find themselves at a loss – one remembers, for instance, Proudhon's fantastic dreams of an 'exchange-bank' – so that it is not difficult to point out their logical fallacies. When Marxism solemnly forbids its adherents to concern themselves with economic problems beyond the expropriation of the expropriators, it adopts no new principle, since the Utopians throughout their descriptions have also neglected all economic considerations, and concentrated attention solely upon painting lurid pictures of existing conditions and glowing pictures of that golden age which is the natural consequence of the New Dispensation.

Whether one regards the coming of socialism as an unavoidable result of human evolution, or considers the socialization of the means of production as the greatest blessing or the worst disaster that can befall mankind, one must at least concede, that investigation into the conditions of society organized upon a socialist basis is of value as something more than 'a good mental exercise, and a means of promoting political clearness and consistency of thought'.[2] In an age in which we are approaching nearer and nearer to socialism, and even, in a certain sense, are dominated by it, research into the problems of the socialist state acquires added significance for the explanation of what is going on around us. Previous analyses of the exchange economy no longer suffice for a proper understanding of social phenomena in Germany and its eastern neighbours to-day. Our task in this connection is to embrace within a fairly wide range the elements of socialistic society. Attempts to achieve clarity on this subject need no further justification.

1. *The Distribution of Consumption-goods in the Socialist Commonwealth*

Under socialism all the means of production are the property of the community. It is the community alone which can dispose of them and which determines their use in production. It goes without saying that the community will only be in a position to employ its powers of disposal through the setting up of a special body for the purpose. The structure of this body and the question of how it will articulate and represent the communal will is for us of subsidiary importance. One may assume that this last will depend upon the choice of personnel, and in cases where the power is not vested in a dictatorship, upon the majority vote of the members of the corporation.

The owner of production-goods, who has manufactured consumption-goods and thus becomes their owner, now has the choice of either consuming them himself or of having them consumed by others. But where the

4

community becomes the owner of consumption-goods, which it has acquired in production, such a choice will no longer obtain. It cannot itself consume; it has perforce to allow others to do so. Who is to do the consuming and what is to be consumed by each is the crux of the problem of socialist distribution.

It is characteristic of socialism that the distribution of consumption-goods must be independent of the question of production and of its economic conditions. It is irreconcilable with the nature of the communal ownership of production-goods that it should rely even for a part of its distribution upon the economic imputation of the yield to the particular factors of production. It is logically absurd to speak of the worker's enjoying the 'full yield' of his work, and then to subject to a separate distribution the shares of the material factors of production. For, as we shall show, it lies in the very nature of socialist production that the shares of the particular factors of production in the national dividend cannot be ascertained, and that it is impossible in fact to gauge the relationship between expenditure and income.

What basis will be chosen for the distribution of consumption-goods among the individual comrades is for us a consideration of more or less secondary importance. Whether they will be apportioned according to individual needs, so that he gets most who needs most, or whether the superior man is to receive more than the inferior, or whether a strictly equal distribution is envisaged as the ideal, or whether service to the State is to be the criterion, is immaterial to the fact that, in any event, the portions will be meted out by the State.

Let us assume the simple proposition that distribution will be determined upon the principle that the State treats all its members alike; It is not difficult to conceive of a number of peculiarities such as age, sex, health, occupation, etc., according to which what each receives will be graded. Each comrade receives a bundle of coupons, redeemable within a certain period against a definite quantity of certain specified goods. And so he can eat several times a day, find permanent lodgings, occasional amusements and a new suit every now and again. Whether such provision for these needs is ample or not, will depend on the productivity of social labour.

Moreover, it is not necessary that every man should consume the whole of his portion. He may let some of it perish without consuming it; he may give it away in presents; he may even in so far as the nature of the goods permit, hoard it for future use. He can, however, also exchange some of them. The beer-tippler will gladly dispose of non-alcoholic drinks allotted to him, if he can get more beer in exchange, whilst the teetotaller will be ready to give up his portion of drink if he can get other goods for it. The art-lover will be willing to dispose of his cinema tickets in order the more

5

often to hear good music; the Philistine will be quite prepared to give up the tickets which admit him to art exhibitions in return for opportunities for pleasure he more readily understands. They will all welcome exchanges. But the material of these exchanges will always be consumption-goods. Production-goods in a socialist commonwealth are exclusively communal; they are an inalienable property of the community, and thus *res extra commercium*.

The principle of exchange can thus operate freely in a socialist state within the narrow limits permitted. It need not always develop in the form of direct exchanges. The same grounds which have always existed for the building-up of indirect exchange will continue in a socialist state, to place advantages in the way of those who indulge in it. It follows that the socialist state will thus also afford room for the use of a universal medium of exchange – that is, of Money. Its rôle will be fundamentally the same in a socialist as in a competitive society; in both it serves as the universal medium of exchange. Yet the significance of Money in a society where the means of production are State-controlled will be different from that which attaches to it one where they are privately owned. It will be, in fact, incomparably narrower, since the material available for exchange will be narrower, inasmuch as it will be confined to consumption-goods. Moreover, just because no production-good will ever become the object of exchange, it will be impossible to determine its monetary value. Money could never fill in a socialist state the rôle it fills in a competitive society in determining the value of production-goods. Calculation in terms of money will here be impossible.

The relationships which result from this system of exchange between comrades cannot be disregarded by those responsible for the administration and distribution of products. They must take these relationships as their basis, when they seek to distribute goods per head in accordance with their exchange value. If, for instance 1 cigar becomes equal to 5 cigarettes, it will be impossible for the administration to fix the arbitrary value of 1 cigar = 3 cigarettes as a basis for the equal distribution of cigars and cigarettes respectively. If the tobacco coupons are not to be redeemed uniformly for each individual, partly against cigars, partly against cigarettes, and if some receive only cigars and others only cigarettes, either because that is their wish or because the coupon office cannot do anything else at the moment, the market conditions of exchange would then have to be observed. Otherwise everybody getting cigarettes would suffer as against those getting cigars. For the man who gets one cigar can exchange it for five cigarettes, and he is only marked down with three cigarettes.

Variations in exchange relations in the dealings between comrades will therefore entail corresponding variations in the administrations' estimates of the representative character of the different consumption-goods. Every such variation shows that a gap has appeared between the particular needs of comrades and their satisfactions because in fact, some one commodity is more strongly desired than another.

The administration will indeed take pains to bear this point in mind also as regards production. Articles in greater demand will have to be produced in greater quantities while production of those which are less demanded will have to suffer a curtailment. Such control may be possible, but one thing it will not be free to do; it must not leave it to the individual comrade to ask the value of his tobacco ticket either in cigars or cigarettes at will. If the comrade were to have the right of choice, then it might well be that the demand for cigars and cigarettes would exceed the supply, or vice versa, that cigars or cigarettes pile up in the distributing offices because no one will take them.

If one adopts the standpoint of the labour theory of value, the problem freely admits of a simple solution. The comrade is then marked up for every hour's work put in, and this entitles him to receive the product of one hour's labour, less the amount deducted for meeting such obligations of the community as a whole as maintenance of the unfit, education etc.

Taking the amount deducted for covering communal expenses as one half of the labour product, each worker who had a full hour would be entitled only to obtain such amount of the product as really answered to half an hour's work. Accordingly, anybody who is in a position to offer twice the labour-time taken in manufacturing an article, could take it from the market and transfer to his own use or consumption. For the clarification of our problem it will be better to assume that the State does not in fact deduct anything from the workers towards meeting its obligations, but instead imposes an income tax upon its working members. In that way every hour of work put in would carry with it the right of taking for oneself such amount of goods as entailed an hour's work.

Yet such a manner of regulating distribution would be unworkable, since labour is not a uniform and homogeneous quantity. Between various types of labour there is necessarily a qualitative difference, which leads to a different valuation according to the difference in the conditions of demand for and supply of their products. For instance, the supply of pictures cannot be increased, *ceteris paribus*, without damage to the quality of the product. Yet one cannot allow the labourer who had put in an hour of the most simple type of labour to be entitled to the product of an hour's higher type of labour. Hence, it becomes utterly impossible in any socialist community to posit a connection between the significance to the community of any type of labour and the apportionment of the yield of the communal process of production. The remuneration of labour cannot

7

but proceed upon an arbitrary basis; it cannot be based upon the economic valuation of the yield as in a competitive state of society, where the means of production are in private hands, since – as we have seen – any such valuation is impossible in a socialist community. Economic realities impose clear limits to the community's power of fixing the remuneration of labour on an arbitrary basis: in no circumstances can the sum expended on wages exceed the income for any length of time.

Within these limits it can do as it will. It can rule forthwith that all labour is to be reckoned of equal worth, so that every hour of work, whatever its quality, entails the same reward; it can equally well make a distinction in regard to the quality of work done. Yet in both cases it must reserve the power to control the particular distribution of the labour product. It will never be able to arrange that he who has put in an hour's labour shall also have the right to consume the product of an hour's labour, even leaving aside the question of differences in the quality of the labour and the products, and assuming moreover that it would be possible to gauge the amount of labour represented by any given article. For, over and above the actual labour, the production of all economic goods entails also the cost of materials. An article in which more raw material is used can never be reckoned of equal value with one in which less is used.

2. The Nature of Economic Calculation

Every man who, in the course of economic life, takes a choice between the satisfaction of one need as against another, *eo ipso* makes a judgment of value. Such judgments of value at once include only the very satisfaction of the need itself; and from this they reflect back upon the goods of a lower, and then further upon goods of a higher order. As a rule, the man who knows his own mind is in a position to value goods of a lower order. Under simple conditions it is also possible for him without much ado to form some judgment of the significance to him of goods of a higher order. But where the state of affairs is more involved and their interconnections not so easily discernible, subtler means must be employed to accomplish a correct[3] valuation of the means of production. It would not be difficult for a farmer in economic isolation to come by a distinction between the expansion of pasture-farming and the development of activity in the hunting field. In such a case the processes of production involved are relatively short and the expense and income entailed can be easily gauged. But it is quite a different matter when the choice lies between the utilization of a water-course for the manufacture of electricity or the extension of a coal-mine or the drawing up of plans for the better employment of the energies latent in raw coal. Here the roundabout processes of production are many and each is very lengthy; here the conditions necessary for the success of the enterprises which are to be initiated are diverse, so that one cannot apply merely vague valuations, but requires rather more exact estimates and some judgment of the economic issues actually involved.

Valuation can only take place in terms of units, yet it is impossible that there should ever be a unit of subjective use-value for goods. Marginal utility does not posit any unit of value, since it is obvious that the value of two units of a given stock is necessarily greater than, but less than double, the value of a single unit. Judgments of value do not measure; they merely establish grades and scales.[4] Even Robinson Crusoe, when he has to make a decision where no ready judgment of value appears and where he has to construct one upon the basis of a more or less exact estimate, cannot operate solely with subjective use-value, but must take into consideration the intersubstitutability of goods on the basis of which he can then form his estimates. In such circumstances it will be impossible for him to refer all things back to one unit. Rather will he, so far as he can, refer all the elements which have to be taken into account in forming his estimate to those economic goods which can be apprehended by an obvious judgment of value – that is to say, to goods of a lower order and to pain-cost. That this is only possible in very simple conditions is obvious. In the case of more complicated and more lengthy processes of production it will, plainly, not answer.

In an exchange economy the objective exchange-value of commodities enters as the unit of economic calculation. This entails a threefold advantage. In the first place, it renders it possible to base the calculation upon the valuations of all participants in trade. The subjective use-value of each is not immediately comparable as a purely individual phenomenon with the subjective use-value of other men. It only becomes so in exchange-value, which arises out of the interplay of the subjective valuations of all who take part in exchange. But in that case calculation by exchange-value furnishes a control over the appropriate employment of goods. Anyone who wishes to make calculations in regard to a complicated process of production will immediately notice whether he has worked more economically than others or not; if he finds, from reference to the exchange relations obtaining in the market, that he will not be able to produce profitably, this shows that others understand how to make a better use of the goods of a higher order in question. Lastly, calculation by exchange-value makes it possible to refer values back to a unit. For this purpose, since goods are mutually substitutable in accordance with the exchange-relations obtaining in the market, any possible good can be chosen. In a monetary economy it is money that is so chosen.

Monetary calculation has its limits. Money is no yardstick of value, nor yet of price. Value is not indeed *measured* in money, nor is price. They merely consist in money. Money as an economic good is not of stable value as has been naïvely, but wrongly, assumed in using it as a 'standard of deferred payments'. The exchange-relationship which obtains between money and goods is subjected to constant, if (as a rule) not too violent, fluctuations originating not only from the side of other economic goods, but also from the side of money. However, these fluctuations disturb value calculations only in the slightest degree, since usually, in view of the ceaseless alternations in other economic data – these calculations will refer only to comparatively short periods of time – periods in which 'good' money, at least normally, undergoes comparatively trivial fluctuations in regard to its exchange-relations. The inadequacy of the monetary calculation of value does not have its mainspring in the fact that value is then calculated in terms of a universal medium of exchange, namely money, but rather in the fact that in this system it is exchange-value and not subjective use-value on which the calculation is based. It can never obtain as a measure for the calculation of those value-determining elements which stand outside the domain of exchange transactions. If, for example, a man were to calculate the profitability of erecting a waterworks, he would not be able to include in his calculation the beauty of the waterfall which the scheme might impair, except that he may pay attention to the diminution of tourist traffic or similar changes, which may be valued in terms of money. Yet these considerations might well prove one of the factors in deciding whether or no the building is to go up at all.

It is customary to term such elements 'extra-economic'. This perhaps is appropriate; we are not concerned with disputes over terminology; yet the considerations themselves can scarcely be termed irrational. In any place where men regard as significant the beauty of a neighbourhood or of a building, the health, happiness and contentment of mankind, the honour of individuals or nations, they are just as much motive-forces of rational conduct as are economic factors in the proper sense of the word, even where they are not substitutable against each other on the market and therefore do not enter into exchange-relationships.

That monetary calculation cannot embrace these factors lies in its very nature; but for the purposes of our everyday economic life this does not detract from the significance of monetary calculation. For all those ideal goods are goods of a lower order, and can hence be embraced straightway within the ambit of our judgment of values. There is therefore no difficulty in taking them into account, even though they must remain outside the sphere of monetary value. That they do not admit of such computation renders their consideration in the affairs of life easier and not harder. Once we see clearly how highly we value, beauty, health, honour and pride, surely nothing can prevent us from paying a corresponding regard to them. It may seem painful to any sensitive spirit to have to balance spiritual goods against material. But that is not the fault of monetary calculation; it lies in the very nature of things themselves. Even where judgments of value can be established directly without computation in value or in money, the necessity of choosing between material and spiritual satisfaction cannot be evaded. Robinson Crusoe and the socialist state have an equal obligation to make the choice.

Anyone with a genuine sense of moral values experiences no hardship in deciding between honour and livelihood. He knows his plain duty. If a man cannot make honour his bread, yet can he renounce his bread for honour's sake. Only they who prefer to be relieved of the agony of this decision, because they cannot bring themselves to renounce material comfort for the sake of spiritual advantage, see in the choice a profanation of true values.

Monetary calculation only has meaning within the sphere of economic organization. It is a system whereby the rules of economics may be applied in the disposition of economic goods. Economic goods only have a part in this system in proportion to the extent to which they may be exchanged for money. Any extension of the sphere of monetary calculation causes misunderstanding. It cannot be regarded as constituting a kind of yardstick for the valuation of goods, and cannot be so treated in historical investigations into the development of social relationships; it cannot be used as a criterion of national wealth and income, nor as a means of gauging the value of goods which stand outside the sphere of exchange, as who should seek to estimate the extent of human losses through emigrations or wars in terms of money?[5] This is mere socialistic tomfoolery, however much it may be indulged in by otherwise perspicacious economists.

Nevertheless within these limits, which in economic life it never oversteps, monetary calculation fulfils all the requirements of economic calculation. It affords us a guide through the oppressive plenitude of economic potentialities. It enables us to extend to all goods of a higher order the judgment of value, which is bound up with and clearly evident in, the case of goods ready for consumption, or at best of production-goods of the lowest order. It renders their value capable of computation and thereby gives us the primary basis for all economic operations with goods of a higher order. Without it, all production involving processes stretching well back in time and all the longer roundabout processes of capitalistic production would be gropings in the dark.

There are two conditions governing the possibility of calculating value in terms of money. Firstly, not only must goods of a lower, but also those of a higher, order come within the ambit of exchange, if they are to be included. If they do not do so, exchange relationships would not arise. True enough, the considerations which must obtain in the case of Robinson Crusoe prepared, within the range of his own hearth, to exchange, by production, labour and flour for bread, are indistinguishable from those which obtain when he is prepared to exchange bread for clothes in the open market, and, therefore, it is to some extent true to say that every economic action, including Robinson Crusoe's own production, can be termed *exchange*.[6] Moreover, the mind of one man alone – be it never so cunning, is too weak to grasp the importance of any single one among the countlessly many goods of a higher order. No single man can ever master all the possibilities of production, innumerable as they are, as to be in a position to make straightway evident judgments of value without the aid of some system of computation. The distribution among a number of individuals of administrative control over economic goods in a community of men who take part in the labour of producing them, and who are economically interested in them, entails a kind of intellectual division of labour, which would not be possible without some system of calculating production and without economy.

The second condition is that there exists in fact a universally employed medium of exchange – namely, money – which plays the same part as a medium, in the exchange of production-goods also. If this were not the case, it would not be possible to reduce all exchange-relationships to a common denominator.

Only under simple conditions can economics dispense with monetary calculation. Within the narrow confines of household economy, for instance, where the father can supervise the entire economic management, it is possible to determine the significance of changes in the processes of production, without such aids to the mind, and yet with more or less of accuracy. In such a case the process develops under a relatively limited use of capital. Few of the capitalistic roundabout processes of production are here introduced: what is manufactured is, as a rule, consumption-goods or at least such goods of a higher order as stand very near to consumption-goods. The division of labour is in its rudimentary stages: one and the same labourer controls the labour of what is in effect, a complete process of production of goods ready for consumption, from beginning to end. All this is different, in developed communal production. The experiences of a remote and bygone period of simple production do not provide any sort of argument for establishing the possibility of an economic system without monetary calculation.

In the narrow confines of a closed household economy, it is possible throughout to review the process of production from beginning to end, and to judge all the time whether one or another mode of procedure yields more consumable goods. This, however, is no longer possible in the incomparably more involved circumstances of our own social economy. It will be evident, even in a socialist society, that 1,000 hectolitres of wine are better than 800, and it is not difficult to decide whether it desires 1,000 hectolitres of wine rather than 500 of oil. There is no need for any system of calculation to establish this fact: the deciding element is the will of the economic subjects involved. But once this decision has been taken, the real task of rational economic direction only commences, i.e. economically, to place the means at the service of the end. That can only be done with some kind of economic calculation. The human mind cannot orientate itself properly among the bewildering mass of intermediate products and potentialities of production without such aid. It would simply stand perplexed before the problems of management and location.[7]

It is an illusion to imagine that in a socialist state calculation *in natura* can take the place of monetary calculation. Calculation *in natura*, in an economy without exchange, can embrace consumption-goods only; it completely fails when it comes to deal with goods of a higher order. And as soon as one gives up the conception of a freely established monetary price for goods of a higher order, rational production becomes completely impossible. Every step that takes us away from private ownership of the means of production and from the use of money also takes us away from rational economics.

It is easy to overlook this fact, considering that the extent to which socialism is in evidence among us constitutes only a socialistic oasis in a society with monetary exchange, which is still a free society to a certain degree. In one sense we may agree with the socialists' assertion which is otherwise entirely untenable and advanced only as a demagogic point, to the effect that the nationalization and municipalization of enterprise is not really socialism, since these concerns in their business organizations are so much dependent upon the environing economic system with its free commerce that they cannot be said to partake to-day of the really essential nature of a socialist economy. In state and municipal undertakings technical improvements are introduced because their effect in similar private enterprises, domestic or foreign, can be noticed, and because those private industries which produce the materials for these improvements give the impulse for their introduction. In these concerns the advantages of reorganization can be established, because they operate within the sphere of a society based upon the private ownership of the means of production and upon the system of monetary exchange, being thus capable of computation and account. This state of affairs, however, could not obtain in the case of socialist concerns operating in a purely socialistic environment.

Without economic calculation there can be no economy. Hence, in a socialist state wherein the pursuit of economic calculation is impossible, there can be – in our sense of the term – no economy whatsoever. In trivial and secondary matters rational conduct might still be possible, but in general it would be impossible to speak of rational production any more. There would be no means of determining what was rational, and hence it is obvious that production could never be directed by economic considerations. What this means is clear enough, apart from its effects on the supply of commodities. Rational conduct would be divorced from the very ground which is its proper domain. Would there, in fact, be any such thing as rational conduct at all, or, indeed, such a thing as rationality and logic in thought itself? Historically, human rationality is a development of economic life. Could it then obtain when divorced therefrom?

For a time the remembrance of the experiences gained in a competitive economy, which has obtained for some thousands of years, may provide a check to the complete collapse of the art of economy. The older methods of procedure might be retained not because of their rationality but because they appear to be hallowed by tradition. Actually, they would meanwhile have become irrational, as no longer comporting with the new conditions. Eventually, through the general reconstruction of economic thought, they will experience alterations which will render them in fact uneconomic. The supply of goods will no longer proceed anarchically of its own accord; that is true. All transactions which serve the purpose of meeting requirements will be subject to the control of a supreme authority. Yet in place of the economy of the 'anarchic' method of production, recourse will be had to the senseless output of an absurd apparatus. The wheels will turn, but will run to no effect.

One may anticipate the nature of the future socialist society. There will be hundreds and thousands of factories in operation. Very few of these will be producing wares ready for use; in the majority of cases what will be manufactured will be unfinished goods and production-goods. All these concerns will be interrelated. Every good will go through a whole series of stages before it is ready for use. In the ceaseless toil and moil of this process, however, the administration will be without means of testing their bearings. It will never be able to determine whether a given good has not been kept for a superfluous length of time in the necessary processes of production, or whether work and material have not been wasted in its completion. How will it be able to decide whether this or that method of production is the more profitable? At best it will only be able to compare the quality and quantity of the consumable end-product produced, but will in the rarest cases be in a position to compare the expenses entailed in production. It will know, or think it knows, the ends to be achieved by

14

economic organization, and will have to regulate its activities accordingly, i.e. it will have to attain those ends with the least experience. It will have to make its computations with a view to finding the cheapest way. This computation will naturally have to be a value-computation. It is eminently clear, and requires no further proof, that it cannot be of a technical character, and that it cannot be based upon the objective use-value of goods and services.

Now, in the economic system of private ownership of the means of production, the system of computation by value is necessarily employed by each independent member of society. Everybody participates in its emergence in a double way: on the one hand as a consumer and on the other as a producer. As a consumer he establishes a scale of valuation for goods ready for use and consumption. As a producer he puts goods of a higher order into such use as produces the greatest return. In this way all goods of a higher order receive a position in the scale of valuations in accordance with the immediate state of social conditions of production and of social needs. Through the interplay of these two processes of valuation, means will be afforded for governing both consumption and production by the economic principle throughout. Every graded system of pricing proceeds from the fact that men always and ever harmonize their own requirements with their estimation of economic facts.

All this is necessarily absent from a socialist state. The administration may know exactly what goods are most urgently needed. But in so doing, it has only found what is, in fact, but one of the two necessary prerequisites for economic calculation. In the nature of the case it must, however, dispense with the other – the valuation of the means of production. It may establish the value attained by the totality of the means of production; this is obviously identical with that of all the needs thereby satisfied. It may also be able to calculate the value of any means of production by calculating the consequence of its withdrawal in relation to the satisfaction of needs. Yet it cannot reduce this value to the uniform expression of a money price, as can a competitive economy, wherein all prices can be referred back to a common expression in terms of money. In a socialist commonwealth which, whilst it need not of necessity dispense with money altogether, yet finds it impossible to use money as an expression of the price of the factors of production (including labour), money can play no role in economic calculation.[8]

Picture the building of a new railroad. Should it be built at all, and if so, which out of a number of conceivable roads should be built? In a competitive and monetary economy, this question would be answered by monetary calculation. The new road will render less expensive the transport of some goods, and it may be possible to calculate whether this reduction of expense transcends that involved in the building and upkeep of the next line. That can only be calculated in money. It is not possible to attain the desired end merely by counterbalancing the various physical expenses and physical savings. Where one cannot express hours of labour, iron, coal, all kinds of building materials, machines and other things necessary for the construction and upkeep of the railroad in a common unit it is not possible to make calculations at all. The drawing up of bills on an economic basis is only possible where all the goods concerned can be referred back to money. Admittedly, monetary calculation has its inconveniences and serious defects, but we have certainly nothing better to put in its place, and for the practical purposes of life monetary calculation as it exists under a sound monetary system always suffices. Were we to dispense with it, any economic system of calculation would become absolutely impossible.

The socialist society would know how to look after itself. It would issue an edict to decide for or against the projected building. Yet this decision would depend at best upon vague estimates; it would never be based upon the foundation of an exact calculation of value.

The static state can dispense with economic calculation. For here the same events in economic life are ever recurring; and if we assume that the first disposition of the static socialist economy follows on the basis of the final state of the competitive economy, we might at all events conceive of a socialist production system which is rationally controlled from an economic point of view. But this is only conceptually possible. For the moment, we leave aside the fact that a static state is impossible in real life, as our economic data are for ever changing, so that the static nature of economic activity is only a theoretical assumption corresponding to no real state of affairs, however necessary it may be for our thinking and for the perfection of our knowledge of economics. Even so, we must assume that the transition to socialism must, as a consequence of the levelling out of the differences in income and the resultant re-adjustments in consumption, and therefore production, change all economic data in such a way that a connecting link with the final state of affairs in the previously existing competitive economy becomes impossible. But then we have the spectacle of a socialist economic order floundering in the ocean of possible and conceivable economic combinations without the compass of economic calculation.

Thus in the socialist commonwealth every economic change becomes an undertaking whose success can be neither appraised in advance nor later retrospectively determined. There is only groping in the dark. Socialism is the abolition of rational economy.

3. *Economic Calculation in the Socialist Commonwealth*

Are we really dealing with the necessary consequences of common owner-ship of the means of production? Is there no way in which some kind of economic calculation might be tied up with a socialist system?

In every great enterprise, each particular business or branch of business is to some extent independent in its accounting. It reckons the labour and material against each other, and it is always possible for each individual group to strike a particular balance and to approach the economic results of its activities from an accounting point of view. We can thus ascertain with what success each particular section has laboured, and accordingly draw conclusions about the reorganization, curtailment, abandonment, or expansion of existing groups and about the institution of new ones. Admit-tedly, some mistakes are inevitable in such a calculation. They arise partly from the difficulties consequent upon an allocation of general expenses. Yet other mistakes arise from the necessity of calculating with what are not from many points of view rigorously ascertainable data, e.g. when in the ascertainment of the profitability of a certain method of procedure we compute the amortization of the machines used on the assumption of a given duration for their usefulness. Still, all such mistakes can be confined within certain narrow limits, so that they do not disturb the net result of the calculation. What remains of uncertainty comes into the calculation of the uncertainty of future conditions, which is an inevitable concomitant of the dynamic nature of economic life.

It seems tempting to try to construct by analogy a separate estimation of the particular production groups in the socialist state also. But it is quite impossible. For each separate calculation of the particular branches of one and the same enterprise depends exclusively on the fact that it is precisely in market dealings that market prices to be taken as the bases of calculation are formed for all kinds of goods and labour employed. Where there is no free market, there is no pricing mechanism; without a pricing mechanism, there is no economic calculation.

We might conceive of a situation, in which exchange between particular branches of business is permitted, so as to obtain the mechanism of exchange relations (prices) and thus create a basis for economic calculation even in the socialist commonwealth. Within the framework of a uniform economy knowing not private ownership of the means of production, individual labour groups are constituted independent and authoritative disposers, which have indeed to behave in accordance with the directions of the supreme economic council, but which nevertheless assign each other material goods and services only against a payment, which would

17

have to be made in the general medium of exchange. It is roughly in this way that we conceive of the organization of the socialist running of business when we nowadays talk of complete socialization and the like. But we have still not come to the crucial point. Exchange relations between production-goods can only be established on the basis of private ownership of the means of production. When the 'coal syndicate' provides the 'iron syndicate' with coal, no price can be formed, except when both syndicates are the owners of the means of production employed in their business. This would not be socialization but workers' capitalism and syndicalism.

The matter is indeed very simple for those socialist theorists who rely on the labour theory of value.

As soon as society takes possession of the means of production and applies them to production in their directly socialised form, each individual's labour, however different its specific utility may be, becomes *a priori* and directly social labour. The amount of social labour invested in a product need not then be established indirectly; daily experience immediately tells us how much is necessary on an average. Society can simply calculate how many hours of labour are invested in a steam engine, a quarter of last harvest's wheat, and a 100 yards of linen of given quality. . . . To be sure, society will also have to know how much labour is needed to produce any consumption-good. It will have to arrange its production plan according to its means of production, to which labour especially belongs. The utility yielded by the various consumption-goods, weighted against each other and against the amount of labour required to produce them, will ultimately determine the plan. People will make everything simple without the mediation of the notorious 'value'.[9]

Here it is not our task once more to advance critical objections against the labour theory of value. In this connection they can only interest us in so far as they are relevant to an assessment of the applicability of labour in the value computations of a socialist community.

On a first impression calculation in terms of labour also takes into consideration the natural non-human conditions of production. The law of diminishing returns is already allowed for in the concept of socially necessary average labour-time to the extent that its operation is due to the variety of the natural conditions of production. If the demand for a commodity increases and worse natural resources must be exploited, then the average socially necessary labour-time required for the production of a unit increases too. If more favourable natural resources are discovered, the amount of socially necessary labour diminishes.[10] The consideration of the natural condition of production suffices only in so far as it is reflected in the amount of labour socially necessary. But it is in this respect that valuation in terms of labour fails. It leaves the employment of material factors of production out of account. Let the amount of socially necessary labour-time required for the production of each of the commodities P and Q be 10 hours. Further, in addition to labour the production of both P and Q requires the raw material a, a unit of which is produced by an hour's socially necessary labour; 2 units of a and 8 hours' labour are used in the production of P, and one unit of a and 9 hours' labour in the production of Q. In terms of labour P and Q are equivalent, but in value terms P is more valuable than Q. The former is false, and only the latter corresponds to the nature and purpose of calculation. True, this surplus, by which according to value calculation P is more valuable than Q, this material sub-stratum 'is given by nature without any addition from man'.[11] Still, the fact that it is only present in such quantities that it becomes an object of economizing, must be taken into account in some form or other in value-calculation.

The second defect in calculation in terms of labour is the ignoring of the different qualities of labour. To Marx all human labour is economically of the same kind, as it is always 'the productive expenditure of human brain, brawn, nerve and hand'.[12]

Skilled labour counts only as intensified, or rather multiplied, simple labour, so that a smaller quantity of skilled labour is equal to a larger quantity of simple labour. Experience shows that skilled labour can always be reduced in this way to the terms of simple labour. No matter that a commodity be the product of the most highly skilled labour, its value can be equated with that of the product of simple labour, so that it represents merely a definite amount of simple labour.

Böhm-Bawerk is not far wrong when he calls this argument 'a theoretical juggle of almost stupefying naïveté'.[13] To judge Marx's view we need not ask if it is possible to discover a single uniform physiological measure of all human labour, whether it be physical or 'mental'. For it is certain that there exist among men varying degrees of capacity and dexterity, which cause the products and services of labour to have varying qualities. What must be conclusive in deciding the question whether reckoning in terms of labour is applicable or not, is whether it is or is not possible to bring different kinds of labour under a common denominator without the mediation of the economic subject's valuation of their products. The proof Marx attempts to give is not successful. Experience indeed shows that goods are consumed under exchange relations without regard of the fact of their being produced by simple or complex labour. But this would only be a proof that given amounts of simple labour are directly made equal to given amounts of complex labour, if it were shown that labour is the source of exchange value. This not only is not demonstrated, but is what Marx is trying to demonstrate by means of these very arguments.

No more is it a proof of this homogeneity that rates of substitution between simple and complex labour are manifested in the wage rate in an exchange economy – a fact to which Marx does not allude in this context. This equalizing process is a result of market transactions and not its antecedent. Calculation in terms of labour would have to set up an arbitrary proportion for the substitution of complex by simple labour, which excludes its employment for purposes of economic administration.

It was long supposed that the labour theory of value was indispensable to socialism, so that the demand for the nationalization of the means of production should have an ethical basis. To-day we know this for the error it is. Although the majority of socialist supporters have thus employed this misconception, and although Marx, however much he fundamentally took another point of view, was not altogether free from it, it is clear that the political call for the introduction of socialized production neither requires nor can obtain the support of the labour theory of value on the one hand, and that on the other those people holding different views on the nature and origin of economic value can be socialists according to their sentiments. Yet the labour theory of value is inherently necessary for the supporters of socialist production in a sense other than that usually intended. In the main socialist production might only appear rationally realizable, if it provided an objectively recognizable unit of value, which would permit of economic calculation in an economy where neither money nor exchange were present. And only labour can conceivably be considered as such.

4. Responsibility and Initiative in Communal Concerns

The problem of responsibility and initiative in socialist enterprises is closely connected with that of economic calculation. It is now universally agreed that the exclusion of free initiative and individual responsibility, on which the successes of private enterprise depend, constitutes the most serious menace to socialist economic organization.[14]

The majority of socialists silently pass this problem by. Others believe they can answer it with an allusion to the directors of companies; in spite of the fact that they are not the owners of the means of production, enterprises under their control have flourished. If society, instead of company shareholders, becomes the owner of the means of production, nothing will have altered. The directors would not work less satisfactorily for society than for shareholders.

We must distinguish between two groups of joint-stock companies and similar concerns. In the first group, consisting for the large part of smaller companies, a few individuals unite in a common enterprise in the legal form of a company. They are often heirs of the founders of the company, or often previous competitors who have amalgamated. Here the actual control and management of business is in the hands of the shareholders themselves or at least some of the shareholders, who do business in their own interest; or in that of closely related shareholders such as wives, minors, etc. The directors in their capacity as members of the board of management or of the board of control, and sometimes also in an attenuated legal capacity, themselves exercise the decisive influence in the conduct of affairs. Nor is this affected by the circumstance that sometimes part of the share-capital is held by a financial consortium or bank. Here in fact the company is only differentiated from the public commercial company by its legal form.

The situation is quite different in the case of large-scale companies, where only a fraction of the shareholders, i.e. the big shareholders, participate in the actual control of the enterprise. And these usually have the same interest in the firm's prosperity as any property holder. Still, it may well be that they have interests other than those of the vast majority of small shareholders, who are excluded from the management even if they own the larger part of the share-capital. Severe collisions may occur, when the firm's business is so handled on behalf of the directors that the shareholders are injured. But be that as it may, it is clear that the real holders of power in companies run the business in their own interest, whether it coincides with that of the shareholders or not. In the long run it will generally be to the advantage of the solid company administrator, who is not merely bent on making a transient profit, to represent the shareholders' interests only in every case and to avoid manipulations which might damage them. This holds good in the first instance for banks and financial groups, which should not trifle at the public's expense with the credit they enjoy. Thus it is not merely on the prescriptiveness of ethical motives that the success of companies depend.

The situation is completely transformed when an undertaking is nationalized. The motive force disappears with the exclusion of the material interests of private individuals, and if State and municipal enterprises thrive at all, they owe it to the taking over of 'management' from private enterprise, or to the fact that they are ever driven to reforms and innovations by the business men from whom they purchase their instruments of production and raw material.

Since we are in position to survey decades of State and socialist endeavour, it is now generally recognized that there is no internal pressure to reform and improvement of production in socialist undertakings, that they cannot be adjusted to the changing conditions of demand, and that in a word they are a dead limb in the economic organism. All attempts to

21

breathe life into them have so far been in vain. It was supposed that a reform in the system of remuneration might achieve the desired end. If the managers of these enterprises were interested in the yield, it was thought they would be in a position comparable to that of the manager of large-scale companies. This is a fatal error. The managers of large-scale companies are bound up with the interests of the businesses they administer in an entirely different way from what could be the case in public concerns. They are either already owners of a not inconsiderable fraction of the share capital, or hope to become so in due course. Further, they are in a position to obtain profits by stock-exchange speculation in the company's shares. They have the prospect of bequeathing their positions to, or at least securing part of their influence for, their heirs. The type to which the success of joint-stock companies is to be attributed, is not that of a complacently prosperous managing director resembling the civil servant in his outlook and experience; rather it is precisely the manager, promoter, and man of affairs, who is himself interested as a shareholder, whom it is the aim of all nationalization and municipalization to exclude.

It is not generally legitimate to appeal in a socialist context to such arguments in order to ensure the success of an economic order built on socialist foundations. All socialist systems, including that of Karl Marx, and his orthodox supporters, proceed from the assumption that in a socialist society a conflict between the interests of the particular and general could not possibly arise. Everybody will act in his own interest in giving of his best because he participates in the product of all economic activity. The obvious objection that the individual is very little concerned whether he himself is diligent and enthusiastic, and that it is of greater moment to him that everybody else should be, is either completely ignored or is insufficiently dealt with by them. They believe they can construct socialist commonwealth on the basis of the Categorical Imperative alone. How lightly it is their wont to proceed in this way is best shown by Kautsky when he says, 'If socialism is a social necessity, then it would be human nature and not socialism which would have to readjust itself, if ever the two clashed.'[15] This is nothing but sheer Utopianism.

But even if we for the moment grant that these Utopian expectations can actually be realized, that each individual in a socialist society will exert himself with the same zeal as he does to-day in a society where he is subjected to the pressure of free competition, there still remains the problem of measuring the result of economic activity in a socialist commonwealth which does not permit of any economic calculation. We cannot act economically if we are not in a position to understand economizing.

A popular slogan affirms that if we think less bureaucratically and more commercially in communal enterprises, they will work just as well as private enterprises. The leading positions must be occupied by merchants, and then income will grow apace. Unfortunately 'commercial-mindedness' is not something external, which can be arbitrarily transferred. A merchant's qualities are not the property of a person depending on inborn aptitude, nor are they acquired by studies in a commercial school or by working in a commercial house, or even by having been a business man oneself for some period of time. The entrepreneur's commercial attitude and activity arises from his position in the economic process and is lost with its disappearance. When a successful business man is appointed the manager of a public enterprise, he may still bring with him certain experiences from his previous occupation, and be able to turn them to good account in a routine fashion for some time. Still, with his entry into communal activity he ceases to be a merchant and becomes as much a bureaucrat as any other placeman in the public employ. It is not a knowledge of bookkeeping, of business organization, or the style of commercial correspondence, or even a dispensation from a commercial highschool, which makes the merchant, but his characteristic position in the production process, which allows of the identification of the firm's and his own interests. It is no solution of the problem when Otto Bauer in his most recently published work proposes that the directors of the National Central Bank, on whom leadership in the economic process will be conferred, should be nominated by a Collegium, to which representatives of the teaching staff of the commercial high schools would also belong.[16] Like Plato's philosophers, the directors so appointed may well be the wisest and best of their kind, but they cannot be merchants in their posts as leaders of a socialist society, even if they should have been previously.

It is a general complaint that the administration of public undertakings lacks initiative. It is believed that this might be remedied by changes in organization. This also is a grievous mistake. The management of a socialist concern cannot entirely be placed in the hands of a single individual, because there must always be the suspicion that he will permit errors inflicting heavy damages on the community. But if the important conclusions are made dependent on the votes of committees, or on the consent of the relevant government offices, then limitations are imposed on the individual's initiative. Committees are rarely inclined to introduce bold innovations. The lack of free initiative in public business rests not on an absence of organization, it is inherent in the nature of the business itself. One cannot transfer free disposal of the factors of production to an employee, however high his rank, and this becomes even less possible, the more strongly he is materially interested in the successful performance of his duties; for in practice the propertyless manager can only be held morally responsible for losses incurred. And so ethical losses are juxtaposed with opportunities for material gain. The property owner on the other hand himself bears responsibility, as he himself must primarily feel the loss arising from unwisely conducted business. It is precisely in this that there is a characteristic difference between liberal and socialist production.

5. *The most Recent Socialist Doctrines and the Problem of Economic Calculation*

Since recent events helped socialist parties to obtain power in Russia, Hungary, Germany and Austria, and have thus made the execution of a socialist nationalization programme a topical issue, Marxist writers have themselves begun to deal more closely with the problems of the regulation of the socialist commonwealth. But even now they still cautiously avoid the crucial question, leaving it to be tackled by the despised 'Utopians'. They themselves prefer to confine their attention to what is to be done in the immediate future; they are for ever drawing up programmes of the path to Socialism and not of Socialism itself. The only possible conclusion from all these writings is that they are not even conscious of the larger problem of economic calculation in a socialist society.

To Otto Bauer the nationalization of the banks appears the final and decisive step in the carrying through of the socialist nationalization programme. If all banks are nationalized and amalgamated into a single central bank, then its administrative board becomes 'the supreme economic authority, the chief administrative organ of the whole economy. Only by nationalization of the banks does society obtain the power to regulate its labour according to a plan, and to distribute its resources rationally among the various branches of production, so as to adapt them to the nation's needs.'[17] Bauer is not discussing the monetary arrangements which will prevail in the socialist commonwealth after the completion of the nationalization of the banks. Like other Marxists he is trying to show how simply and obviously the future socialist order of society will evolve from the conditions prevailing in a developed capitalist economy. 'It suffices to transfer to the nation's representatives the power now exercised by bank shareholders through the Administrative Boards they elect,'[18] in order to socialize the banks and thus to lay the last brick on the edifice of socialism. Bauer leaves his readers completely ignorant of the fact that the nature of the banks is entirely changed in the process of nationalization and amalgamation into one central bank. Once the banks merge into a single bank, their essence is wholly transformed; they are then in a position to issue credit without any limitation.[19] In this fashion the monetary system as we know it to-day disappears of itself. When in addition the single central bank is nationalized in a society, which is otherwise already completely socialized, market dealings disappear and all exchange transactions are abolished. At the same time the Bank ceases to be a bank, its specific functions are extinguished, for there is no longer any place for it in such a society. It may be that the name 'Bank' is retained, that the Supreme Economic Council of the socialist community is called the Board of Directors of the Bank, and that they hold their meetings in a building formerly occupied by a bank. But it is no longer a bank, it fulfils none of those functions which a bank fulfils in an economic system resting on the private ownership of the means of production and the use of a general medium of exchange-money. It no longer distributes any credit, for a socialist society makes credit of necessity impossible. Bauer himself does not tell us what a bank is, but he begins his chapter on the nationalization of the banks with the sentence: 'All disposable capital flows into a common pool in the banks.'[20] As a Marxist must he not raise the question of what the banks' activities will be after the abolition of capitalism?

All other writers who have grappled with the problems of the organization of the socialist commonwealth are guilty of similar confusions. They do not realize that the bases of economic calculation are removed by the exclusion of exchange and the pricing mechanism, and that something must be substituted in its place, if all economy is not to be abolished and a hopeless chaos is not to result. People believe that socialist institutions might evolve without further ado from those of a capitalist economy. This is not at all the case. And it becomes all the more grotesque when we talk of banks, bank management, etc. in a socialist commonwealth.

Reference to the conditions that have developed in Russia and Hungary under Soviet rule proves nothing. What we have there is nothing but a picture of the destruction of an existing order of social production, for which a closed peasant household economy has been substituted. All branches of production depending on social division of labour are in a state of entire dissolution. What is happening under the rule of Lenin and Trotsky is merely destruction and annihilation. Whether, as the liberals hold, socialism must inevitably draw these consequences in its train, or whether, as the socialists retort, this is only a result of the fact that the Soviet Republic is attacked from without, is a question of no interest to us in this context. All that has to be established is the fact that the Soviet socialist commonwealth has not even begun to discuss the problem of economic calculation, nor has it any cause to do so. For where things are still produced for the market in Soviet Russia in spite of governmental prohibitions, they are valued in terms of money, for there exists to that extent private ownership of the means of production, and goods are sold against money. Even the Government cannot deny the necessity, which it confirms by increasing the amount of money in circulation, of retaining a monetary system for at least the transition period.

That the essence of the problem to be faced has not yet come to light in Soviet Russia, Lenin's statements in his essay on *Die nächsten Aufgaben der Sowjetmacht* best show. In the dictator's deliberations there ever recurs the thought that the immediate and most pressing task of Russian Communism is 'the organization of bookkeeping and control of those concerns, in which the capitalists have already been expropriated, and of all other economic concerns'.[21] Even so Lenin is far from realizing that an entirely new problem is here involved which it is impossible to solve with the conceptual instruments of 'bourgeois' culture. Like a real politician, he does not bother with issues beyond his nose. He still finds himself surrounded by monetary transactions, and does not notice that with progressive socialization money also necessarily loses its function as the medium of exchange in general use, to the extent that private property and with it exchange disappear. The implication of Lenin's reflections is that he would like to re-introduce into Soviet business 'bourgeois' bookkeeping carried on on a monetary basis. Therefore he also desires to restore 'bourgeois experts' to a state of grace.[22] For the rest Lenin is as little aware as Bauer of the fact that in a socialist commonwealth the functions of the bank are unthinkable in their existing sense. He wishes to go farther with the 'nationalization of the banks' and to proceed 'to a transformation of the banks into the nodal point of social bookkeeping under socialism'.[23]

Lenin's ideas on the socialist economic system, to which he is striving to lead his people, are generally obscure.

'The socialist state', he says 'can only arise as a net of producing and consuming communes, which conscientiously record their production and consumption, go about their labour economically, uninterruptedly raise their labour productivity and thus attain the possibility of lowering the working day to seven or six hours or even lower.'[24] 'Every factory, every village appears as a production and consumption commune having the right and obligation to apply the general Soviet legislation in its own way ("in its own way" not in the sense of its violation but in the sense of the variety of its forms of realisation), and to solve in its own way the problem of calculating the production and distribution of products.'[25]

'The chief communes must and will serve the most backward ones as educators, teachers, and stimulating leaders.' The successes of the chief communes must be broadcast in all their details in order to provide a good example. The communes 'showing good business results' should be immediately rewarded by a curtailment of the working day and with an increase in wages, and by allowing more attention to be paid to cultural and aesthetic goods and values'.[26]

We can infer that Lenin's ideal is a state of society in which the means of production are not the property of a few districts, municipalities, or even of the workers in the concern, but of the whole community. His ideal is socialist and not syndicalist. This need not be specially stressed for a Marxist such as Lenin. It is not extraordinary of Lenin the theorist, but of Lenin the statesman, who is the leader of the syndicalist and small-holding peasant Russian revolution. However, at the moment we are engaged with the writer Lenin and may consider his ideals separately, without letting ourselves be disturbed by the picture of sober reality. According to Lenin the theorist, every large agricultural and industrial concern is a member of the great commonwealth of labour. Those who are active in this commonwealth have the right of self-government; they exercise a profound influence on the direction of production and again on the distribution of the goods they are assigned for consumption. Still labour is the property of the whole society, and as its product belongs to society also, it therefore disposes of its distribution. How, we must now ask, is calculation in the economy carried on in a socialist commonwealth which is so organized? Lenin gives us a most inadequate answer by referring us back to statistics. We must

bring statistics to the masses, make it popular, so that the active population will gradually learn by themselves to understand and realise how much and what kind of work must be done, how much and what kind of recreation should be taken, so that the comparison of the economy's industrial results in the case of individual communes becomes the object of general interest and education.[27]

From these scanty allusions it is impossible to infer what Lenin understands by statistics and whether he is thinking of monetary or *in natura* computation. In any case, we must refer back to what we have said about the impossibility of learning the money prices of production-goods in a socialist commonwealth and about the difficulties standing in the way of *in natura* valuation.[28] Statistics would only be applicable to economic calculation, whose ill-suitedness for this purpose we have demonstrated. It is naturally impossible where no exchange relations are formed between goods in the process of trade.

CONCLUSION

It must follow from what we have been able to establish in our previous arguments that the protagonists of a socialist system of production claim preference for it on the ground of greater rationality as against an economy so constituted as to depend on private ownership of the means of production.

27

We have no need to consider this opinion within the framework of the present essay, in so far as it falls back on the assertion that rational economic activity necessarily cannot be perfect, because certain forces are operative which hinder its pursuance. In this connection we may only pay attention to the economic and technical reason for this opinion. There hovers before the holders of this tenet a muddled conception of technical rationality, which stands in antithesis to economic rationality, on which also they are not very clear. They are wont to overlook the fact that 'all technical rationality of production is identical with a low level of specific expenditure in the processes of production'.[29] They overlook the fact that technical calculation is not enough to realize the 'degree of general and teleological expediency'[30] of an event; that it can only grade individual events according to their significance; but that it can never guide us in those judgments which are demanded by the economic complex as a whole. Only because of the fact that technical considerations can be based on profitability can we overcome the difficulty arising from the complexity of the relations between the mighty system of present-day production on the one hand and demand and the efficiency of enterprises and economic units on the other; and can we gain the complete picture of the situation in its totality, which rational economic activity requires.[31]

These theories are dominated by a confused conception of the primacy of objective use-value. In fact, so far as economic administration is concerned, objective use-value can only acquire significance for the economy through the influence it derives from subjective use-value on the formation of the exchange-relations of economic goods. A second confused idea is inexplicably involved – the observer's personal judgment of the utility of goods as opposed to the judgments of the people participating in economic transactions. If anyone finds it 'irrational' to spend as much as is expended in society on smoking, drinking , and similar enjoyments, then doubtless he is right from the point of view of his own personal scale of values. But in so judging, he is ignoring the fact that economy is a means, and that, without prejudice to the rational considerations influencing its pattern, the scale of ultimate ends is a matter for conation and not for cognition.

The knowledge of the fact that rational economic activity is impossible in a socialist commonwealth cannot, of course, be used as an argument either for or against socialism. Whoever is prepared himself to enter upon socialism on ethical grounds on the supposition that the provision of goods of a lower order for human beings under a system of a common ownership of the means of production is diminished, or whoever is guided by ascetic ideals in his desire for socialism, will not allow himself to be influenced in his endeavours by what we have said. Still less will those 'culture' socialists

28

be deterred who, like Muckle, expect from socialism primarily 'the dissolution of the most frightful of all barbarisms – capitalist rationality'.[32] But he who expects a rational economic system from socialism will be forced to re-examine his views.

NOTES

1. [This article appeared originally under the title 'Die Wirtschaftsrechnung im sozialistischen Gemeinwesen' in the *Archiv für Sozialwissenschaften*, vol. 47 (1920). – Ed.]
2. *v.* Kautsky, *The Social Revolution and on the Morrow of the Social Revolution* (London, 1907), pt ii, p. 1.
3. Using that term, of course, in the sense only of the valuating subject, and not in an objective and universally applicable sense.
4. Čuhel, *Zur Lehre von den Bedürfnissen* (Innsbruck, 1907), pp. 198 ff.
5. Cf. Wieser, *Über den Ursprung und die Hauptgesetze des wirtschaftlichen Wertes* (Vienna, 1884), pp. 185 ff.
6. Cf. Mises, *Theorie des Geldes u. der Umlaufsmittel* (Munich and Leipzig, 1912), p. 16, with the references there given.
7. Gottl-Ottlilienfeld, *Wirtschaft u. Technik* (*Grundriss d. Sozialökonomik*, sect. ii (Tübingen, 1914)), p. 216.
8. This fact is also recognized by Neurath (*Durch die Kriegswirtschaft zur Naturalwirtschaft* (Munich, 1919), pp. 216 f.). He advances the view that every complete administrative economy is, in the final analysis, a natural economy. 'Socialization', he says, 'is thus the pursuit of natural economy.' Neurath merely overlooks the insuperable difficulties that would have to develop with economic calculation in the socialist commonwealth.
9. Engels, *Dührings Umwälzung des Wissenschaft*, 7th edn, pp. 335 f.
10. Marx, *Capital*, trans. Eden Cedar Paul, p. 9.
11. Marx, ibid., p. 12.
12. Marx, ibid., pp. 13 et seq.
13. Cf. Böhm-Bawerk, *Capital and Interest*, p. 384.
14. Cf. *Vorläufiger Bericht der Sozialisierungskommission über die Frage der Sozialisierung des Kohlenbergbaues*, concluded 15th February, 1919 (Berlin, 1919), p. 13.
15. Cf. Kautsky, Preface to Atlanticus (Ballod), *Produktion und Konsum im Sozialstaat* (Stuttgart, 1898), p. 14.
16. Cf. Bauer, *Der Weg zum Sozialismus* (Vienna, 1919), p. 25.
17. Bauer, op. cit., pp. 26 f.

18. Ibid., p. 25.
19. Mises, op. cit., pp. 474 ff.
20. Bauer, op. cit., p. 24.
21. Cf. Lenin, *Die nächsten Aufgaben der Sowjetmacht* (Berlin, 1918), pp. 12 f., 22 ff.
22. Op. cit., p. 15.
23. Ibid., pp. 21 and 26. Compare also Bucharin, *Das Programm der Kommunisten* (Zürich, 1918), pp. 27 ff.
24. Cf. Lenin, op. cit., pp. 24 f.
25. Ibid., p. 32.
26. Ibid., p. 33.
27. Op. cit., p. 33.
28. Neurath, too (cf. op. cit., pp. 212 et seq.) imputes great importance to statistics for the setting up of the socialist economic plan.
29. Cf. Gottl, op. cit., p. 220.
30. Ibid., p. 219.
31. Ibid., p. 225.
32. Cf. Muckle, *Das Kulturideal des Sozialismus* (Munich and Leipzig), p. 213. On the other hand, Muckle demands the 'highest degree of rationalisation of economic life in order to curtail hours of labour, and to permit man to withdraw to an island where he can listen to the melody of his being'.

E63 E52 32 - 111 [1978]

Ludwig von Mises, 'Monetary Stabilization and Cyclical Policy', Percy L. Greaves (ed.), *On the Manipulation of Money and Credit* (Dobbs Ferry, N.Y.: Free Market Books, 1978), pp. 59–171.

This paper was originally published as a monograph, *Geldwertsta-bilisierung und Konjunkturpolitik* (Jena: Gustav Fischer, 1928); translated for the above edition by Bettina Bien Greaves. The paper is an important statement of Mises's position on cyclical theory and policy, developing ideas concisely adumbrated in Mises's 1912 work on monetary theory (translated in 1934 as *The Theory of Money and Credit*).

It should be noted that only the footnotes to which the initials LvM are appended are from the original. All other notes are by the editor of the book cited above (Percy L. Greaves, Jr) and/or the translator. Occasionally these latter notes contain cross-references to papers in the book, other than the paper presented here. Where notes cite MME, the refererence is to Percy L. Greaves, Jr, *Mises Made Easy: A Glossary for Ludwig von Mises' Human Action* (Dobbs Ferry, N.Y.: Free Market Books, 1974).

33 -

not on
Econt

23

Monetary Stabilization and Cyclical Policy

LUDWIG von MISES

Preface

In recent years the problems of monetary and banking policy have been approached more and more with a view to both stabilizing the value of the monetary unit and eliminating fluctuations in the economy. Thanks to serious attempts at explaining and publicizing these most difficult economic problems, they have become familiar to almost everyone. It may perhaps be appropriate to speak of fashions in economics, and it is undoubtedly the 'fashion' today to establish institutions for the study of business trends.

This has certain advantages. Careful attention to these problems has eliminated some of the conflicting doctrines which had handicapped economics. There is only one theory of monetary value today – the Quantity Theory. There is also only one trade cycle theory – the Circulation Credit Theory, developed out of the Currency Theory and usually called the 'Monetary Theory of the Trade Cycle.'[1] These theories, of course, are no longer what they were in the days of Ricardo and Lord Overstone. They have been revised and made consistent with modern subjective economics. Yet the basic principle remains the same. The underlying thesis has merely been elaborated upon. So despite all its defects, which are now recognized, due credit should be given the Currency School for its achievement.

In this connection, just as in all other aspects of economics, it becomes apparent that scientific development goes steadily forward. Every single step in the development of a doctrine is necessary. No intellectual effort applied to these problems is in vain. A continuous, unbroken line of

33

scientific progress runs from the Classical authors down to the modern writers. The accomplishment of Gossen, Menger, Walras and Jevons, in overcoming the apparent antinomy of value during the third quarter of the last century, permits us to divide the history of economics into two large subdivisions – the Classical,[2] and the Modern or Subjective.[3] Still it should be remembered that the contributions of the Classical School have not lost all value. They live in modern science and continue to be effective.

Whenever an economic problem is to be seriously considered, it is necessary to expose the violent rejection of economics which is carried on everywhere for political reasons, especially on German soil. Nothing concerning the problems involved in either the creation of the purchasing power of money or economic fluctuations can be learned from Historicism or Nominalism.[4] Adherents of the Historical-Empirical-Realistic School and of Institutionalism[5] either say nothing at all about these problems, or else they depend on the very same methodological and theoretical grounds which they otherwise oppose. The Banking Theory, until very recently certainly the leading doctrine, at least in Germany, has been justifiably rejected. Hardly anyone who wishes to be taken seriously dares to set forth the doctrine of the elasticity of the circulation of fiduciary media – its principal thesis and cornerstone.[6]

However, the popularity attained by the two political problems of stabilization – the value of the monetary unit and fiduciary media – also brings with it serious disadvantages. The popularization of a theory always contains a threat of distorting it, if not of actually demolishing its very essence. Thus the results expected of measures proposed for stabilizing the value of the monetary unit and eliminating business fluctuations have been very much overrated. This danger, especially in Germany, should not be underestimated. During the last ten years, the systematic neglect of the problems of economic theory has meant that no attention has been paid to accomplishments abroad. Nor has any benefit been derived from the experiences of other countries.

The fact is ignored that proposals for the creation of a monetary unit with 'stable value' have already had a hundred year history. Also ignored is the fact that an attempt to eliminate economic crises was made more than eighty years ago – in England – through Peel's Bank Act (1844). It is not necessary to put all these proposals into practice to see their inherent difficulties. However, it is simply inexcusable that so little attention has been given during recent generations to the understanding gained, or which might have been gained if men had not been so blind, concerning monetary policy and fiduciary media.

Current proposals for a monetary unit of 'stable value' and for a non-fluctuating economy are, without doubt, more refined than were the first attempts of this kind. They take into consideration many of the less important objections raised against earlier projects. However, the basic shortcomings, which are necessarily inherent in all such schemes, cannot be overcome. As a result, the high hopes for the proposed reforms must be frustrated.

If we are to clarify the possible significance – for economic science, public policy and individual action – of the cyclical studies and price statistics so widely and avidly pursued today, they must be thoroughly and critically analyzed. This can, by no means, be limited to considering cyclical changes only. 'A theory of crises,' as Böhm-Bawerk said, 'can never be an inquiry into just one single phase of economic phenomena. If it is be to more than an amateurish absurdity, such an inquiry must be the last, or the next last, chapter of a written or unwritten economic system. In other words, it is the final fruit of knowledge of all economic events and their interconnected relationships.'[7]

Only on the basis of a comprehensive theory of indirect exchange, i.e., a theory of money and banking, can a trade cycle theory be erected. This is still frequently ignored. Cyclical theories are carelessly drawn up and cyclical policies are even more carelessly put into operation. Many a person believes himself competent to pass judgment, orally and in writing, on the problem of the formulation of monetary value and the rate of interest. If given the opportunity – as legislator or manager of a country's monetary and banking policy – he feels called upon to enact radical measures without having any clear idea of their consequences. Yet, nowhere is more foresight and caution necessary than precisely in this area of economic knowledge and policy. For the superficiality and carelessness, with which social problems are wont to be handled, soon misfire if applied in this field. Only by serious thought, directed at understanding the interrelationship of all market phenomena, can the problems we face here be satisfactorily solved.

PART I

Stabilization of the purchasing power
of the monetary unit

I. *The Problem*

1. *'Stable Value' Money*

Gold and silver had already served mankind for thousands of years as generally accepted media of exchange – that is, as money – before there was any clear idea of the formation of the exchange relationship between these metals and consumers' goods, i.e., before there was an understanding as to how money prices for goods and services are formed. At best, some attention was given to fluctuations in the mutual exchange relationships of the two precious metals. But so little understanding was achieved that men clung, without hesitation, to the naive belief that the precious metals were 'stable in value' and hence a useful measure of the value of goods and prices. Only much later did the recognition come that supply and demand determine the exchange relationship between money, on the one hand, and consumers' goods and services, on the other. With this realization, the first versions of the Quantity Theory, still somewhat imperfect and vulnerable, were formulated. It was known that violent changes in the volume of production of the monetary metals led to all-round shifts in money prices. When 'paper money' was used alongside 'hard money,' this connection was still easier to see. The consequences of a tremendous paper inflation could not be mistaken.

From this insight, the doctrine of monetary policy emerged that the issue of 'paper money' should be avoided completely. However, before long other authors made still further stipulations. They called the attention of politicians and businessmen to the fluctuations in the purchasing power of the precious metals and proposed that the substance of monetary claims be made independent of these variations. Side by side with money as the standard of deferred payments,[8] or in place of it, there should be a tabular, index, or multiple commodity standard. Cash transactions, in which the terms of both sides of the contract are fulfilled simultaneously,

37

would not be altered. However, a new procedure would be introduced for credit transactions. Such transactions would not be completed in the sum of money indicated in the contract. Instead, either by means of a universally compulsory legal regulation or else by specific agreement of the two parties concerned, they would be fulfilled by a sum with the purchasing power deemed to correspond to that of the original sum at the time the contract was made. The intent of this proposal was to prevent one party to a contract from being hurt to the other's advantage. These proposals were made more than one hundred years ago by Joseph Lowe (1822) and repeated shortly thereafter by G. Poulett Scrope (1833).[9] Since then, they have cropped up repeatedly but without any attempt having been made to put them into practice anywhere.

2. Recent Proposals

One of the proposals, for a multiple commodity standard, was intended simply to supplement the precious metals standard. Putting it into practice would have left metallic money as a universally acceptable medium of exchange for all transactions not involving deferred monetary payments. (For the sake of simplicity in the discussion that follows, when referring to metallic money we shall speak only of gold.) Side by side with gold as the universally acceptable medium of exchange, the index or multiple commodity standard would appear as a standard of deferred payments.

Proposals have been made in recent years, however, which go still farther. These would introduce a 'tabular,' or 'multiple commodity,' standard for *all* exchanges when one commodity is not exchanged directly for another. This is essentially Keynes' proposal. Keynes wants to oust gold from its position as money. He wants gold to be replaced by a paper standard, at least for trade within a country's borders. The government, or the authority entrusted by the government with the management of monetary policy, should regulate the quantity in circulation so that the purchasing power of the monetary unit would remain unchanged.[10]

The American, Irving Fisher, wants to create a standard under which the paper dollar in circulation would be redeemable, not in a previously specified weight of gold, but in a weight of gold which has the same purchasing power the dollar had at the moment of the transition to the new currency system. The dollar would then cease to represent a fixed amount of gold with changing purchasing power and would become a changing amount of gold supposedly with unchanging purchasing power. It was Fisher's idea that the amount of gold which would correspond to a dollar should be determined anew from month to month, according to variations detected by the index number.[11] Thus, in the view of both these reformers, in place of monetary gold, the value of which is independent of the influence of government, a standard should be adopted which the government 'manipulates' in an attempt to hold the purchasing power of the monetary unit stable.

However, these proposals have not as yet been put into practice anywhere, although they have been given a great deal of careful consideration. Perhaps no other economic question is debated with so much ardour or so much spirit and ingenuity in the United States, as that of stabilizing the purchasing power of the monetary unit. Members of the House of Representatives have dealt with the problem in detail. Many scientific works are concerned with it. Magazines and daily papers devote lengthy essays and articles to it, while important organizations seek to influence public opinion in favour of carrying out Fisher's ideas.

II. *The Gold Standard*

1. *The Demand for Money*
Under the gold standard, the formation of the value of the monetary unit is not *directly* subject to the action of the government. The production of gold is free and responds only to the opportunity for profit. All gold not introduced into trade for consumption or for some other purpose flows into the economy as money, either as coins in circulation or as bars or coins in bank reserves. Should the increase in the quantity of money exceed the increase in the demand for money, then the purchasing power of the monetary unit must fall. Likewise, if the increase in the quantity of money lags behind the increase in the demand for money, the purchasing power of the monetary unit will rise.[12]

There is no doubt about the fact that, in the last generation, the purchasing power of gold has declined. Yet earlier, during the two decades following the German monetary reform and the great economic crisis of 1873, there was widespread complaint over the decline of commodity prices. Governments consulted experts for advice on how to eliminate this generally prevailing 'evil.' Powerful political parties recommended measures for pushing prices up by increasing the quantity of money. In place of the gold standard, they advocated the silver standard, the double standard [bimetallism] or even a paper standard, for they considered the annual production of gold too small to meet the growing demand for money without increasing the purchasing power of the monetary unit. However, these complaints died out in the last five years of the 19th century, and soon men everywhere began to grumble about the opposite situation, i.e., the increasing cost of living. Just as they had proposed monetary reforms in the 1880s and 1890s to counteract the *drop* in prices, they *now* suggested measures to stop prices from rising.

The general advance of the prices of all goods and services in terms of gold is due to the state of gold production and the demand for gold, both for use as money as well as for other purposes. There is little to say about the production of gold and its influence on the ratio of the value of gold to that of other commodities. It is obvious that a small increase in the available quantity of gold might have counteracted the depreciation of gold. Nor need anything special be said about the industrial uses of gold. But the third factor involved, the way demand is created for gold as money, is quite another matter. Very careful attention should be devoted to this problem, especially as the customary analysis ignores most unfairly this monetary demand for gold.

During the period for which we are considering the development of the purchasing power of gold, various parts of the world, which formerly used silver or credit money ('paper money') domestically, have changed over to the gold standard. Everywhere, the volume of money transactions has increased considerably. The division of labour has made great progress. Economic self-sufficiency and barter have declined. Monetary exchanges now play a role in phases of economic life where earlier they were completely unknown. The result has been a decided increase in the demand for money. There is no point in asking whether this increase in the demand for cash holdings by individuals, together with the demand for gold for non-monetary uses, was sufficient to counteract the effect on prices of the new gold flowing into the market from production. Statistics on the height and fluctuations of cash holdings are not available. Even if they could be known, they would tell us little because the changes in prices do not correspond with changes in the relationship between supply and demand for cash holdings. Of greater importance, however, is the observation that the increase in the demand for money is not the same thing as an increase in the demand for gold for monetary purposes.

As far as the individual's cash holding is concerned, claims payable in money, which may be redeemed at any time and are universally considered safe, perform the service of money. These money substitutes – small coins, banknotes and bank deposits subject to check or similar payment on demand (checking accounts) – may be used just like money itself for the settlement of all transactions. Only a part of these money substitutes, however, is fully covered by stocks of gold on deposit in the banks' reserves. In the decades of which we speak, the use of money substitutes has increased considerably more than has the rise in demand for money and, at the same time, its reserve ratio has worsened. As a result, in spite of an appreciable increase in the demand for money, the demand for gold has not risen enough for the market to absorb the new quantities of gold flowing from production without lowering its purchasing power.

2. Economizing on Money

If one complains of the decline in the purchasing power of gold today, and contemplates the creation of a monetary unit whose purchasing power shall be more constant than that of gold in recent decades, it should not be forgotten that the principal cause of the decline in the value of gold during this period is to be found in monetary policy and not in gold production itself. Money substitutes not covered by gold, which we call fiduciary media, occupy a relatively more important position today in the world's total quantity of money[13] than in earlier years. But this is not a development which would have taken place without the cooperation, or even without the express support, of governmental monetary policies. As a matter of fact, it was monetary policy itself which was deliberately aimed at a 'saving' of gold and, which created, thereby, the conditions that led inevitably to the depreciation of gold.

The fact that we use as money a commodity like gold, which is produced only with a considerable expenditure of capital and labour, saddles mankind with certain costs. If the amount of capital and labour spent for the production of monetary gold could be released and used in other ways, people could be better supplied with goods for their immediate needs. There is no doubt about that! However, it should be noted that, in return for this expenditure, we receive the advantage of having available, for settling transactions, a money with a relatively steady value and, what is more important, the value of which is not directly influenced by governments and political parties. However, it is easy to understand why men began to ponder the possibility of creating a monetary system that would combine all the advantages offered by the gold standard with the added virtue of lower costs.

Adam Smith drew a parallel between the gold and silver which circulated in a land as money and a highway on which nothing grew, but over which fodder and grain were brought to market. The substitution of notes for the precious metals would create, so to speak, a 'waggon-way through the air,' making it possible to convert a large part of the roads into fields and pastures and, thus, to increase considerably the yearly output of the economy. Then in 1816, Ricardo devised his famous plan for a gold exchange standard. According to his proposal, England should retain the gold standard, which had proved its value in every respect. However, gold coins should be replaced in domestic trade by banknotes, and these notes should be redeemable, not in gold coins, but in bullion only. Thus the

41

notes would be assured of a value equivalent to that of gold and the country would have the advantage of possessing a monetary standard with all the attributes of the gold standard but at a lower cost.

Ricardo's proposals were not put into effect for decades. As a matter of fact, they were even forgotten. Nevertheless, the gold exchange standard was adopted by a number of countries during the 1890s – in the beginning usually as a temporary expedient only, without intending to direct monetary policy on to a new course. Today it is so widespread that we would be fully justified in describing it as 'the monetary standard of our age.'[14] However, in a majority, or at least in quite a number of these countries, the gold exchange standard has undergone a development which entitles it to be spoken of rather as a flexible gold exchange standard.[15] Under Ricardo's plan, savings would be realized not only by avoiding the costs of coinage and the loss from wearing coins thin in use, but also because the amount of gold required for circulation and bank reserves would be less than under the 'pure' gold standard.

Carrying out this plan in a single country must obviously, *ceteris paribus*, reduce the purchasing power of gold. And the more widely the system was adopted, the more must the purchasing power of gold decline. If a single land adopts the gold exchange standard, while others maintain a 'pure' gold standard, then the gold exchange standard country can gain an immediate advantage over costs in the other areas. The gold, which is surplus under the gold exchange standard as compared with the gold which would have been called for under the 'pure' gold standard, may be spent abroad for other commodities. These additional commodities represent an improvement in the country's welfare as a result of introducing the gold exchange standard. The gold exchange standard renders all the services of the gold standard to this country and also brings an additional advantage in the form of this increase of goods.

However, should every country in the world shift at the same time from the 'pure' gold standard to a similar gold exchange standard, no gain of this kind would be possible. The distribution of gold throughout the world would remain unchanged. There would be no country where one could exchange a quantity of gold, made superfluous by the adoption of the new monetary system, for other goods. Embracing the new standard would result only in a universally more severe reduction in the purchasing power of gold. This monetary depreciation, like every change in the value of money, would bring about dislocations in the relationships of wealth and income of the various individuals in the economy. As a result, it could also lead indirectly, under certain circumstances, to an increase in capital accumulation. However, this indirect method will make the world richer only insofar as (1) the demand for gold for other uses (industrial and similar purposes) can be better satisfied and (2) a decline in profitability leads to a restriction of gold production and so releases capital and labour for other purposes.

3. Interest on 'Idle' Reserves

In addition to these attempts toward 'economy' in the operation of the gold standard, by reducing the domestic demand for gold, other efforts have also aimed at the same objective. Holding gold reserves is costly to the banks of issue because of the loss of interest. Consequently, it was but a short step to the reduction of these costs by permitting non-interest bearing gold reserves in bank vaults to be replaced by interest-bearing credit balances abroad, payable in gold on demand, and by bills of exchange payable in gold. Assets of this type enable the banks of issue to satisfy demands for gold in foreign trade just as the possession of a stock of gold coins and bars would. As a matter of fact, the dealer in arbitrage who presents notes for redemption will prefer payment in the form of cheques, and bills of exchange – foreign financial paper – to redemption in gold because the costs of shipping foreign financial papers are lower than those for the transport of gold. The banks of smaller and poorer lands especially converted a part of their reserves into foreign bills of exchange. The inducement was particularly strong in countries on the gold exchange standard, where the banks did not have to consider a demand for gold for use in domestic circulation. In this way, the gold exchange standard [Goldkernwährung] became the flexible gold exchange standard [Golddevisenkernwährung], i.e., the flexible standard. [See note 15 at the end of this paper.].

Nevertheless, the goal of this policy was not only to reduce the costs involved in the maintenance and circulation of an actual stock of gold. In many countries, including Germany and Austria, this was thought to be a way to reduce the rate of interest. The influence of the Currency Theory had led, decades earlier, to banking legislation intended to avoid the consequences of a paper money inflation. These laws, limiting the issue of banknotes not covered by gold, were still in force. Reared in the Historical-Realistic School of economic thinking, the new generation, insofar as it dealt with these problems, was under the spell of the Banking Theory, and thus no longer understood the meaning of these laws.

Lack of originality prevented the new generation from embarking upon any startling reversal in policy. In line with currently prevailing opinion, it abolished the limitation on the issue of banknotes not covered by metal. The old laws were allowed to stay on the books essentially unchanged. However, various attempts were made to reduce their effect. The most noteworthy of these measures was to encourage, systematically and purposefully, the settlement of transactions without the use of cash. By supplanting cash transactions with cheques and other transfer payments, it was expected not only that there would be a reduction in the demand for banknotes but also a flow of gold coins back to the bank and, consequently, a strengthening of the bank's cash position. As German, and also Austrian, banking legislation prescribed a certain percentage of gold cover for notes issued, gold flowing back to the bank meant that more notes could be issued – up to three times their gold value in Germany and two and a half times in Austria. During recent decades, the banking theory has been characterized by a belief that this should result in a reduction in the rate of interest.

4. Gold Still Money

If we glance, even briefly, at the efforts of monetary and banking policy, in recent years, it becomes obvious that the depreciation of gold may be traced in large part to political measures. The decline in the purchasing power of gold and the continual increase in the gold price of all goods and services were not natural phenomena. They were consequences of an economic policy which aimed, to be sure, at other objectives, but which necessarily led to these results. As has already been mentioned, accurate quantitative observations about these matters can never be made. Nevertheless, it is obvious that the increase in gold production has certainly not been the cause, or at least not the only cause, of the depreciation of gold that has been observed since 1896. The policy directed toward displacing gold in actual circulation, which aimed at substituting the gold exchange standard and the flexible standard for the older 'pure' gold standard, forced the value of gold down or at least helped to depress it. Perhaps, if this policy had not been followed, we would hear complaints today over the increase, rather than the depreciation, in the value of gold.

Gold has not been demonetized by the new monetary policy, as silver was a short time ago, for it remains the basis of our entire monetary system. Gold is still, as it was formerly, our money. There is no basis for saying that it has been de-throned, as suggested by scatterbrained innovators of catchwords and slogans who want to cure the world of the 'money illusion.' Nevertheless, gold has been removed from actual use in transactions by the public at large. It has disappeared from view and has been concentrated in bank vaults and monetary reserves. Gold has been taken out of common use and this must necessarily tend to lower its value.

It is wrong to point to the general price increases of recent years to illustrate the inadequacy of the gold standard. It is not the old style gold standard, as recommended by advocates of the gold standard in England and Germany, which has given us a monetary system that has led to rising prices in recent years. Rather these price increases have been the results of monetary and banking policies which permitted the 'pure' or 'classical' gold standard to be replaced by the gold exchange and flexible standards, leaving in circulation only notes and small coins and concentrating the gold stocks in bank and currency reserves.

III. *'The Manipulation'* of the Gold Standard

1. Monetary Policy and Purchasing Power of Gold
Most important for the old, 'pure,' or classical gold standard, as originally formulated in England and later, after the formation of the Empire, adopted in Germany, was the fact that it made the formation of prices independent of political influence and the shifting views which sway political action. This feature especially recommended the gold standard to liberals[16] who feared that economic productivity might be impaired as a result of the tendency of governments to favour certain groups of persons at the expense of others.

However, it should certainly not be forgotten that under the 'pure' gold standard governmental measures may also have a significant influence on the formation of the value of gold. In the first place, governmental actions determine whether to adopt the gold standard, abandon it, or return to it. However, the effect of these governmental actions, which we need not consider any further here is conceived as very different from those described by the various 'state theories of money' – theories which, now at long last, are generally recognized as absurd. The continual displacement of the silver standard by the gold standard and the shift in some countries from credit money to gold added to the demand for monetary gold in the years before the World War [1914–1918]. War measures resulted in monetary policies that led the belligerent nations, as well as some neutral states, to release large parts of their gold reserves, thus releasing more gold for world markets. Every political act in this area, insofar as it affects the demand for, and the quantity of, gold as money, represents a 'manipulation' of the gold standard and affects all countries adhering to the gold standard.

Just as the 'pure' gold, the gold exchange and the flexible standards do not differ in principle, but only in the degree to which money substitutes are actually used in circulation, so is there no basic difference in their susceptibility to manipulation. The 'pure' gold standard is subject to the influence of monetary measures – on the one hand, insofar as monetary policy may affect the acceptance or rejection of the gold standard in a political area and, on the other hand, insofar as monetary policy, while still clinging to the gold standard in principle, may bring about changes in the demand for gold through an increase or decrease in actual gold circulation or by changes in reserve requirements for banknotes and checking accounts. The influence of monetary policy on the formation of the value [i.e., the purchasing power] of gold also extends just that far and no farther under the gold exchange and flexible standards. Here again, governments and those agencies responsible for monetary policy can influence the formation of the value of gold by changing the course of monetary policy. The extent of this influence depends on how large the increase or decrease in the demand for gold is nationally, in relation to the total world demand for gold.

If advocates of the old 'pure' gold standard spoke of the independence of the value of gold from governmental influences, they meant that once the gold standard had been adopted everywhere (and gold standard advocates of the last three decades of the 19th century had not the slightest doubt that this would soon come to pass, for the gold standard had already been almost universally accepted) no further political action would affect the formation of monetary value. This would be equally true for both the gold exchange and flexible standards. It would by no means disturb the logical assumptions of the perceptive 'pure' gold standard advocate to say that the value of gold would be considerably affected by a change in United States Federal Reserve Board policy, such as the resumption of the circulation of gold or the retention of larger gold reserves in European countries. In this sense, all monetary standards may be 'manipulated' under today's economic conditions. The advantage of the gold standard – whether 'pure' or 'gold exchange' – is due solely to the fact that, if once generally adopted in a definite form, and adhered to, it is no longer subject to specific political interferences.

War and postwar actions, with respect to monetary policy, have radically changed the monetary situation throughout the entire world. One by one, individual countries are now [1928] reverting to a gold basis and it is likely that this process will soon be completed. Now, this leads to a second problem: Should the exchange standard, which generally prevails today, be retained? Or should a return be made once more to the actual use of gold in moderate-sized transactions as before under the 'pure' gold standard? Also, if it is decided to remain on the exchange standard, should reserves actually be maintained in gold? And at what height? Or could individual countries be satisfied with reserves of foreign exchange payable in gold? (Obviously, the flexible standard cannot become entirely universal. At least one country must continue to invest its reserves in real gold, even if it does not use gold in actual circulation.) Only if the state of affairs prevailing at a given instant in every single area is maintained and, also, only if matters are left just as they are, including of course the ratio of bank reserves, can it be said that the gold standard cannot be manipulated in the manner described above. If these problems are dealt with in such a way as to change markedly the demand for gold for monetary purposes, then the purchasing power of gold must undergo corresponding changes.

To repeat for the sake of clarity, this represents no essential disagreement with the advocates of the gold standard as to what they considered its special superiority. Changes in the monetary system of any large and wealthy land will necessarily influence substantially the creation of monetary value. Once these changes have been carried out and have worked their effect on the purchasing power of gold, the value of money will necessarily be affected again by a return to the previous monetary system. However, this detracts in no way from the truth of the statement that the creation of value under the gold standard is independent of politics, so long as no essential changes are made in its structure, nor in the size of the area where it prevails.

2. Changes in Purchasing Power of Gold

Irving Fisher, as well as many others, criticize the gold standard because the purchasing power of gold has declined considerably since 1896, and especially since 1914. In order to avoid misunderstanding, it should be pointed out that this drop in the purchasing power of gold must be traced back to monetary policy – monetary policy which fostered the reduction in the purchasing power of gold through measures adopted between 1896 and 1914, to 'economize' gold and, since 1914, through the rejection of gold as the basis for money in many countries. If others denounce the gold standard because the imminent return to the actual use of gold in circulation and the strengthening of gold reserves in countries on the exchange standard would bring about an increase in the purchasing power of gold, then it becomes obvious that we are dealing with the consequences of political changes in monetary policy which transform the structure of the gold standard.

The purchasing power of gold is not 'stable.' It should be pointed out that there is no such thing as 'stable' purchasing power, and never can be. The concept of 'stable value' is vague and indistinct. Strictly speaking, only an economy in the final state of rest – where all prices remain unchanged – could have a money with fixed purchasing power. However, it is a fact which no one can dispute that the gold standard, once generally adopted and adhered to without changes, makes the formation of the purchasing power of gold independent of the operations of shifting political efforts.

As gold is obtained only from a few sources, which sooner or later will be exhausted, the fear is repeatedly expressed that there may someday be a scarcity of gold and, as a consequence, a continuing decline in commodity prices. Such fears became especially great in the late 1870s and the 1880s. Then they quieted down. Only in recent years have they been revived again. Calculations are made indicating that the placers and mines currently being worked will be exhausted within the foreseeable future. No prospects are seen that any new rich sources of gold will be opened up. Should the demand for money increase in the future, to the same extent as it has in the recent past, then a general price drop appears inevitable, if we remain on the gold standard.[17]

Now one must be very cautious with forecasts of this kind. A half century ago, Eduard Suess, the geologist, claimed – and he sought to establish this scientifically – that an unavoidable decline in gold production should be expected.[18] Facts very soon proved him wrong. And it may be that those who express similar ideas today will also be refuted just as quickly and just as thoroughly. Still we must agree that they are right in the final analysis, that prices are tending to fall [1928] and that all the social consequences of an increase in purchasing power are making their appearance. What may be ventured, given the circumstances, in order to change the economic pessimism, will be discussed at the end of the second part of this study.

IV. 'Measuring' Changes in the Purchasing Power of The Monetary Unit

1. Imaginary Constructions

All proposals to replace the commodity money, gold, with a money thought to be better, because it is more 'stable' in value, are based on the vague idea that changes in purchasing power can somehow be measured. Only by starting from such an assumption is it possible to conceive of a monetary unit with unchanging purchasing power as the ideal and to consider seeking ways to reach this goal. These proposals, vague and basically contradictory, are derived from the old, long since exploded, objective theory of value. Yet they are not even completely consistent with that theory. They now appear very much out of place in the company of modern subjective economics.

The prestige which they still enjoy can be explained only by the fact that, until very recently, studies in subjective economics have been restricted to the theory of direct exchange (barter). Only later have such studies been expanded to include also the theory of intermediate (indirect) exchange, i.e., the theory of a generally accepted medium of exchange (monetary theory) and the theory of fiduciary media (banking theory) with all their relevant problems.[19] It is certainly high time to expose conclusively the errors and defects of the basic concept that purchasing power can be measured.

Exchange ratios on the market are constantly subject to change. If we imagine a market where no generally accepted medium of exchange, i.e., no money, is used, it is easy to recognize how nonsensical the idea is of trying to measure the changes taking place in exchange ratios. It is only if we resort to the fiction of completely stationary exchange ratios among all commodities, other than money, and then compare these other commodities with money, that we can envisage exchange relationships between money and each of the other individual exchange commodities changing uniformly. Only then can we speak of a uniform increase or decrease in the monetary price of all commodities and of a uniform rise or fall of the 'price level.' Still, we must not forget that this concept is pure fiction, what Vaihinger termed an 'as if.'[20] It is a deliberate imaginary construction, indispensable for scientific thinking.

Perhaps the necessity for this imaginary construction will become somewhat more clear if we express it, not in terms of the objective exchange value of the market, but in terms of the subjective exchange valuation of the acting individual. To do that, we must imagine an unchanging man with never-changing values. Such an individual could determine, from his never-changing scale of values, the purchasing power of money. He could say precisely how the quantity of money, which he must spend to attain a certain amount of satisfaction, had changed. Nevertheless, the idea of a definite structure of prices, a 'price level,' which is raised or lowered uniformly, is just as fictitious as this. However, it enables us to recognize clearly that every change in the exchange ratio between a commodity, on the one side, and money, on the other, must necessarily lead to shifts in the disposition of wealth and income among acting individuals. Thus, each such change acts as a dynamic agent also. In view of this situation, therefore, it is not permissible to make such an assumption as a uniformly changing 'level' of prices.

This imaginary construction is necessary, however, to explain that the exchange ratios of the various economic goods may undergo a change from the side of one individual commodity. This fictional concept is the *ceteris paribus* of the theory of exchange relationships. It is just as fictitious and, at the same time, just as indispensable as any *ceteris paribus*. If extraordinary circumstances lead to exceptionally large and hence conspicuous changes in exchange ratios, data on market phenomena may help to facilitate sound thinking on these problems. However, then even more than ever, if we want to see the situation at all clearly, we must resort to the imaginary construction necessary for an understanding of our theory.

The expressions, 'inflation' and 'deflation,' scarcely known in German economic literature several years ago, are in daily use today. In spite of their inexactness, they are undoubtedly suitable for general use in public discussions of economic and political problems.[21] But in order to understand them precisely, one must elaborate with rigid logic that fictional concept [the imaginary construction of completely stationary exchange ratios among all commodities other than money], the falsity of which is clearly recognized.

Among the significant services performed by this fiction is that it enables us to distinguish and determine whether changes in exchange relationships between money and other commodities arise on the money side or the commodity side. In order to understand the changes which take place constantly on the market, this distinction is urgently needed. It is still more indispensable for judging the significance of measures proposed or adopted in the field of monetary and banking policy. Even in these cases, however, we can never succeed in constructing a fictional representation that coincides with the situation which actually appears on the market. The imaginary construction makes it easier to understand reality, but we must remain conscious of the distinction between fiction and reality.[22]

2. Index Numbers

Attempts have been made to measure changes in the purchasing power of money by using data derived from changes in the money prices of individual economic goods. These attempts rest on the theory that, in a carefully selected index of a large number, or of all, consumers' goods, influences from the commodity side affecting commodity prices cancel each other out. Thus, so the theory goes, the direction and extent of the influence on prices and factors arising on the money side may be discovered from such an index. Essentially, therefore, by computing an arithmetical mean, this method seeks to convert the price changes emerging among the various consumers' goods into a figure which may then be considered an index to the change in the value of money. In this discussion, we shall disregard the practical difficulties which arise in assembling the price quotations necessary to serve as the basis for such calculations and restrict ourselves to commenting on the fundamental usefulness of this method for the solution of our problem.

First of all it should be noted that there are various arithmetical means. Which one should be selected? That is an old question. Reasons may be advanced for, and objections raised against, each. From our point of view, the only important thing to be learned in such a debate is that the question cannot be settled conclusively so that everyone will accept any single answer as 'right.'

The other fundamental question concerns the relative importance of the various consumer goods. In developing the index, if the price of each and every commodity is considered as having the same weight, a 50% increase in the price of bread, for instance, would be offset in calculating the arithmetical average by a drop of one-half in the price of diamonds. The index would then indicate no change in purchasing power, or 'price level.' As such a conclusion is obviously preposterous, attempts are made in fabricating index numbers, to use the prices of various commodities according to their relative importance. Prices should be included in the calculations according to the coefficient of their importance. The result is then known as a 'weighted' average.

This brings us to the second arbitrary decision necessary for developing such an index. What is 'importance'? Several different approaches have been tried and arguments pro and con each have been raised. Obviously, a clear-cut, all-round satisfactory solution to the problem cannot be found. Special attention has been given the difficulty arising from the fact that, if the usual method is followed, the very circumstances involved in determining 'importance' are constantly in flux; thus the coefficient of importance itself is also continuously changing.

As soon as one starts to take into consideration the 'importance' of the various goods, one forsakes the assumption of objective exchange value – which often leads to nonsensical conclusions as pointed out above – and enters the area of subjective values. Since there is no generally recognized immutable 'importance' to various goods, since, 'subjective' value has meaning only from the point of view of the acting individual, further reflection leads eventually to the subjective method already discussed – namely the inexcusable fiction of a never-changing man with never-changing values. To avoid arriving at this conclusion, which is also obviously absurd, one remains indecisively on the fence, midway between two equally nonsensical methods – on the one side the un-weighted average and on the other the fiction of a never-changing individual with never-changing values. Yet one believes he has discovered something useful. Truth is not the halfway point between two untruths. The fact that each of these two methods, if followed to its logical conclusion, is shown to be preposterous, in no way proves that a combination of the two is the correct one.

All index computations pass quickly over these unanswerable objections. The calculations are made with whatever coefficients of importance are selected. However, we have established that even the problem of

51

determining 'importance' is not capable of solution, with certainty, in such a way as to be recognized by everyone as 'right.'

Thus the idea that changes in the purchasing power of money may be measured is scientifically untenable. This will come as no surprise to anyone who is acquainted with the fundamental problems of modern subjectivistic catallactics and has recognized the significance of recent studies with respect to the measurement of value[23] and the meaning of monetary calculation.[24]

One can certainly try to devise index numbers. Nowadays nothing is more popular among statisticians than this. Nevertheless, all these computations rest on a shaky foundation. Disregarding entirely the difficulties which, from time to time, even thwart agreement as to the commodities whose prices will form the bases of these calculations, these computations are arbitrary in two ways – first, with respect to the arithmetical mean chosen and, secondly, with respect to the coefficient of importance selected. There is no way to characterize one of the many possible methods as the only 'correct' one and the others as 'false.' Each is equally legitimate or illegitimate. None is scientifically meaningful.

It is small consolation to point out that the results of the various methods do not differ substantially from one another. Even if that is the case, it cannot in the least affect the conclusions we must draw from the observations we have made. The fact that people can conceive of such a scheme at all, that they are not more critical, may be explained only by the eventuality of the great inflations, especially the greatest and most recent one.[25]

Any index method is good enough to make a rough statement about the extremely severe depreciation of the value of a monetary unit, such as that wrought in the German inflation. There, the index served an instructional task, enlightening a people who were inclined to the 'State Theory of Money' idea. Nevertheless, a method that helps to open the eyes of the people is not necessarily either scientifically correct or applicable in actual practice.

V. *Fisher's Stabilization Plan*

1. *Political Problem*

The superiority of the gold standard consists in the fact that the value of gold develops independent of political actions. It is clear that its value is not 'stable.' There is not, and never can be, any such thing as stability of value. If, under a 'manipulated' monetary standard, it was government's task to influence the value of money, the question of how this influence was to be exercised would soon become the main issue among political and economic interests. Government would be asked to influence the purchasing power of money so that certain politically powerful groups would be favoured by its intervention, at the expense of the rest of the population. Intense political battles would rage over the direction and scope of the edicts affecting monetary policy. At times, steps would be taken in one direction, and at other times in other directions – in response to the momentary balance of political power. The steady, progressive development of the economy would continually experience disturbances from the side of money. The result of the manipulation would be to provide us with a monetary system which would certainly not be any more stable than the gold standard.

If the decision were made to alter the purchasing power of money so that the index number always remained unchanged, the situation would not be any different. We have seen that there are many possible ways, not just one single way, to determine the index number. No single one of these methods can be considered the only correct one. Moreover, each leads to a different conclusion. Each political party would advocate the index method which promised results consistent with its political aims at the time. Since it is not scientifically possible to find one of the many mthods objectively right and to reject all others as false, no judge could decide impartially among groups disputing the correct method of calculation.

In addition, however, there is still one more very important consideration. The early proponents of the Quantity Theory believed that changes in the purchasing power of the monetary unit caused by a change in the quantity of money were exactly inversely proportional to one another. According to this Theory, a doubling of the quantity of money would cut the monetary unit's purchasing power in half. It is to the credit of the more recently developed monetary theory that this version of the Quantity Theory has been proved untenable. An increase in the quantity of money must, to be sure, lead *ceteris paribus* to a decline in the purchasing power of the monetary unit. Still the extent of this decrease in no way corresponds to the extent of the increase in the quantity of money. No fixed quantitative relationship can be established between the changes in the quantity of money and those of the unit's purchasing power.[26] Hence, every manipulation of the monetary standard will lead to serious difficulties. Political controversies would arise not only over the 'need' for a measure, but also over the degree of inflation or restriction, even after agreement had been reached on the purpose the measure was supposed to serve.

All this is sufficient to explain why proposals for establishing a manipulated standard have not been popular. It also explains – even if one disregards the way finance ministers have abused their authority – why credit money[27] (commonly known as 'paper money') is considered 'bad' money. Credit money is considered 'bad money' precisely because it may be manipulated.

2. Multiple Commodity Standard

Proposals that a multiple commodity standard replace, or supplement, monetary standards based on the precious metals – in their role as standards of deferred payments – are by no means intended to create a manipulated money. They are not intended to change the precious metals standard itself nor its effect on value. They seek merely to provide a way to free all transactions involving future monetary payments from the effect of changes in the value of the monetary unit. It is easy to understand why these proposals were not put into practice. Relying as they do on the shaky foundation of index number calculations, which cannot be scientifically established, they would not have produced a stable standard of value for deferred payments. They would only have created a different standard with different changes in value from those under the gold metallic standard.

To some extent Fisher's proposals parallel the early ideas of advocates of a multiple commodity standard. These forerunners also tried to eliminate only the influence of the social effects of changes in monetary value on the content of future monetary obligations. Like most Anglo-American students of this problem, as well as earlier advocates of a multiple commodity standard, Fisher took little notice of the fact that changes in the value of money have *other* social effects also.

Fisher, too, based his proposals entirely on index numbers. What seems to recommend *his* scheme, as compared with proposals for introducing a 'multiple standard,' is the fact that he does not use index numbers directly to determine changes in purchasing power over a long period of time. Rather he uses them primarily to understand changes taking place from month to month only. Many objections raised against the use of the index method for analyzing longer periods of time will perhaps appear less justified when considering only shorter periods. But there is no need to discuss this question here, for Fisher did *not* confine the application of his plan to short periods only. Also, even if adjustments are always made from month to month only, they were to be carried forward, on and on, until eventually calculations were being made, with the help of the index number, which extended over long periods of time. Because of the imperfection of the index number, these calculations would necessarily lead in time to errors of very considerable proportions.

3. Price Premium

Fisher's most important contribution to monetary theory is the emphasis he gave to the previously little noted effect of changes in the value of money on the formation of the interest rate.[28] Insofar as movements in the purchasing power of money can be foreseen, they find expression in the gross interest rate – not only as to the direction they will take but also as to their approximate magnitude. That portion of the gross interest rate which is demanded, and granted, in view of anticipated changes in purchasing power is known as the purchasing-power-change premium or price-change premium. In place of these clumsy expressions we shall use a shorter term – 'price premium.' Without any further explanation, this terminology leads to an understanding of the fact that, given an anticipation of general price increases, the price premium is 'positive,' thus raising the gross rate of interest. On the other hand, with an anticipation of general price *decreases*, the price premium becomes 'negative' and so reduces the gross interest rate.

The individual businessman is not generally aware of the fact that monetary value is affected by changes from the side of money. Even if he were, the difficulties, which hamper the formation of a halfway reliable judgment, as to the direction and extent of anticipated changes, are tremendous, if not outright insurmountable. Consequently, monetary units used in credit transactions are generally regarded rather naively as being 'stable' in value. So, with agreement as to conditions under which credit will be applied for and granted, a price premium is not generally considered in the calculation. This is practically always true, even for long-term credit. If opinion is shaken as to the 'stability of value' of a certain kind of money, this money is not used at all in long-term credit transactions. Thus, in all nations using credit money, whose purchasing power fluctuated violently, long-term credit obligations were drawn up in gold, whose value was held to be 'stable.'

However, because of obstinacy and pro-government bias, this course of action was not employed in Germany, nor in other countries during the recent inflation. Instead, the idea was conceived of making loans in terms of rye and potash. If there had been no hope at all of a later compensating revaluation of these loans, their price on the exchange in German marks, Austrian crowns and similarly inflated currencies would have been so high that a positive price premium corresponding to the magnitude of the anticipated further depreciation of these currencies would have been reflected in the actual interest payment.

The situation is different with respect to short-term credit transactions. Every businessman estimates the price changes anticipated in the immediate future and guides himself accordingly in making sales and purchases.

If he expects an increase in prices, he will make purchases and postpone sales. To secure the means for carrying out this plan, he will be ready to offer higher interest than otherwise. If he expects a drop in prices, then he will seek to sell and to refrain from purchasing. He will then be prepared to lend out, at a cheaper rate, the money made available as a result. Thus, the expectation of price increases leads to a positive price premium, that of price declines to a negative price premium.

To the extent that this process correctly anticipates the price movements that actually result, with respect to short-term credit, it cannot very well be maintained that the content of contractual obligations are transformed by the change in the purchasing power of money in a way which was neither foreseen nor contemplated by the parties concerned. Nor can it be maintained that, as a result, shifts take place in the wealth and income relationship between creditor and debtor. Consequently, it is unnecessary, so far as short-term credit is concerned, to look for a more perfect standard of deferred payments.

Thus we are in a position to see that Fisher's proposal actually offers no more than was offered by any previous plan for a multiple standard. In regard to the role of money as a standard of deferred payments, the verdict must be that, for long-term contracts, Fisher's scheme is inadequate. For short-term commitments, it is both inadequate and superfluous.

4. Changes in Wealth and Income

However, the social consequences of changes in the value of money are not limited to altering the content of future monetary obligations. In addition to these social effects, which are generally the only ones dealt with in Anglo-American literature, there are still others. Changes in money prices never reach all commodities at the same time, and they do not affect the prices of the various goods to the same extent. Shifts in relationships between the demand for, and the quantity of, money for cash holdings generated by changes in the value of money from the money side do not appear simultaneously and uniformly throughout the entire economy. They must necessarily appear on the market at some definite point, affecting only one group in the economy at first, influencing only *their* judgments of value in the beginning and, as a result, only the prices of commodities these particular persons are demanding. Only gradually does the change in the purchasing power of the monetary unit make its way throughout the entire economy.

For example, if the quantity of money increases, the additional new quantity of money must necessarily flow first of all into the hands of certain definite individuals – gold producers, for example, or, in the case of paper money inflation, the coffers of the government. It changes only *their* incomes and fortunes at first and, consequently, only *their* value judgments. Not all goods go up in price in the beginning, but only those goods which are demanded by these first beneficiaries of the inflation. Only later are prices of the remaining goods raised, as the increased quantity of money progresses step by step throughout the land and eventually reaches every participant in the economy.[29] But even then, when finally the upheaval of prices due to the new quantity of money has ended, the prices of all goods and services will not have increased to the same extent. Precisely because the price increases have not affected all commodities at one time, shifts in the relationships in wealth and income are effected which affect the supply and demand of individual goods and services differently. Thus, these shifts must lead to a new orientation of the market and of market prices.

Suppose we ignore the consequences of changes in the value of money on future monetary obligations. Suppose further that changes in the purchasing power of money occur simultaneously and uniformly with respect to all commodities in the entire economy. Then, it becomes obvious that changes in the value of money would produce no changes in the wealth of the individual entrepreneurs. Changes in the value of the monetary unit would then have no more significance for them than changes in weights and measures or in the calendar.

It is only because changes in the purchasing power of money never affect all commodities everywhere simultaneously that they bring with them (in addition to their influence on debt transactions) still other shifts in wealth and income. The groups which produce and sell the commodities that go up in price first are benefited by the inflation, for they realize higher profits in the beginning and yet they can still buy the commodities they need at lower prices, reflecting the previous stock of money. So during the inflation of the World War [1914–1918], the producers of war material and the workers in war industries, who received the output of the printing presses earlier than other groups of people, benefited from the monetary depreciation. At the same time, those whose incomes remained nominally the same suffered from the inflation, as they were forced to compete in making purchases with those receiving war inflated incomes. The situation became especially clear in the case of government employees. There was no mistaking the fact that they were losers. Salary increases came to them too late. For some time they had to pay prices, already affected by the increase in the quantity of money, with money incomes related to previous conditions.

5. Uncompensatable Changes

In the case of foreign trade, it was just as easy to see the consequences of the fact that price changes of the various commodities did not take place simultaneously. The deterioration in the value of the monetary unit encourages exports because a part of the raw materials, semi-produced factors of production and labour needed for the manufacture of export commodities, were procured at the old lower prices. At the same time the change in purchasing power, which for the time being has affected only a part of the domestically-produced commodities, has already had an influence on the rate of exchange on the Bourse. The result is that the exporter realizes a specific monetary gain.

The changes in purchasing power arising on the money side are considered disturbing not merely because of the transformation they bring about in the content of future monetary obligations. They are also upsetting because of the uneven timing of the price changes of the various goods and services. Can Fisher's dollar of 'stable value' eliminate *these* price changes?

In order to answer this question, it must be restated that Fisher's proposal does not eliminate changes in the value of the monetary unit. It attempts instead to compensate for these changes continuously – from month to month. Thus the consequences associated with the step-by-step emergence of changes in purchasing power are not eliminated. Rather they materialize during the course of the month. Then, when the correction is made at the end of the month the course of monetary depreciation is still not ended. The adjustment calculated at that time is based on the index number of the *previous* month when the full extent of that month's monetary depreciation had not then been felt because all prices had not yet been affected. However, the prices of goods for which demand was forced up first by the additional quantity of money undoubtedly reached heights that may not be maintained later.

Whether or not these two deviations in prices correspond in such a way that their effects cancel each other out will depend on the specific data in each individual case. Consequently, the monetary depreciation will continue in the following month, even if no further increase in the quantity of money were to appear in that month. It would continue to go on until the process finally ended with a general increase in commodity prices, in terms of gold, and thus with an increase in the value of the gold dollar on the basis of the index number. The social consequences of the uneven timing of price changes would, therefore, not be avoided because the unequal timing of the price changes of various commodities and services would not have been eliminated.[30]

So there is no need to go into more detail with respect to the technical difficulties that stand in the way of realizing Fisher's Plan. Even if it could be put into operation successfully, it would not provide us with a monetary system that would leave the disposition of wealth and income undisturbed.

VI. *Goods-Induced and Cash-Induced changes in the Purchasing Power of the Monetary Unit*

1. The Inherent Instability of Market Ratios

Changes in the exchange ratios between money and the various other commodities may originate either from the money side or from the commodity side of the transaction. Stabilization policy does not aim only at eliminating changes arising on the side of money. It also seeks to prevent all future price changes, even if this is not always clearly expressed and may sometimes be disputed.

It is not necessary for our purposes to go any further into the market phenomena which an increase or decrease in commodities must set in motion if the quantity of money remains unchanged.[31] It is sufficient to point out that, in addition to changes in the exchange ratios among individual commodities, shifts would also appear in the exchange ratios between money and the majority of the other commodities in the market. A decrease in the quantity of other commodities would weaken the purchasing power of the monetary unit. An increase would enhance it. It should be noted, however, that the social adjustments which must result from these changes in the quantity of other commodities will lead to a reorganization in the demand for money and hence cash holdings. These shifts can occur in such a way as to counteract the immediate effect of the change in the quantity of goods on the purchasing power of the monetary unit. Still for the time being, we may ignore this situation.

The goal of all stabilization proposals, as we have seen, is to maintain unchanged the original content of future monetary obligations. Creditors and debtors should neither gain nor lose in purchasing power. This is assumed to be 'just.' Of course, what is 'just' or 'unjust' cannot be scientifically determined. That is a question of ultimate purpose and ethical judgment. It is not a question of fact.

It is impossible to know just why the advocates of purchasing power stabilization see as 'just' only the maintenance of an unchanged purchasing power for *future* monetary obligations. However, it is easy to understand that they do not want to permit either debtor or creditor to gain or lose. They want contractual liabilities to continue in force as little altered as possible in the midst of the constantly changing world economy. They want to transplant contractual liabilities out of the flow of events, so to speak, and into a timeless existence.

Now let us see what this means. Imagine that all production has become more fruitful. Goods flow more abundantly than ever before. Where only one unit was available for consumption before, there are now two. Since the quantity of money has not been increased, the purchasing power of the monetary unit has risen and with one monetary unit it is possible to buy, let us say, 1½ times as much merchandise as before. Whether this actually means, if no 'stabilization policy' is attempted, that the debtor now has a disadvantage and the creditor an advantage is not immediately clear.

If you look at the situation from the viewpoint of the prices of the factors of production, it is easy to see why this is the case. For the debtor could use the borrowed sum to buy at lower prices factors of production whose output has not gone up; or if their output has gone up, their prices have not risen correspondingly. It might now be possible to buy *for less money*, factors of production with a productive capacity comparable to that of the factors of production one could have bought with the borrowed money at the time of the loan. There is no point in exploring the uncertainties of theories which do not take into consideration the influence that ensuing changes exert on entrepreneurial profit, interest and rent.

However, if we consider changes in real income due to increased production, it becomes evident that the situation may be viewed very differently from the way it appears to those who favour 'stabilization.' If the creditor gets back the same nominal sum, he can obviously buy more goods. Still, his economic situation is not improved as a result. He is not benefited relative to the general increase of real income which has taken place. If the multiple commodity standard were to reduce in part the nominal debt, his economic situation would be worsened. He would be deprived of something that, in his view, in all fairness belonged to him. Under a multiple commodity standard, interest payable over time, life annuities, subsistence allowances, pensions, and the like, would be increased or decreased according to the index number. Thus, these considerations cannot be summarily dismissed as irrelevant from the viewpoint of consumers.

We find, on the one hand, that neither the multiple commodity standard nor Irving Fisher's specific proposal is capable of eliminating the economic concomitants of changes in the value of the monetary unit due to the unequal timing in appearance and the irregularity in size of price changes. On the other hand, we see that these proposals seek to eliminate the repercussions on the content of debt agreements, circumstances permitting, in such a way as to cause definite shifts in wealth and income relations, shifts which appear obviously 'unjust,' at least to those on whom their burden falls. The 'justice' of these proposed reforms, therefore, is somewhat more doubtful than their advocates are inclined to assume.

2. The Misplaced Partiality to Debtors
It is certainly regrettable that this worthy goal cannot be attained, at least not by this particular route. These and similar efforts are usually

acknowledged with sympathy by many who recognize their fallacy and their unworkability. This sympathy is based ultimately on the intellectual and physical inclination of men to be both lazy and resistant to change at the same time. Surely everyone wants to see his situation improved with respect to his supply of goods and the satisfaction of his wants. Surely everyone hopes for changes which would make him richer. Many circumstances make it appear that the old and the traditional, being familiar, are preferable to the new. Such circumstances would include distrust of the individual's own powers and abilities, aversion to being forced to adapt in thought and action to new situations and, finally, the knowledge that one is no longer able, in advanced years of life, to meet his obligations with the vitality of youth.

Certainly, something new is welcomed and gratefully accepted, if the something new is beneficial to the individual's welfare. However, any change which brings disadvantages or merely appears to bring them, whether or not the change is to blame, is considered 'unjust.' Those favoured by the new state of affairs through no special merit on their part quietly accept the increased prosperity as a matter of course and even as something already long due. Those hurt by the change, however, complain vociferously. From such observations, there developed the concepts of a 'just price' and a 'just wage.' Whoever fails to keep up with the times and is unable to comply with its demands, becomes a eulogist of the past and an advocate of the status quo. However, the ideal of stability, of the stationary economy, is directed opposed to that of continual progress.

For some time popular opinion has been in sympathy with the debtor. The picture of the rich creditor, demanding payment from the poor debtor, and the vindictive teachings of moralists dominate popular thinking on indebtedness. A by-product of this is to be found in the contrast, made by the contemporaries of the Classical School and their followers, between the 'idle rich' and the 'industrious poor.' However, with the development of bonds and savings deposits, and with the decline of small-scale enterprise and the rise of big business, a reversal of the former situation took place. It then became possible for the masses, with their increasing prosperity, to become creditors. The 'rich man' is no longer the typical creditor, nor the 'poor man' the typical debtor. In many cases, perhaps even in the majority of cases, the relationship is completely reversed. Today, except in the lands of farmers and small property owners, the debtor viewpoint is no longer that of the masses. Consequently it is also no longer the view of the political demagogues.[32] Once upon a time inflation may have found its strongest support among the masses, who were burdened with debts. But the situation is now very different. A policy of monetary restriction would not be unwelcome among the masses today, for they would hope to reap a sure gain from it as creditors. They would expect the decline in their wages and salaries to lag behind, or at any rate not to exceed, the drop in commodity prices.

It is understandable, therefore, that proposals for the creation of a 'stable value' standard of deferred payments, almost completely forgotten in the years when commodity prices were declining, have been revived again in the twentieth century. Proposals of this kind are always primarily intended for the prevention of losses to creditors, hardly ever to safeguard jeopardized debtor interests. They cropped up in England when she was the great world banker. They turned up again in the United States at the moment when she started to become a creditor nation instead of a land of debtors, and they became quite popular there when America became the great world creditor.

Many signs seem to indicate that the period of monetary depreciation is coming to an end. Should this actually be the case, then the appeal which the idea of a manipulated standard now enjoys among creditor nations also would abate.

VII. The Goal of Monetary Policy

1. Liberalism[33] and the Gold Standard
Monetary policy of the preliberal era was either crude coin debasement, for the benefit of financial administration (only rarely intended as Seisachtheia,[34] i.e., to nullify outstanding debts), or still more crude paper money inflation. However, in addition to, sometimes even instead of, its fiscal goal, the driving motive behind paper money inflation very soon became the desire to favour the debtor at the expense of the creditor.

In opposing the depreciated paper standard, liberalism frequently took the position that after an inflation the value of paper money should be raised, through contraction, to its former parity with metallic money. It was only when men had learned that such a policy could not undo or reverse the 'unfair' changes in wealth and income brought about by the previous inflationary period and that an increase in the purchasing power per unit [by contraction or deflation] also brings other unwanted shifts of wealth and income, that the demand for return to a metallic standard at the debased monetary unit's *current* parity gradually replaced the demand for restoration at the *old* parity.

In opposing a single precious metal standard, monetary policy exhausted itself in the fruitless attempt to make bimetallism an actuality. The results which must follow the establishment of a legal exchange ratio between the two precious metals, gold and silver, have long been known, even before Classical economics developed an understanding of the regularity of market phenomena. Again and again Gresham's Law, which applied the general theory of price controls to the special case of money, demonstrated its validity. Eventually, efforts were abandoned to reach the ideal of a bimetallic standard. The next goal then became to free international trade, which was growing more and more important, from the effects of fluctuations in the ratio between the prices of the gold standard and the suppression of the alternating [bimetallic] and silver standards. Gold then became the world's money.

With the attainment of gold monometallism, liberals believed the goal of monetary policy had been reached. (The fact that they considered it necessary to supplement monetary policy through banking policy will be examined later in considerable detail.) The value of gold was then independent of any *direct* manipulation by governments, political policies, public opinion or Parliaments. So long as the gold standard was maintained, there was no need to fear severe price disturbances from the side of money. The adherents of the gold standard wanted no more than this, even though it was not clear to them at first that this was all that *could* be attained.

2. 'Pure' Gold Standard Disregarded
We have seen how the purchasing power of gold has continuously declined since the turn of the century. That was not, as frequently maintained, simply the consequence of increased gold production. There is no way to know whether the increased production of gold would have been sufficient to satisfy the increased demand for money without increasing its purchasing power, if monetary policy had not intervened as it did. The gold exchange and flexible standards were adopted in a number of countries, not the 'pure' gold standard as its advocates had expected. 'Pure' gold standard countries embraced measures which were thought to be, and actually were, steps toward the exchange standard. Finally, since 1914, gold has been withdrawn from actual circulation almost everywhere. It is primarily due to these measures that gold declined in value, thus generating the current debate on monetary policy.

The fault found with the gold standard today is not, therefore, due to the gold standard itself. Rather, it is the result of a policy which deliberately seeks to undermine the gold standard in order to lower the costs of using money and especially to obtain 'cheap money,' i.e., lower interest rates for loans. Obviously, this policy cannot attain the goal it sets for itself. It must eventually bring not low interest on loans but rather price increases and distortion of economic development. In view of this, then, isn't it simply enough to abandon all attempts to use tricks of banking and monetary policy to lower interest rates, to reduce the costs of using and circulating money and to satisfy 'needs' by promoting paper inflation?

The 'pure' gold standard formed the foundation of the monetary system in the most important countries of Europe and America, as well as in Australia. This system remained in force until the outbreak of the World War [1914]. In the literature on the subject, it was also considered the ideal monetary policy until very recently. Yet the champions of this 'pure' gold standard undoubtedly paid too little attention to changes in the purchasing power of monetary gold originating on the side of money. They scarcely noted the problem of the 'stabilization' of the purchasing power of money, very likely considering it completely impractical. Today we may pride ourselves on having grasped the basic questions of price and monetary theory more thoroughly and on having discarded many of the concepts which dominated works on monetary policy of the recent past. However, precisely because we believe we have a better understanding of the problem of value today, we can no longer consider acceptable the proposals to construct a monetary system based on index numbers.

3. The Index Standard

It is characteristic of current political thinking to welcome every suggestion which aims at enlarging the influence of government. If the Fisher and Keynes[35] proposals are approved on the grounds that they are intended to use government to make the formation of monetary value directly subservient to certain economic and political ends, this is understandable. However, anyone who approves of the index standard, because he wants to see purchasing power 'stabilized,' will find himself in serious error.

Abandoning the pursuit of the chimera of a money of unchanging purchasing power calls for neither resignation nor disregard of the social consequences of changes in monetary value. The necessary conclusion from this discussion is that stability of the purchasing power of the monetary unit presumes stability of all exchange relationships and, therefore, the absolute abandonment of the market economy.

The question has been raised again and again: What will happen if, as a result of a technological revolution, gold production should increase to such an extent as to make further adherence to the gold standard impossible? A change-over to the index standard *must* follow then, it is asserted, so that it would only be expedient to make this change voluntarily now. However, it is futile to deal with monetary problems today which may or may not arise in the future. We do not know under what conditions steps will have to be taken toward solving them. It could be that, under certain circumstances, the solution may be to adopt a system based on an index number. However, this would appear doubtful. Even so, an index standard would hardly be a more suitable monetary standard than the one we now have. In spite of all its defects, the gold standard is a useful and not inexpedient standard.

PART II

Cyclical Policy to Eliminate Economic Fluctuations

I. *Stabilization of the Purchasing Power of the Monetary Unit and Elimination of the Trade Cycle*

1. *Currency School's Contribution*

'Stabilization' of the purchasing power of the monetary unit would also lead, at the same time, to the ideal of an economy without any changes. In the stationary economy[36] there would be no 'ups' and 'downs' of business. Then, the sequence of events would flow smoothly and steadily. Then, no unforeseen event would interrupt the provisioning of goods. Then, the acting individual would experience no disillusionment because events did not develop as he had assumed in planning his affairs to meet future demands.

First, we have seen that this ideal cannot be realized. Secondly, we have seen that this ideal is generally proposed as a goal only because the problems involved in the formation of purchasing power have not been thought through completely. Finally, we have seen that even if a stationary economy *could* actually be realized, it would certainly not accomplish what had been expected. Yet neither these facts nor the limiting of monetary policy to the maintenance of a 'pure' gold standard means that the political slogan, 'Eliminate the business cycle,' is without value.

It is true that some authors, who dealt with these problems, had a rather vague idea that the 'stabilization of the price level' was the way to attain the goals they set for cyclical policy. Yet cyclical policy was not completely spent on fruitless attempts to fix the purchasing power of money. Witness the fact that steps were undertaken to curb the boom through banking policy, and thus to prevent the decline, which inevitably follows the upswing, from going as far as it would if matters were allowed to run their course. These efforts – undertaken with enthusiasm at a time when people did not realize that anything like stabilization of monetary value would

65

ever be conceived of and sought after – led to measures that had far-reaching consequences.

We should not forget for a moment the contribution which the Currency School made to the clarification of our problem. Not only did it contribute theoretically and scientifically but it contributed also to practical policy. The recent theoretical treatment of the problem – in the study of events and statistical data and in politics – rests entirely on the accomplishments of the Currency School. We have not surpassed Lord Overstone[37] so far as to be justified in disparaging his achievement.

Many modern students of cyclical movements are contemptuous of theory – not only of this or that theory but of *all* theories – and profess to let the facts speak for themselves. The delusion that theory must be distilled from the results of an impartial investigation of facts is more popular in cyclical theory than in any other field of economics. Yet, nowhere else is it clearer that there can be no understanding of the facts without theory.

Certainly it is no longer necessary to expose once more the errors in logic of the Historical-Empirical-Realistic approach to the 'social sciences.'[38] Only recently has this task been most thoroughly undertaken once more by competent scholars. Nevertheless, we continually encounter attempts to deal with the business cycle problem while presumably rejecting theory.

In taking this approach one falls prey to a delusion which is incomprehensible. It is assumed that data on economic fluctuations are given clearly, directly and in a way that cannot be disputed. Thus it remains for science merely to interpret these fluctuations – and for the art of politics simply to find ways and means to eliminate them.

2. Early Trade Cycle Theories

All business establishments do well at times and badly at others. There are times when the entrepreneur sees his profits increase daily more than he had anticipated and when, emboldened by these 'windfalls,' he proceeds to expand his operations. Then, due to an abrupt change in conditions, severe disillusionment follows this upswing, serious losses materialize, long established firms collapse, until widespread pessimism sets in which may frequently last for years. Such were the experiences which had already been forced on the attention of the businessman in capitalistic economies, long before discussions of the crisis problem began to appear in the literature. The sudden turn from the very sharp rise in prosperity – at least what appeared to be prosperity – to a very severe drop in profit opportunities was too conspicuous not to attract general attention. Even those who wanted to have nothing to do with the business world's 'worship of filthy lucre' could not ignore the fact that people who were, or had been considered, rich yesterday were suddenly reduced to poverty, that factories were shut down, that construction projects were left uncompleted, and that workers could not find work. Naturally, nothing concerned the businessman more intimately than this very problem.

If an entrepreneur is asked what is going on here – leaving aside changes in the prices of individual commodities due to recognizable causes – he may very well reply that at times the entire 'price level' tends upward and then at other times it tends downward. For inexplicable reasons, he would say, conditions arise under which it is impossible to dispose of all commodities, or almost all commodities, except at a loss. And what is most curious is that these depressing times always come when least expected, just when all business had been improving for some time so that people finally believed that a new age of steady and rapid progress was emerging.

Eventually, it must have become obvious to the more keenly thinking businessman that the genesis of the crisis should be sought in the preceding boom. The scientific investigator, whose view is naturally focused on the longer period, soon realized that economic upswings and downturns, alternated with seeming regularity. Once this was established, the problem was half-way exposed and scientists began to ask questions as to how this apparent regularity might be explained and understood.

Theoretical analysis was able to reject, as completely false, two attempts to explain the crisis – the theories of general overproduction and of underconsumption. These two doctrines have disappeared from serious scientific discussion. They persist today only outside the realm of science – the theory of general overproduction, among the ideas held by the average citizen; and the underconsumption theory, in Marxist literature.

It was not so easy to criticize a third group of attempted explanations, those which sought to trace economic fluctuations back to periodical changes in natural phenomena affecting agricultural production. These doctrines cannot be reached by theoretical inquiry alone. Conceivably such events may occur and reoccur at regular intervals. Whether this actually is the case can be shown only by attempts to verify the theory through observation. So far, however, none of these 'weather theories'[39] has successfully passed this test.

A whole series of a very different sort of attempts to explain the crisis are based on a definite irregularity in the psychological and intellectual talents of people. This irregularity is expressed in the economy by a change from confidence over the future, which inspires the boom, to despondency, which leads to the crisis and to stagnation of business. Or else this irregularity appears as a shift from boldly striking out in new directions to quietly following along already well-worn paths.

What should be pointed out about these doctrines and about the many other similar theories based on psychological variations is, first of all, that they do not explain. They merely pose the problem in a different way. They are not able to trace the change in business conditions back to a previously established and identified phenomenon. From the periodical fluctuations in psychological and intellectual data alone, without any further observation concerning the field of labour in the social or other sciences, we learn that such economic shifts as these may also be conceived of in a different way. So long as the course of such changes appears plausible only because of economic fluctuations between boom and bust, psychological and other related theories of the crisis amount to no more than tracing one unknown factor back to something else equally unknown.

3. The Circulation Credit Theory

Of all the theories of the trade cyle, only one has achieved and retained the rank of a fully-developed economic doctrine. That is the theory advanced by the Currency School, the theory which traces the cause of changes in business conditions to the phenomenon of circulation credit.[40] All other theories of the crisis, even when they try to differ in other respects from the line of reasoning adopted by the Currency School, return again and again to follow in its footsteps. Thus, our attention is constantly being directed to observations which seem to corroborate the Currency School's interpretation.

In fact, it may be said that the Circulation Credit Theory of the Trade Cycle[41] is now accepted by all writers in the field and that the other theories advanced today aim only at explaining why the volume of circulation credit granted by the banks varies from time to time. All attempts to study the course of business fluctuations empirically and statistically, as well as all efforts to influence the shape of changes in business conditions by political action, are based on the Circulation Credit Theory of the Trade Cycle.

To show that an investigation of business cycles is not dealing with an imaginary problem, it is necessary to formulate a cycle theory that recognizes a cyclical regularity of changes in business conditions. If we could not find a satisfactory theory of cyclical changes, then the question would remain as to whether or not each individual crisis arose from a special cause which we would have to track down first. Originally, economics approached the problem of the crisis by trying to trace all crises back to specific 'visible' and 'spectacular' causes such as war, cataclysms of nature, adjustments of new economic data – for example, changes in consumption and technology, or the discovery of easier and more favourable methods of production. Crises which could not be explained in this way became the specific 'problem of the crisis.'

Neither the fact that unexplained crises still recur again and again nor the fact that they are always preceded by a distinct boom period is sufficient to prove with certainty that the problem to be dealt with is a unique phenomenon originating from one specific cause. Recurrences do not appear at regular intervals. And it is not hard to believe that the more a crisis contrasts with conditions in the immediately preceding period, the more severe it is considered to be. It might be assumed, therefore, that there is no specific 'problem of the crisis' at all, and that the still unexplained crises must be explained by various special causes somewhat like the 'crisis' which Central European agriculture has faced since the rise of competition from the tilling of richer soil in Eastern Europe and overseas, or the 'crisis' of the European cotton industry at the time of the American Civil War. What is true of the crisis can also be applied to the boom. Here again, instead of seeking a general boom theory we could look for special causes for each individual boom.

Neither the connection between boom and bust nor the cyclical change of business conditions is a fact that can be established independent of theory. Only theory, business cycle theory, permits us to detect the wavy outline of a cycle in the tangled confusion of events.[42]

II. *Circulation Credit Theory*

1. *The Banking School Fallacy*

If notes are issued by the banks, or if bank deposits subject to check or other claim are opened, in excess of the amount of money kept in the vaults as cover, the effect on prices is similar to that obtained by an increase in the quantity of money. Since these fiduciary media, as notes and bank deposits not backed by metal are called, render the service of money as safe and generally accepted, payable on demand monetary claims, they may be used as money in all transactions. On that account, they are genuine money substitutes. Since they are in excess of the given total quantity of money in the narrower sense, they represent an increase in the quantity of money in the broader sense.

The practical significance of these undisputed and indisputable conclusions in the formation of prices is denied by the Banking School with its contention that the issue of such fiduciary media is strictly limited by the demand for money in the economy. The Banking School doctrine maintains that if fiduciary media are issued by the banks only to discount short-term commodity bills, then no more would come into circulation than were 'needed' to liquidate the transactions. According to this doctrine, bank management could exert no influence on the volume of the commodity transactions activated. Purchases and sales from which short-term commodity bills originate would, by this very transaction, already have brought into existence paper credit which can be used, through further negotiation, for the exchange of goods and services. If the bank discounts the bill and, let us say, issues notes against it, that is, according to the Banking School, a neutral transaction as far as the market is concerned. Nothing more is involved than replacing one instrument which is technically less suitable for circulation, the bill of exchange, with a more suitable one, the note. Thus, according to this School, the effect of the issue of notes need not be to increase the quantity of money in circulation. If the bill of exchange is retired at maturity, then notes would flow back to the bank and new notes could enter circulation again only when new commodity bills came into being once more as a result of new business.

The weak link in this well-known line of reasoning lies in the assertion that the volume of transactions completed, as sales and purchases from which commodity bills can derive, is independent of the behaviour of the banks. If the banks discount at a lower, rather than a higher, interest rate, then more loans are made. Enterprises which are unprofitable at 5%, and hence are not undertaken, may be profitable at 4%. Therefore, by lowering the interest rate they charge, banks can intensify the demand for credit. Then, by satisfying this demand, they can increase the quantity of fiduciary media in circulation. Once this is recognized, the Banking Theory's only argument, that prices are not influenced by the issue of fiduciary media, collapses.

One must be careful not to speak simply of the effects of credit in general on prices, but to specify clearly the effects of 'increased credit' or 'credit expansion.' A sharp distinction must be made between (1) credit which a bank grants by lending its own funds or funds placed at its disposal by depositors, which we call 'commodity credit,'[43] and (2) that which is granted by the creation of fiduciary media, i.e., notes and deposits not covered by money, which we call 'circulation credit.'[44] It is only through the granting of circulation credit that the prices of all commodities and services are directly affected.

If the banks grant circulation credit by discounting a three month bill of exchange, they exchange a future good – a claim payable in three months – for a present good that they produce out of nothing. It is not correct, therefore, to maintain that it is immaterial whether the bill of exchange is discounted by a bank of issue or whether it remains in circulation, passing from hand to hand. Whoever takes the bill of exchange in trade can do so only if he has the resources. But the bank of issue discounts by creating the necessary funds and putting them into circulation. To be sure, the fiduciary media flow back again to the bank at expiration of the note. If the bank does not give the fiduciary media out again, precisely the same consequences appear as those which come from a decrease in the quantity of money in its broader sense.

2. Early Effects of Credit Expansion

The fact that in the regular course of banking operations the banks issue fiduciary media only as loans to producers and merchants means that they are not used directly for purposes of consumption.[45] Rather, these fiduciary media are used first of all for production, that is to buy factors of production and pay wages. The first prices to rise, therefore, as a result of an increase of the quantity of money in the broader sense, caused by the issue of such fiduciary media, are those of raw materials, semimanufactured products, other goods of higher orders, and wage rates. Only later do the prices of goods of the first order [consumers' goods] follow. Changes in the purchasing power of a monetary unit, brought about by the issue of fiduciary media, follow a different path and have different accompanying social side effects from those produced by a new discovery of precious metals or by the issue of paper money. Still in the last analysis, the effect on prices is similar in both instances.

Changes in the purchasing power of the monetary unit do not directly affect the height of the rate of interest. An indirect influence on the height of the interest rate can take place as a result of the fact that shifts in wealth and income relationships, appearing as a result of the change in the value of the monetary unit, influence savings and, thus, the accumulation of capital. If a depreciation of the monetary unit favours the wealthier members of society at the expense of the poorer, its effect will probably be an increase in capital accumulation since the well-to-do are the more important savers. The more they put aside, the more their incomes and fortunes will grow.

If monetary depreciation is brought about by an issue of fiduciary media, and if wage rates do not promptly follow the increase in commodity prices, then the decline in purchasing power will certainly make this effect much more severe. This is the 'forced savings' which is quite properly stressed in recent literature.[46] However, three things should not be forgotten. First, it always depends upon the data of the particular case whether shifts of wealth and income, which lead to increased saving, are actually set in motion. Secondly, under circumstances which need not be discussed further here, by falsifying economic calculation, based on monetary bookkeeping calculations, a very substantial devaluation can lead to capital consumption (such a situation did take place temporarily during the recent inflationary period). Thirdly, as advocates of inflation through credit expansion should observe, any legislative measure which transfers

71

resources to the 'rich' at the expense of the 'poor' will also foster capital formation.

Eventually, the issue of fiduciary media in such manner can also lead to increased capital accumulation within narrow limits and, hence, to a further reduction of the interest rate. In the beginning, however, an immediate and direct decrease in the loan rate appears with the issue of fiduciary media, but this immediate decrease in the loan rate is distinct in character and degree from the later reduction. The new funds offered on the money market by the banks must obviously bring pressure to bear on the rate of interest. The supply and demand for loan money were adjusted at the interest rate prevailing *before* the issue of any additional supply of fiduciary media. Additional loans can be placed only if the interest rate is lowered. Such loans are profitable for the banks because the increase in the supply of fiduciary media calls for no expenditure except for the mechanical costs of banking (i.e., printing the notes and bookkeeping). The banks can, therefore, undercut the interest rates which would otherwise appear on the loan market, in the absence of their intervention. Since competition from them compels other money lenders to lower *their* interest charges, the market interest rate must therefore decline. But can this reduction be maintained? *That* is the problem.

3. Inevitable Effects of Credit Expansion on Interest Rates

In conformity with Wicksell's terminology, we shall use 'natural interest rate' to describe that interest rate which would be established by supply and demand if real goods were loaned *in natura* [directly, as in barter] without the intermediary of money. 'Money rate of interest' will be used for that interest rate asked on loans made in money or money substitutes. Through continued expansion of fiduciary media, it is possible for the banks to force the money rate down to the actual cost of the banking operations, practically speaking that is almost to zero. As a result, several authors have concluded that interest could be completely abolished in this way. Whole schools of reformers have wanted to use banking policy to make credit gratuitous and thus to solve the 'social question.' No reasoning person today, however, believes that interest can ever be abolished, nor doubts but what, if the 'money interest rate' is depressed by the expansion of fiduciary media, it must sooner or later revert once again to the 'natural interest rate.' The question is only how this inevitable adjustment takes place. The answer to this will explain at the same time the fluctuations of the business cycle.

The Currency Theory limited the problem too much. It only considered the situation that was of practical significance for the England of its time – that is, when the issue of fiduciary media is increased in one country while remaining unchanged in others. Under these assumptions, the situation is quite clear: General price increases at home; hence an increase in imports, a drop in commodity exports; and with this, as notes can circulate only within the country, an outflow of metallic money. To obtain metallic money for export, holders of notes present them for redemption; the metallic reserves of the banks decline; and consideration for their own solvency then forces them to restrict the credit offered.

That is the instant at which the business upswing, brought about by the availability of easy credit, is demonstrated to be illusory prosperity. An abrupt reaction sets in. The 'money rate of interest' shoots up; enterprises from which credit is withdrawn collapse and sweep along with them the banks which are their creditors. A long persisting period of business stagnation now follows. The banks, warned by this experience into observing restraint, not only no longer underbid the 'natural interest rate' but exercise extreme caution in granting credit.

4. The Price Premium

In order to complete this interpretation, we must, first of all, consider the price premium. As the banks start to expand the circulation credit, the anticipated upward movement of prices results in the appearance of a positive price premium. Even if the banks do not lower the actual interest rate any more, the gap widens between the 'money interest rate' and the 'natural interest rate' which would prevail in the absence of their intervention. Since loan money is now cheaper to acquire than circumstances warrant, entrepreneurial ambitions expand.

New businesses are started in the expectation that the necessary capital can be secured by obtaining credit. To be sure, in the face of growing demand, the banks now raise the 'money interest rate.' Still they do not discontinue granting further credit. They expand the supply of fiduciary media issued, with the result that the purchasing power of the monetary unit must decline still further. Certainly the actual 'money interest rate' increases during the boom, but it continues to lag behind the rate which would conform to the market, i.e., the 'natural interest rate' augmented by the positive price premium.

So long as this situation prevails, the upswing continues. Inventories of goods are readily sold. Prices and profits rise. Business enterprises are overwhelmed with orders because everyone anticipates further price increases and workers find employment at increasing wage rates. However, this situation cannot last forever!

5. Malinvestment of Available Capital Goods

The 'natural interest rate' is established at that height which tends toward equilibrium[47] on the market. The tendency is toward a condition where no capital goods are idle, no opportunities for starting profitable enterprises remain unexploited and the only projects not undertaken are those which no longer yield a profit at the prevailing 'natural interest rate.' Assume, however, that the equilibrium, toward which the market is moving, is disturbed by the interference of the banks. Money may be obtained below the 'natural interest rate.' As a result businesses may be started which weren't profitable before, and which become profitable only through the lower than 'natural interest rate' which appears with the expansion of circulation credit.

Here again, we see the difference which exists between a drop in purchasing power, caused by the expansion of circulation credit, and a loss of purchasing power, brought about by an increase in the quantity of money. In the latter case [i.e., with an increase in the quantity of money in the narrower sense] the prices first affected are either (1) those of consumers' goods only or (2) the prices of both consumers' *and* producers' goods. Which it will be depends on whether those first receiving the new quantitites of money use this new wealth for consumption or production. However, if the decrease in purchasing power is caused by an increase in bank created fiduciary media, then it is the prices of producers' goods which are first affected. The prices of consumers' goods follow only to the extent that wages and profits rise.

Since it always requires some time for the market to reach full 'equilibrium,' the 'static' or 'natural'[48] prices, wage rates and interest rates never actually appear. The process leading to their establishment is never completed before changes occur which once again indicate a new 'equilibrium.' At times, even on the unhampered market, there are some unemployed workers, unsold consumers' goods and quantities of unused factors of production, which would not exist under 'static equilibrium.'[49] With the revival of business and productive activity, these reserves are in demand right away. However, once they are gone, the increase in the supply of fiduciary media necessarily leads to disturbances of a special kind.

In a given economic situation, the opportunities for production, which may actually be carried out, are limited by the supply of capital goods available. Roundabout methods of production can be adopted only so far as the means for subsistence exist to maintain the workers during the entire period of the expanded process. All those projects, for the completion of which means are not available, must be left uncompleted, even though they may appear technically feasible – that is, if one disregards the supply of capital. However, such businesses, because of the lower loan rate offered by the banks, appear for the moment to be profitable and are, therefore, initiated. However, the existing resources are insufficient. Sooner or later this must become evident. Then it will become apparent that production has gone astray, that plans were drawn up in excess of the economic means available, that speculation, i.e., activity aimed at the provision of future goods, was misdirected.

6. 'Forced Savings'

In recent years, considerable significance has been attributed to the fact that 'forced savings,' which may appear as a result of the drop in purchasing power that follows an increase of fiduciary media, lead to an increase in the supply of capital. The subsistence fund is made to go farther, due to the fact that (1) the workers consume less because wage rates tend to lag behind the rise in the prices of commodities,[50] and (2) those who reap the advantage of this reduction in the workers' incomes save at least a part of their gain. Whether 'forced savings' actually appear depends, as noted above, on the circumstances in each case. There is no need to go into this any further.

Nevertheless, establishing the existence of 'forced savings' does not mean that bank expansion of circulation credit does not lead to the initiation of more roundabout production than available capabilities would warrant. To prove that, one must be able to show that the banks are only in a position to depress the 'money interest rate' and expand the issue of fiduciary media to the extent that the 'natural interest rate' declines as a result of 'forced savings.' This assumption is simply absurd and there is no point in arguing it further. It is almost inconceivable that anyone should want to maintain it.

What concerns us is the problem brought about by the banks, in reducing the 'money rate of interest' *below* the 'natural rate.' For our problem, it is immaterial how much the 'natural interest rate' may also decline under certain circumstances and within narrow limits, as a result of this action by the banks. No one doubts that 'forced savings' can reduce the 'natural interest rate' only fractionally, as compared with the reduction in the 'money interest rate' which produces the 'forced savings.'[51]

The resources which are claimed for the newly initiated longer time consuming methods of production are unavailable for those processes where they would otherwise have been put to use. The reduction in the loan rate benefits all producers, so that all producers are now in a position to pay higher wage rates and higher prices for the material factors of production. Their competition drives up wage rates and the prices of the other factors of production. Still, except for the possibilities already discussed, this does not increase the size of the labour force or the supply of available goods of the higher order. The means of subsistence are not sufficient to provide for the workers during the extended period of production. It becomes apparent that the proposal for the new, longer, roundabout production was not adjusted with a view to the actual capital situation. For one thing, the enterprises realize that the resources available to them are not sufficient to continue their operations. They find that 'money' is scarce.

That is precisely what has happened. The general increase in prices means that all businesses need more funds than had been anticipated at their 'launching.' More resources are required to complete them. However, the increased quantity of fiduciary media loaned out by the banks is already exhausted. The banks can no longer make additional loans at the same interest rates. As a result, they must raise the loan rate once more for two reasons. In the first place, the appearance of the positive price premium forces them to pay higher interest for outside funds which they borrow. Then also, they must discriminate among the many applicants for credit. Not all enterprises can afford this increased interest rate. Those which cannot run into difficulties.

7. A Habit-forming Policy

Now, in extending circulation credit, the banks do not proceed by pumping a limited dosage of new fiduciary media into circulation and then stop. They expand the fiduciary media continuously for some time, sending, so to speak, after the first offering, a second, third, fourth, and so on. They do not simply undercut the 'natural interest rate' once, and then adjust promptly to the new situation. Instead they continue the practice of making loans below the 'natural interest rate' for some time. To be sure, the increasing volume of demands on them for credit may cause them to raise the 'money rate of interest.' Yet, even if the banks revert to the former 'natural rate,' the rate which prevailed before their credit expansion affected the market, they still lag behind the rate which would now exist on the market if they were not continuing to expand credit. This is because a positive price premium must now be included in the new 'natural rate.' With the help of this new quantity of fiduciary media, the banks now take care of the businessmen's intensified demand for credit. Thus, the crisis does not appear yet. The enterprises using more roundabout methods of production, which have been started, are continued. Because prices rise still further, the earlier calculations of the entrepreneurs are realized. They make profits. In short, the boom continues.

8. The Inevitable Crisis and Cycle

The crisis breaks out only when the banks alter their conduct to the extent that they discontinue issuing any more new fiduciary media and stop undercutting the 'natural interest rate.' They may even take steps to restrict circulation credit. *When* they actually do this, and *why*, is still to be examined. First of all, however, we must ask ourselves whether it is possible for the banks to stay on the course upon which they have embarked, permitting new quantities of fiduciary media to flow into circulation continuously and proceeding always to make loans below the rate of interest which would prevail on the market in the absence of their interference with newly created fiduciary media.

If the banks could proceed in this manner, with businesses improving continually, could they then provide for lasting good times? Would they then be able to make the boom eternal?

They cannot do this. The reason they cannot is that inflationism carried on *ad infinitum* is not a workable policy. If the issue of fiduciary media is expanded continuously, prices rise ever higher and at the same time the positive price premium also rises. (We shall disregard the fact that consideration for (1) the continually declining monetary reserves relative to fiduciary media and (2) the banks' operating costs must sooner or later compel them to discontinue the further expansion of circulation credit.) It is precisely because, and only because, no end to the prolonged 'flood' of expanding fiduciary media is foreseen, that it leads to still sharper price increases and, finally, to a panic in which prices and the loan rate move erratically upward.

Suppose the banks still did not want to give up the race? Suppose, in order to depress the loan rate, they wanted to satisfy the continuously expanding desire for credit by issuing still more circulation credit? Then they would only hasten the end, the collapse of the entire system of fiduciary media. The inflation can continue only so long as the conviction persists that it will one day cease. Once people are persuaded that the inflation will *not* stop, they turn from the use of this money. They flee then to 'real values,' foreign money, the precious metals, and barter.

Sooner or later, the crisis *must* inevitably break out as the result of a change in the conduct of the banks. The later the crack-up comes, the longer the period in which the calculation of the entrepreneurs is misguided by the issue of additional fiduciary media. The greater this additional quantity of fiduciary money, the more factors of production have been firmly committed in the form of investments which appeared profitable only because of the artificially reduced interest rate and which prove to be unprofitable now that the interest rate has again been raised. Great losses are sustained as a result of misdirected capital investments. Many new structures remain unfinished. Others, already completed, close down operations. Still others are carried on because, after writing off losses which represent a waste of capital, operation of the existing structure pays at least something.[52]

The crisis, with its unique characteristics, is followed by stagnation.

The misguided enterprises and businesses of the boom period are already liquidated. Bankruptcy and adjustment have cleared up the situation. The banks have become cautious. They fight shy of expanding circulation credit. They are not inclined to give an ear to credit applications from schemers and promoters. Not only is the artificial stimulus to business, through the expansion of circulation credit, lacking, but even businesses which *would* be feasible, considering the capital goods available, are not attempted because the general feeling of discouragement makes every innovation appear doubtful. Prevailing 'money interest rates' fall *below* the 'natural interest rates.'

When the crisis breaks out, loan rates bound sharply upward because threatened enterprises offer extremely high interest rates for the funds to acquire the resources, with the help of which they hope to save themselves. Later, as the panic subsides, a situation develops, as a result of the restriction of circulation credit and attempts to dispose of large inventories, causing prices [and the 'money interest rate'] to fall steadily and leading to the appearance of a negative price premium. This reduced rate of loan interest is adhered to for some time, even after the decline in prices comes to a standstill, when a negative price premium no longer corresponds to conditions. Thus, it comes about that the 'money interest rate' is lower than the 'natural rate.' Yet, because the unfortunate experiences of the recent crisis have made everyone uneasy, the incentive to business activity is not as strong as circumstances would otherwise warrant. Quite a time passes before capital funds, increased once again by savings accumulated in the meantime, exert sufficient pressure on the loan interest rate for an expansion of entrepreneurial activity to resume. With this development, the low point is passed and the new boom begins.

III. *The Reappearance of Cycles*

1. *Metallic Standard Fluctuations*
From the instant when the banks start expanding the volume of circulation credit, until the moment they stop such behaviour, the course of events is substantially similar to that provoked by any increase in the quantity of money. The difference results from the fact that fiduciary media generally come into circulation through the banks, i.e., as loans, while increases in the quantity of money appear as additions to the wealth and income of specific individuals. This has already been mentioned and will not be further considered here. Considerably more significant for us is another distinction between the two.

Such increases and decreases in the quantity of money have no connection with increases or decreases in the demand for money. If the demand grows in the wake of a population increase or a progressive reduction of barter and self-sufficiency resulting in increased monetary transactions, there is absolutely no need to increase the quantity of money. It might even decrease. In any event, it would be most extraordinary if changes in the demand for money were balanced by reciprocal changes in its quantity so that both changes were concealed and no change took place in the monetary unit's purchasing power.

Changes in the value of the monetary unit are always taking place in the economy. Periods of declining purchasing power alternate with those of increasing purchasing power. Under a metallic standard, these changes are usually so slow and so insignificant that their effect is not at all violent. Nevertheless, we must recognize that even under a precious metal standard periods of ups and downs would still alternate at irregular intervals. In addition to the standard metallic money, such a standard would recognize only token coins for petty transactions. There would, of course, be no paper money or any other currency (i.e., either notes or bank accounts subject to check which are not fully covered). Yet even then, one would be able to speak of economic 'ups,' 'downs' and 'waves.' However, one would hardly be inclined to refer to such minor alternating 'ups' and 'downs' as regularly recurring cycles. During these periods when purchasing power moved in one direction, whether up or down, it would probably move so slightly that businessmen would scarcely notice the changes. Only economic historians would become aware of them. Moreover, the fact is that the transition from a period of rising prices to one of falling prices would be so slight that neither panic nor crisis would appear. This would also mean that businessmen and news reports of market activities would be less occupied with the 'long waves' of the trade cycle[53]

2. Infrequent Recurrences of Paper Money Inflations
The effects of inflations brought about by increases in paper money are quite different. They also produce price increases and hence 'good business conditions,' which are further intensified by the apparent encouragement of exports and the hampering of imports. Once the inflation comes to an end, whether by a providential halt to further increases in the quantity of money (as for instance recently in France and Italy) or through complete debasement of the paper money due to inflationary policy carried to its final conclusions (as in Germany in 1923), then the 'stabilization crisis'[54] appears. The cause and appearance of this crisis correspond precisely to those of the crisis which comes at the close of a period of circulation credit expansion. One must clearly distinguish *this* crisis [i.e.,

79

when increases in the quantity of money are simply halted] from the consequences which must result when the cessation of inflation is followed by deflation.

There is no regularity as to the recurrence of paper money inflations. They generally originate in a certain political attitude, not from events within the economy itself. One can only say, with certainty, that after a country has pursued an inflationist policy to its end or, at least, to substantial lengths, it cannot soon use this means again successfully to serve its financial interests. The people, as a result of their experience, will have become distrustful and would resist any attempt at a renewal of inflation.

Even at the very beginning of a new inflation, people would reject the notes or accept them only at a far greater discount than the actual increased quantity would otherwise warrant. As a rule, such an unusually high discount is characteristic of the final phases of an inflation. Thus an early attempt to return to a policy of paper money inflation must either fail entirely or come very quickly to a catastrophic conclusion. One can assume – and monetary history confirms this, or at least does not contradict it – that a new generation must grow up before consideration can be given to bolstering the government's finances with the printing press.

Many states have never pursued a policy of paper money inflation. Many have resorted to it only once in their history. Even the states traditionally known for their printing press money have not repeated the experiment often. Austria waited almost a generation after the banknote inflation of the Napoleonic era before embarking on an inflation policy again. Even then, the inflation was in more modest proportions than at the beginning of the 19th century. Almost a half century passed between the end of her second and the beginning of her third and most recent period of inflation. It is by no means possible to speak of cyclical reappearances of paper money inflations.

3. The Cyclical Process of Credit Expansions[55]

Regularity can be detected only with respect to the phenomena originating out of circulation credit. Crises have reappeared every few years since banks issuing fiduciary media began to play an important role in the economic life of people. Stagnation followed crisis, and following these came the boom again. More than ninety years ago Lord Overstone described the sequence in a remarkably graphic manner:

We find it [the 'state of trade'] subject to various conditions which are periodically returning; it revolves apparently in an established cycle. First we find it in a state of quiescence, – next improvement, – growing confidence, – prosperity, – excitement, – overtrading, – convulsion, – pressure, – stagnation, – distress, – ending again in quiescence.[56]

This description, unrivalled for its brevity and clarity, must be kept in mind to realize how wrong it is to give later economists credit for transforming the problem of the crisis into the problem of general business conditions.

Attempts have been made, with little success, to supplement the observation that business cycles recur by attributing a definite time period to the sequence of events. Theories which sought the source of economic change in recurring cosmic events have, as might be expected, leaned in this direction. A study of economic history fails to support such assumptions. It shows recurring ups and downs in business conditions, but not ups and downs of equal length.

The problem to be solved is the recurrence of fluctuations in business activity. The Circulation Credit Theory shows us, in rough outline, the typical course of a cycle. However, so far as we have as yet analyzed the theory, it still does not explain why the cycle always recurs.

According to the Circulation Credit Theory, it is clear that the direct stimulus which provokes the fluctuations is to be sought in the conduct of the banks. Insofar as they start to reduce the 'money rate of interest' below the 'natural rate of interest,' they expand circulation credit, and thus divert the course of events away from the path of normal development. They bring about changes in relationships which must necessarily lead to boom and crisis. Thus, the problem consists of asking what leads the banks again and again to renew attempts to expand the volume of circulation credit.

Many authors believe that the instigation of the banks' behaviour comes from outside, that certain events induce them to pump more fiduciary media into circulation and that they would behave differently if these circumstances failed to appear. I was also inclined to this view in the first edition of my book on monetary theory.[57] I could not understand why the banks didn't learn from experience. I thought they would certainly persist in a policy of caution and restraint, if they were not led by outside circumstances to abandon it. Only later did I become convinced that it was useless to look to an outside stimulus for the change in the conduct of the banks. Only later did I also become convinced that fluctuations in general business conditions were completely dependent on the relationship of the quantity of fiduciary media in circulation to demand.

Each new issue of fiduciary media has the consequences described above. First of all, it depresses the loan rate and then it reduces the monetary unit's purchasing power. Every subsequent issue brings the same result. The establishment of new banks of issue and their step-by-step expansion of circulation credit provides the means for a business boom and, as a result, leads to the crisis with its accompanying decline.

81

We can readily understand that the banks issuing fiduciary media, in order to improve their chances for profit, may be ready to expand the volume of credit granted and the number of notes issued. What calls for special explanation is why attempts are made again and again to improve general economic conditions by the expansion of circulation credit in spite of the spectacular failure of such efforts in the past.

The answer must run as follows: According to the prevailing ideology of businessman and economist-politician, the reduction of the interest rate is considered an essential goal of economic policy. Moreover, the expansion of circulation credit is assumed to be the appropriate means to achieve this goal.

4. The Mania for Lower Interest Rates

The naive inflationist theory of the 17th and 18th centuries could not stand up in the long run against the criticism of economics. In the 19th century, that doctrine was held only by obscure authors who had no connection with scientific inquiry or practical economic policy. For purely political reasons, the school of empirical and historical 'Realism' did not pay attention to problems of economic theory. It was due only to this neglect of theory that the naive theory of inflation was once more able to gain prestige temporarily during the World War, especially in Germany.

The doctrine of inflationism by way of fiduciary media was more durable. Adam Smith had battered it severely, as had others even before him, especially the American William Douglass.[58] Many, notably in the Currency School, had followed. But then came a reversal. The Banking School confused the situation. Its founders failed to see the error in their doctrine. They failed to see that the expansion of circulation credit lowered the interest rate. They even argued that it was impossible to expand credit beyond the 'needs of business.' So there are seeds in the Banking Theory which need only to be developed to reach the conclusion that the interest rate can be reduced by the conduct of the banks. At the very least, it must be admitted that those who dealt with those problems did not sufficiently understand the reasons for opposing credit expansion to be able to overcome the public clamour for the banks to provide 'cheap money.'

In discussions of the rate of interest, the economic press adopted the questionable jargon of the business world, speaking of a 'scarcity' or an 'abundance' of money and calling the short term loan market the 'money market.' Banks issuing fiduciary media, warned by experience to be cautious, practiced discretion and hesitated to indulge the universal desire of the press, political parties, parliaments, governments, entrepreneurs, landowners and workers for cheaper credit. Their reluctance to expand credit was falsely attributed to reprehensible motives. Even newspapers, that knew better, and politicians, who should have known better, never tired of asserting that the banks of issue could certainly discount larger sums more cheaply if they were not trying to hold the interest rate as high as possible out of concern for their own profitability and the interests of their controlling capitalists.

Almost without exception, the great European banks of issue on the continent were established with the expectation that the loan rate could be reduced by issuing fiduciary media. Under the influence of the Currency School doctrine, at first in England and then in other countries where old laws did not restrict the issue of notes, arrangements were made to limit the expansion of circulation credit, at least of that part granted through the issue of uncovered banknotes. Still, the Currency Theory lost out as a result of criticism by Tooke (1774–1858) and his followers. Although it was considered risky to abolish the laws which restricted the issue of notes, no harm was seen in circumventing them. Actually, the letter of the banking laws provided for a concentration of the nation's supply of precious metals in the vaults of banks of issue. This permitted an increase in the issue of fiduciary media and played an important role in the expansion of the gold exchange standard.

Before the war [1914], there was no hesitation in Germany in openly advocating withdrawal of gold from trade so that the Reichsbank might issue sixty marks in notes for every twenty marks in gold added to its stock. Propaganda was also made for expanding the use of payments by check with the explanation that this was a means to lower the interest rate substantially.[59] The situation was similar elsewhere, although perhaps more cautiously expressed.

Every single fluctuation in general business conditions – the upswing to the peak of the wave and the decline into the trough which follows – is prompted by the attempt of the banks of issue to reduce the loan rate and thus expand the volume of circulation credit through an increase in the supply of fiduciary media (i.e., banknotes and checking accounts not fully backed by money). The fact that these efforts are resumed again and again in spite of their widely deplored consequences, causing one business cycle after another, can be attributed to the predominance of an ideology – an ideology which regards rising commodity prices and especially a low rate of interest as goals of economic policy. The theory is that even this second goal may be attained by the expansion of fiduciary media. Both crisis and depression are lamented. Yet, because the causal connection between the behaviour of the banks of issue and the evils complained about is not correctly interpreted, a policy with respect to interest is advocated which, in the last analysis, must necessarily always lead to crisis and depression.

5. Free Banking

Every deviation from the prices, wage rates and interest rates which would prevail on the unhampered market must lead to disturbances of the economic 'equilibrium.'[60] This disturbance, brought about by attempts to depress the interest rate artificially, is precisely the cause of the crisis.

The ultimate cause, therefore, of the phenomenon of wave after wave of economic ups and downs is ideological in character. The cycles will not disappear so long as people believe that the rate of interest may be reduced, not through the accumulation of capital, but by banking policy.

Even if governments had never concerned themselves with the issue of fiduciary media, there would still be banks of issue and fiduciary media in the form of notes as well as checking accounts. There would then be no legal limitation on the issue of fiduciary media. Free banking would prevail. However, banks would have to be especially cautious because of the sensitivity to loss of reputation of their fiduciary media, which no one would be forced to accept. In the course of time, the inhabitants of capitalistic countries would learn to differentiate between good and bad banks. Those living in 'undeveloped' countries would distrust all banks. No government would exert pressure on the banks to discount on easier terms than the banks themselves could justify. However, the managers of solvent and highly respected banks, the only banks whose fiduciary media would enjoy the general confidence essential for money-substitute quality, would have learned from past experiences. Even if they scarcely detected the deeper correlations, they would nevertheless know how far they might go without precipitating the danger of a breakdown.

The cautious policy of restraint on the part of respected and well-established banks would compel the more irresponsible managers of other banks to follow suit, however much they might want to discount more generously. For the expansion of circulation credit can never be the act of one individual bank alone, nor even of a group of individual banks. It always requires that the fiduciary media be *generally* accepted as a money substitute. If several banks of issue, each enjoying equal rights, existed side by side, and if some of them sought to expand the volume of circulation credit while others did not alter their conduct, then at every bank clearing, demand balances would regularly appear in favour of the conservative enterprises. As a result of the presentation of notes for redemption and withdrawal of their cash balances, the expanding banks would very quickly be compelled once more to limit the scale of their emissions.

In the course of the development of a banking system with fiduciary media, crises could not have been avoided. However, as soon as bankers recognized the dangers of expanding circulation credit, they would have done their utmost, in their own interests, to avoid the crisis. They would then have taken the only course leading to this goal: extreme restraint in the issue of fiduciary media.

6. Government Intervention in Banking

The fact that the development of fiduciary media banking took a different turn may be attributed entirely to the circumstance that the issue of banknotes (which for a long time were the only form of fiduciary media and are today [1928] still the more important, even in the United States and England) became a public concern. The private bankers and joint-stock banks were supplanted by the politically privileged banks of issue because the governments favoured the expansion of circulation credit for reasons of fiscal and credit policy. The privileged institutions could proceed unhesitatingly in the granting of credit, not only because they usually held a monopoly in the issue of notes, but also because they could rely on the government's help in an emergency. The private banker would go bankrupt, if he ventured too far in the issue of credit. The privileged bank received permission to suspend payments and its notes were made legal tender at face value.

If the knowledge derived from the Currency Theory had led to the conclusion that fiduciary media should be deprived of all special privileges and placed, like other claims, under general law in every respect and without exception, this would probably have contributed more toward eliminating the threat of crises than was actually accomplished by establishing rigid proportions[61] for the issue of fiduciary media in the form of notes and restricting the freedom of banks to issue fiduciary media in the form of checking accounts. The principle of free banking was limited to the field of checking accounts. In fact, it could not function here to bring about restraint on the part of banks and bankers. Public opinion decreed that government should be guided by a different policy – a policy of coming to the assistance of the central banks of issue in times of crises. To permit the Bank of England to lend a helping hand to banks which had gotten into trouble by expanding circulation credit, the Peel Act was suspended in 1847, 1857 and 1866. Such assistance, in one form or another, had been offered time and again everywhere.

In the United States, national banking legislation made it technically difficult, if not entirely impossible, to grant such aid. The system was considered especially unsatisfactory, precisely because of the legal obstacles it placed in the path of helping grantors of credit who became insolvent and of supporting the value of circulation credit they had granted. Among the reasons leading to the significant revision of the American banking system [i.e., the Federal Reserve Act of 1913], the most important was the belief that provisions must be made for times of crises. In other words, just as the emergency institution of Clearing House Certificates was able to save expanding banks, so should technical expedients be used to prevent the breakdown of the banks and bankers whose conduct had led to the crisis. It was usually considered especially important to shield the banks which expanded circulation credit from the consequences of their conduct. One of the chief tasks of the central banks of issue was to jump into this breach. It was also considered the duty of those other banks who, thanks to foresight, had succeeded in preserving their solvency, even in the general crisis, to help fellow banks in difficulty.

7. Intervention No Remedy

It may well be asked whether the damage inflicted by misguiding entrepreneurial activity by artificially lowering the loan rate would be greater if the crisis were permitted to run its course. Certainly many saved by the intervention would be sacrificed in the panic, but if such enterprises were permitted to fail, others would prosper. Still the total loss brought about by the 'boom' (which the crisis did not produce, but only made evident) is largely due to the fact that factors of production were expended for fixed investments which, in the light of economic conditions, were not the most urgent. As a result, these factors of production are now lacking for more urgent uses. If intervention prevents the transfer of goods from the hands of imprudent entrepreneurs to those who would now take over because they have evidenced better foresight, this imbalance becomes neither less significant nor less perceptible.

In any event, the practice of intervening for the benefit of banks, rendered insolvent by the crisis, and of the customers of these banks, has resulted in suspending the market forces which could serve to prevent a return of the expansion, in the form of a new boom, and the crisis which inevitably follows. If the banks emerge from the crisis unscathed, or only slightly weakened, what remains to restrain them from embarking once more on an attempt to reduce artificially the interest rate on loans and expand circulation credit? If the crisis were ruthlessly permitted to run its course, bringing about the destruction of enterprises which were unable to meet their obligations, then all entrepreneurs – not only banks but also other businessmen – would exhibit more caution in granting and using credit in the future. Instead, public opinion approves of giving assistance in the crisis. Then, no sooner is the worst over, than the banks are spurred on to a new expansion of circulation credit.

To the businessman, it appears most natural and understandable that the banks should satisfy his demand for credit by the creation of fiduciary media. The banks, he believes, should have the task and the duty to 'stand by' business and trade. There is no dispute but what the expansion of circulation credit furthers the accumulation of capital within the narrow limits of the 'forced savings' it brings about and to that extent permits an increase in productivity. Still it can be argued that, given the situation, each step in this direction steers business activity, in the manner described above, on a 'wrong' course. The discrepancy between what the entrepreneurs do and what the unhampered market would have prescribed becomes evident in the crisis. The fact that each crisis, with its unpleasant consequences, is followed once more by a new 'boom,' which must eventually expend itself as another crisis, is due only to the circumstances that the ideology which dominates all influential groups – political economists, politicians, statesmen, the press and the business world – not only sanctions, but also demands, the expansion of circulation credit.

IV. The Crisis Policy
of the Currency School

1. The Inadequacy of the Currency School
Every advance toward explaining the problem of business fluctuations to date is due to the Currency School. We are also indebted to this School alone for the ideas responsible for policies aimed at eliminating business fluctuations. The fatal error of the Currency School consisted in the fact that it failed to recognize the similarity between banknotes and bank demand deposits as money substitutes and, thus, as money certificates and fiduciary media. In their eyes, only the banknote was a money substitute. In their view, therefore, the circulation of pure metallic money could only be adulterated by the introduction of a banknote not covered by money.

Consequently, they thought that the only thing that needed to be done to prevent the periodic return of crises was to set a rigid limit for the issue of banknotes not backed by metal. The issue of fiduciary media in the form of demand deposits not covered by metal was left free.[62] Since nothing stood in the way of granting circulation credit through bank deposits, the policy of expanding circulation credit could be continued even in England. When technical difficulties limited further bank loans and precipitated a crisis, it became customary to come to the assistance of the banks and their customers with special issues of notes. The practice of restricting the notes in circulation not covered by metal, by limiting the ratio of such notes to metal, systematized this procedure. Banks could expand the volume of credit with ease if they could not count on the support of the bank of issue in an emergency.

If all further expansion of fiduciary media had been forbidden in any form, that is, if the banks had been obliged to hold full reserves for both the additional notes issued and increases in customers' demand deposits subject to check or similar claim – or at least had not been permitted to increase the quantity of fiduciary media beyond a strictly limited ratio – prices would have declined sharply, especially at times when the increased demand for money surpassed the increase in its quantity. The economy would then not only have lacked the drive contributed by any 'forced savings,' it would also have temporarily suffered from the consequences of a rise in the monetary unit's purchasing power [i.e., falling prices]. Capital accumulation would then have been slowed down, although certainly not stopped. In any case, the economy surely would not then have experienced periods of stormy upswings followed by dramatic reversals of the upswings into crises and declines.

There is little sense in discussing whether it would have been better to restrict, in this way, the issue of fiduciary media by the banks than it was to pursue the policy actually followed. The alternatives are not merely restriction or freedom in the issue of fiduciary media. The alternatives are, or at least were, privilege in the granting of fiduciary media or true free banking.

The possibility of free banking has scarcely even been suggested. Intervention cast its first shadow over the capitalistic system when banking policy came to the forefront of economic and political discussion. To be sure, some authors, who defended free banking, appeared on the scene. However, their voices were overpowered. The desired goal was to protect the noteholders against the banks. It was forgotten that those hurt by the dangerous suspension of payments by the banks of issue are always the very ones the law was intended to help. No matter how severe the consequences one may anticipate from a breakdown of the banks under a system of absolutely free banking, one would have to admit that they could never even remotely approach the severity of those brought about by the war and postwar banking policies of the three European empires.[63]

2. 'Booms' Favoured

In the last two generations, hardly anyone, who has given this matter some thought, can fail to know that a crisis follows a boom. Nevertheless, it would have been impossible for even the sharpest and cleverest banker to suppress in time the expansion of circulation credit. Public opinion stood in the way. The fact that business conditions fluctuated violently was generally assumed to be inherent in the capitalistic system. Under the influence of the Banking Theory, it was thought that the banks merely went along with the upswing and that their conduct had nothing to do with bringing it about or advancing it. If, after a long period of stagnation, the banks again began to respond to the general demand for easier credit, public opinion was always delighted by the signs of the start of a boom.

In view of the prevailing ideology, it would have been completely unthinkable for the banks to apply the brakes at the start of such a boom. If business conditions continued to improve, then, in conformity with the principles of Lord Overstone, prophecies of a reaction certainly increased in number. However, even those who gave this warning usually did not call for a rigorous halt to all further expansion of circulation credit. They asked only for moderation and for restricting newly granted credits to 'non-speculative' businesses.

Then finally, if the banks changed their policy and the crisis came, it was always easy to find culprits. But there was no desire to locate the real offender – the false theoretical doctrine. So no changes were made in traditional procedures. Economic waves continued to follow one another.

The managers of the banks of issue have carried out their policy without reflecting very much on its basis. If the expansion of circulation credit began to alarm them, they proceeded, not always very skillfully, to raise the discount rate. Thus, they exposed themselves to public censure for having initiated the crisis by their behaviour. It is clear that the crisis must come sooner or later. It is also clear that the crisis must always be caused, primarily and directly, by the change in the conduct of the banks. If we speak of error on the part of the banks, however, we must point to the wrong they do in encouraging the upswing. The fault lies, not with the policy of raising the interest rate, but only with the fact that it was raised too late.

V. Modern[64] Cyclical Policy

1. Pre World War I Policy

The cyclical policy recommended today, in most of the literature dealing with the problem of business fluctuations and toward which considerable strides have already been made in the United States, rests entirely on the reasoning of the Circulation Credit Theory.[65] The aim of much of this literature is to make this theory useful in practice by studying business conditions with precise statistical methods.

There is no need to explain further that there is only one business cycle theory – the Circulation Credit Theory. All other attempts to cope with the problem have failed to withstand criticism. Every crisis policy and every cyclical policy have been derived from this theory. Its ideas have formed the basis of those cyclical and crisis policies pursued in the decades preceding the war. Thus, the Banking Theory, then recognized in literature as the only correct explanation, as well as all those interpretations which related the problem to the theory of direct exchange, were already disregarded. It may have still been popular to speak of the elasticity of notes in circulation as depending on the discounting of commodity bills of exchange. However, in the world of the bank managers, who made cyclical policy, other views prevailed.

To this extent, therefore, one cannot say that the theory behind today's cyclical policy is new. The Circulation Credit Theory has, to be sure, come a long way from the old Currency Theory. The studies which Walras, Wicksell and I have devoted to the problem have conceived of it as a more general phenomenon. These studies have related it to the whole economic process. They have sought to deal with it especially as a problem of interest rate formulation and of 'equilibrium' on the loan market. To recognize the extent of the progress made, compare, for instance, the famous controversy over free credit between Bastiat and Proudhon.[66] Or compare the usual criticism of the Quantity Theory in prewar German literature with recent discussions on the subject. However, no matter how significant this progress may be considered for the development of our understanding, we should not forget that the Currency Theory had already offered policy making every assistance in this regard that a theory can.

It is certainly not to be disputed that substantial progress was made when the problem was considered, not only from the point of view of fiduciary media, but from that of the entire problem of the purchasing power of money. The Currency School paid attention to price changes only insofar as they were produced by an increase or decrease of circulation credit – but they considered only the circulation credit granted by the issue of notes. Thus, the Currency School was a long way from striving for stabilization of the purchasing power of the monetary unit.

2. Post World War I Policies

Today these two problems, the issuance of fiduciary media and the purchasing power of the monetary unit, are seen as being closely linked to the Circulation Credit Theory. One of the tendencies of modern cyclical policy is that these two problems are treated as one. Thus, one aim of cyclical policy is no more nor less than the stabilization of the purchasing power of money. For a discussion of this see Part I of this study.

Like the Currency School, the other aim is not to stabilize purchasing power but only to avoid the crisis. However, a still further goal is contemplated – similar to that sought by the Peel Act and by prewar cyclical olicy. It is proposed to counteract a boom, whether caused by an expansion of fiduciary media or by a monetary inflation (for example, an increase in the production of gold). Then, again, depression is to be avoided when there is restriction irrespective of whether it starts with a contraction in the quantity of money or of fiduciary media. The aim is not to keep prices stable, but to prevent the free market interest rate from being reduced temporarily by the banks of issue or by monetary inflation.

In order to explain the essence of this new policy, we shall now explore two specific cases in more detail:

1. The production of gold increases and prices rise. A price premium appears in the interest rate that would limit the demand for loans to the supply of lendable funds available. The banks, however, have no reason to raise their lending rate. As a matter of fact, they become more willing to discount at a lower rate as the relationship between their obligations and their stock of gold had been improved. It has certainly not deteriorated. The actual loan rate they are asking lags behind the interest rate that would prevail on a free market, thus providing the initiative for a boom. In this instance, prewar crisis policy would not have intervened since it considered only the ratio of the bank's cover which had not deteriorated. As prices and wages rise [resulting in an increased demand for business loans], modern theory maintains that the interest rates should rise and circulation credit be restricted.

2. The inducement to the boom had been given by the banks in response, let us say, to the general pressure to make credit cheaper in order to combat depression, without any change in the quantity of money in the narrower sense.[67] Since the cover ratio deteriorates as a result, even the older crisis policy would have called for increasing the interest rate as a brake.

Only in the first of these two instances does a fundamental difference exist between old and new policies.

3. Empirical Studies

Many now engaged in cyclical research maintain that the special superiority of current crisis policy in America rests on the use of more precise statistical methods than those previously available. Presumably, means for eliminating seasonal fluctuations and the secular general trend have been developed from statistical series and curves. Obviously, it is only with such manipulations that the findings of a market study may become a study of the business cycle. However, even if one should agree with the American investigators in their evaluation of the success of this effort, the question remains as to the usefulness of index numbers. Nothing more can be added to what has been said above on the subject, in Part I of this study.

The development of the Three Market Barometer[68] is considered the most important accomplishment of the Harvard investigations. Since it is is not possible to determine Wicksell's natural rate of interest or the 'ideal' price premium, we are advised to compare the change in the interest rate with the movement of prices and other data indicative of business conditions, such as production figures, the number of unemployed, etc. This has been done for decades. One need only glance at reports in the daily papers, economic weeklies, monthlies and annuals of the last two generations to discover that the many claims, made so proudly today, of being the first to recognize the significance of such data for understanding the course of business conditions, are unwarranted. The Harvard institute, however, has performed a service in that it has sought to establish an empirical regularity in the timing of the movements in the three curves.

There is no need to share the exuberant expectations for the practical usefulness of the Harvard barometer which has prevailed in the American business world for some time. It can readily be admitted that this barometer has scarcely contributed anything toward increasing and deepening our knowledge of cyclical movements. Nevertheless, the significance of the Harvard barometer for the investigation of business conditions may still be highly valued, for it does provide statistical substantiation of the Circulation Credit Theory. Twenty years ago, it would not have been thought possible to arrange and manipulate statistical material so as to make it useful for the study of business conditions. Here real success has crowned the ingenious work done by economists and statisticians together.

Upon examining the curves developed by institutes using the Harvard method, it becomes apparent that the movement of the money market curve (C Curve) in relation to the stock market curve (A Curve) and the commodity market curve (B Curve) corresponds exactly to what the Circulation Credit Theory asserts. The fact that the movements of A Curve generally anticipate those of B Curve is explained by the greater sensitivity of stock, as opposed to commodity, speculation. The stock market reacts more promptly than does the commodity market. It sees more and it sees farther. It is quicker to draw coming events (in this case, the changes in the interest rate) into the sphere of its conjectures.

4. Arbitrary Political Decisions

However, the crucial question still remains: What does the Three Market Barometer offer the man who is actually making bank policy? Are modern methods of studying business conditions better suited than the former, to be sure less thorough, ones for laying the groundwork for decisions on a discount policy aimed at reducing as much as possible the ups and downs of business? Even prewar [World War I] banking policy had this for its goal. There is no doubt but that government agencies responsible for financial policy, directors of the central banks of issue and also of the large private banks and banking houses, were frankly and sincerely interested in attaining this goal. Their efforts in this direction – only when the boom was already in full swing to be sure – were supported at least by a segment of public opinion and of the press. They knew well enough what was needed to accomplish the desired effect. They knew that nothing but a timely and sufficiently far-reaching increase in the loan rate could counteract what was usually referred to as 'excessive speculation.'

They failed to recognize the fundamental problem. They did not understand that every increase in the amount of circulation credit (whether brought about by the issue of banknotes or expanding bank deposits) causes a surge in business and thus starts the cycle which leads once more, over and beyond the crisis, to the decline in business activity. In short, they embraced the very ideology responsible for generating business fluctuations. However, this fact did not prevent them, once the cyclical upswing became obvious, from thinking about its unavoidable outcome. They did not know that the upswing had been generated by the conduct of the banks. If they had, they might well have seen it only as a blessing of banking policy, for to them the most important task of economic policy was to overcome the depression, at least so long as the depression lasted. Still they knew that a progressing upswing must lead to crisis and then to stagnation.

As a result, the trade boom evoked misgivings at once. The immediate problem became simply how to counteract the onward course of the 'unhealthy' development. There was no question of 'whether,' but only of 'how.' Since the method – increasing the interest rate – was already settled, the question of 'how' was only a matter of timing and degree: When and how much should the interest rate be raised?

The critical point was that this question could not be answered precisely, on the basis of undisputed data. As a result, the decision must always be left to discretionary judgment. Now, the more firmly convinced those responsible were that their interference, by raising the interest rate, would put an end to the prosperity of the boom, the more cautiously they must act. Might not those voices be correct which maintained that the upswing was *not* 'artificially' produced, that there wasn't any 'overspeculation' at all, that the boom was only the natural outgrowth of technical progress, the development of means of communication, the discovery of new supplies of raw materials, the opening up of new markets? Should this delightful and happy state of affairs be rudely interrupted? Should the government act in such a way that the economic improvement, for which it took credit, gives way to crisis?

93

The hesitation of officials to intervene is sufficient to explain the situation. To be sure, they had the best of intentions for stopping in time. Even so, the steps they took were usually 'too little and too late.' There was always a time lag before the interest rate reached the point at which prices must start down again. In the interim, capital had become frozen in investments for which it would have been used if the interest rate on money had not been held below its 'natural rate.'

This drawback to cyclical policy is not changed in any respect if it is carried out in accordance with the business barometer. No one who has carefully studied the conclusions, drawn from observations of business conditions made by institutions working with modern methods, will dare to contend that these results may be used to establish, incontrovertibly, when and how much to raise the interest rate in order to end the boom in time before it has led to to capital malinvestment. The accomplishment of economic journalism in reporting regularly on business conditions during the last two generations should not be *under*rated. Nor should the contributions of contemporary business cycle research institutes, working with substantial means, be *over*rated. Despite all the improvements which the preparation of statistics and graphic interpretations have undergone, their use in the determination of interest rate policy still leaves a wide margin for judgment.

5. Sound Theory Essential

Moreover, it should not be forgotten that it is impossible to answer in a straightforward manner not only how seasonal variations and growth factors are to be eliminated, but also how to decide unequivocally from what data and by what method the curves of each of the Three Markets should be constructed. Arguments which cannot be easily refuted may be raised on every point with respect to the business barometer. Also, no matter how much the business barometer may help us to survey the many heterogeneous operations of the market and of production, they certainly do not offer a solid basis for weighing contingencies. Business barometers are not even in a position to furnish clear and certain answers to the questions concerning cyclical policy which are crucial for their operation. Thus, the great expectations generally associated with recent cyclical policy today are not justified.

For the future of cyclical policy more profound theoretical knowledge concerning the nature of changes in business conditions would inevitably be of incomparably greater value than any conceivable manipulation of statistical methods. Some business cycle research institutes are imbued with the erroneous idea that they are conducting impartial factual research, free of any prejudice due to theoretical considerations. In fact, all their work rests on the groundwork of the Circulation Credit Theory. In spite of the reluctance which exists today against logical reasoning in economics and against thinking problems and theories through to their ultimate conclusions, a great deal would be gained if it were decided to base cyclical policy deliberately on this theory. Then, one would know that every expansion of circulation credit must be counteracted in order to even out the waves of the business cycle. Then, a force operating on one side to reduce the purchasing power of money would be offset from the other side. The difficulties, due to the impossibility of finding any method for measuring changes in purchasing power, cannot be overcome. It is impossible to realize the ideal of either a monetary unit of unchanging value or economic stability. However, once it is resolved to forego the artificial stimulation of business activity by means of banking policy, fluctuations in business conditions will surely be substantially reduced. To be sure this will mean giving up many a well-loved slogan, for example, 'easy money' to encourage credit transactions. However, a still greater ideological sacrifice than that is called for. *The desire to reduce the interest rate in any way must also be abandoned.*

It has already been pointed out that events would have turned out very differently if there had been no deviation from the principle of complete freedom in banking and if the issue of fiduciary media had been in no way exempted from the rules of commercial law. It may be that a final solution of the problem can be arrived at only through the establishment of completely free banking. However, the credit structure which has been developed by the continued effort of many generations cannot be transformed with one blow. Future generations, who will have recognized the basic absurdity of all interventionist attempts, will have to deal with this question also. However, the time is not yet ripe – not now nor in the immediate future.

VI. *Control of the Money Market*

1. *International Competition or Cooperation*

There are many indications that public opinion has recognized the significance of the role banks play in initiating the cycle by their expansion of circulation credit. If this view should actually prevail, then the previous popularity of efforts aimed at artificially reducing the interest rate on loans would disappear. Banks that wanted to expand their issue of fiduciary media would no longer be able to count on public approval or government support. They would become more careful and more temperate. That would smooth out the waves of the cycle and reduce the severity of the sudden shift from rise to fall.

However, there are some indications which seem to contradict this view of public opinion. Most important among these are the attempts or, more precisely, the reasoning which underlies the attempts to bring about international cooperation among the banks of issue.

In speculative periods of the past, the very fact that the banks of the various countries did not work together systematically, and according to agreement, constituted a most effective brake. With closely-knit international economic relations, the expansion of circulation credit could only become universal if it were an international phenomenon. Accordingly, lacking any international agreement, individual banks, fearing a large outflow of capital, took care in setting their interest rates not to lag far below the rates of the banks of other countries. Thus, in response to interest rate arbitrage and any deterioration in the balance of trade, brought about by higher prices, an exodus of loan money to other countries would, for one thing, have impaired the ratio of the bank's cover, as a result of foreign claims on their gold and foreign exchange which such conditions impose on the bank of issue. The bank, obliged to consider its solvency, would then be forced to restrict credit. In addition, this impairment of the ever-shifting balance of payments would create a shortage of funds on the money market which the banks would be powerless to combat. The closer the economic connections among peoples become, the less possible it is to have a *national* boom. The business climate becomes an *international* phenomenon.

However, in many countries, especially in the German Reich, the view has frequently been expressed by friends of 'cheap money' that it is only the gold standard that forces the bank of issue to consider interest rates abroad in determining its own interest policy. According to this view, if the bank were free of this shackle, it could then better satisfy the demands of the domestic money market, to the advantage of the national economy. With this view in mind, there were in Germany advocates of bimetallism, as well as of a gold premium policy.[69] In Austria, there was resistance to formalizing legally the *de facto* practice of redeeming its notes.

It is easy to see the fallacy in this doctrine that only the tie of the monetary unit to gold keeps the banks from reducing interest rates at will. Even if all ties with the gold standard were broken, this would not have given the banks the power to lower the interest rate, below the height of the 'natural' interest rate, with impunity. To be sure, the paper standard would have permitted them to continue the expansion of circulation credit without hesitation, because a bank of issue, relieved of the obligation of redeeming its notes, need have no fear with respect to its solvency. Still, the increase in notes would have led first to price increases and consequently to a deterioration in the rate of exchange. Secondly, the crisis would have come – later, to be sure, but all the more severely.

If the banks of issue were to consider seriously making agreements with respect to discount policy, this would eliminate one effective check. By acting in unison, the banks could extend more circulation credit than they do now, without any fear that the consequences would lead to a situation which produces an external drain of funds from the money market. To be sure, if this concern with the situation abroad is eliminated, the banks are still not always in a position to reduce the money rate of interest below its 'natural' rate in the long run. However, the difference between the two interest rates can be maintained longer, so that the inevitable result – malinvestment of capital – appears on a larger scale. This must then intensify the unavoidable crisis and deepen the depression.

So far, it is true, the banks of issue have made no significant agreements on cyclical policy. Nevertheless, efforts aimed at such agreements are certainly being proposed on every side.

2. 'Boom' Promotion Problems
Another dangerous sign is that the slogan concerning the need to 'control the money market,' through the banks of issue, still retains its prestige.

Given the situation, especially as it has developed in Europe, only the central banks are entitled to issue notes. Under that system, attempts to expand circulation credit universally can only originate with the central bank of issue. Every venture on the part of private banks, against the wish or the plan of the central bank, is doomed from the very beginning. Even banking techniques, learned from the Anglo-Saxons, are of no service to private banks, since the opportunity for granting credit, by opening bank deposits, is insignificant in countries where the use of cheques (except for central bank clearings and the circulation of postal cheques) is confined to a narrow circle in the business world. However, if the central bank of issue embarks upon a policy of credit expansion and thus begins to force down the rate of interest, it may be advantageous for the largest private banks to follow suit and expand the volume of circulation credit *they* grant too. Such a procedure has still a further advantage for them. It involves them in no risk. If confidence is shaken during the crisis, they can survive the critical stage with the aid of the bank of issue.

However, the bank of issue's credit expansion policy certainly offers a large number of banks a profitable field for speculation – arbitrage in the loan rates of interest. They seek to profit from the shifting ratio between domestic and foreign interest rates by investing domestically obtained funds in short term funds abroad. In this process, they are acting in opposition to the discount policy of the bank of issue and hurting the alleged interests of those groups which hope to benefit from the artificial reduction of the interest rate and from the boom it produces. The ideology, which sees salvation in every effort to lower the interest rate and regards expansion of circulation credit as the best method of attaining this goal, is consistent with the policy of branding the actions of the interest rate arbitrageur as scandalous and disgraceful, even as a betrayal of the interests of his own people to the advantage of foreigners. The policy of granting the banks of issue every possible assistance in the fight against these speculators is also consistent with this ideology. Both government and bank of issue seek to intimidate the malefactors with threats, to dissuade them from their plan. In the liberal[70] countries of western Europe, at least in the past, little could be accomplished by such methods. In the interventionist countries of middle and eastern Europe, attempts of this kind have met with greater success.

It is easy to see what lies behind this effort of the bank of issue to 'control' the money market. The bank wants to prevent its credit expansion policy, aimed at reducing the interest rate, from being impeded by consideration of relatively restrictive policies followed abroad. It seeks to promote a domestic boom without interference from international reactions.

3. Drive for Tighter Controls

According to the prevailing ideology, however, there are still other occasions when the banks of issue should have stronger control over the money market. If the interest rate arbitrage, resulting from the expansion of circulation credit, had led, for the time being, only to a withdrawal of funds from the reserves of the issuing bank, and that bank, disconcerted by the deterioration of the security behind its notes, has proceeded to raise its discount rate, there may still be, under certain conditions, no cause for the loan rate to rise on the open money market. As yet no funds have been withdrawn from the domestic market. The gold exports came from the bank's reserves, and the increase in the discount rate has not led to a reduction in the credits granted by the bank. It takes time for loan funds to become scarce as a result of the fact that some commercial paper, which would otherwise have been offered to the bank for discount, is disposed of on the open market. The issuing bank, however, does not want to wait so long for its manoeuvre to be effective. Alarmed at the state of its gold and foreign exchange assets, it wants prompt relief. To accomplish this, it must try to make money scarce on the market. It generally tries to bring this about by appearing itself as a borrower on the market.

Another case, when control of the money market is contested, concerns the utilization of funds made available to the market by the generous discount policy. The dominant ideology favours 'cheap money.' It also favours high commodity prices, but not always high stock market prices.

The moderated interest rate is intended to stimulate production and not to cause a stock market boom. However, stock prices increase first of all. At the outset, commodity prices are not caught up in the boom. There are stock exchange booms and stock exchange profits. Yet, the 'producer' is dissatisfied. He envies the 'speculator' his 'easy profit.' Those in power are not willing to accept this situation. They believe that production is being deprived of money which is flowing into the stock market. Besides, it is precisely in the stock market boom that the serious threat of a crisis lies hidden.

Therefore, the aim is to withdraw money from stock exchange loans in order to inject it into the 'economy.' Trying to do this simply by raising the interest rate offers no special attraction. Such a rise in the interest rate is certainly unavoidable in the end. It is only a question of whether it comes sooner or later. Whenever the interest rate rises sufficiently, it brings an end to the business boom. Therefore, other measures are tried to transfer funds from the stock market into production, without changing the cheap rate for loans. The bank of issue exerts pressure on borrowers to influence the use made of the sums loaned out. Or else it proceeds directly to set different terms for credit depending on its use.

Thus we can see what it means if the central bank of issue aims at domination of the money market. Either the expansion of circulation credit is freed from the limitations which would eventually restrict it. Or the boom is shifted by certain measures along a course different from the one it would otherwise have followed. Thus, the pressure for 'control of the money market' specifically envisions the encouragement of the boom – the boom which must end in a crisis. If a cyclical policy is to be followed to eliminate crises, this desire, the desire to control and dominate the money market, must be abandoned.

If it were seriously desired to counteract price increases resulting from an increase in the quantity of money – due to an increase in the mining of gold, for example – by restricting circulation credit, the central banks of issue would borrow more on the market. Paying off these obligations later could hardly be described as 'controlling the money market.' For the bank of issue, the restriction of circulation credit means the renunciation of profits. It may even mean losses.

Morever, such a policy can be successful only if there is agreement among the banks of issue. If restriction were practiced by the central bank of one country only, it would result in relatively high costs of borrowing money within that country. The chief consequence of this would then be that gold would flow in from abroad. Insofar as this is the goal sought by the cooperation of the banks, it certainly cannot be considered a dangerous step in the attempt toward a policy of evening out the waves of the business cycle.

VII. *Business Forecasting for Cyclical Policy and the Businessman*

1. *Contributions of Business Cycle Research*

The popularity enjoyed by contemporary business cycle research, the development of which is due above all to American economic researchers, derives from exaggerated expectations as to its usefulness in practice. With its help, it had been hoped to mechanize banking policy and business activity. It had been hoped that a glance at the business barometer would tell businessmen and those who determine banking policy how to act.

At present, this is certainly out of the question. It has already been emphasized often enough that the results of business cycle studies have only described past events and that they may be used for predicting future developments only on the basis of extremely inadequate principles. However – and this is not sufficiently noted – these principles apply solely on the assumption that the ideology calling for expansion of circulation credit has not lost its standing in the field of economic and banking policy. Once a serious start is made at directing cyclical policy toward the *elimination* of crises, the power of this ideology is already dissipated.

Nevertheless, one broad field remains for the employment of the contemporary business cycle studies. They should indicate to the makers of banking policy when the interest rate must be raised to avoid instigating credit expansion. If the study of business conditions were clear on this point and gave answers admitting of only one interpretation, so that there could be only one opinion, not only as to *whether* but also as to *when* and *how much* to increase the discount rate, then the advantage of such studies could not be rated highly enough. However, this is not the case. Everything that the observation of business conditions contributes in the form of manipulated data and material can be interpreted in various ways.

Even before the development of business barometers, it was already known that increases in stock market quotations and commodity prices, a rise in profits on raw materials, a drop in unemployment, an increase in business orders, the selling off of inventories, and so on, signified a boom. The question is, when should, or when must, the brakes be applied. However, no business cycle institute answers this question straightforwardly and without equivocation. What should be done will always depend on an examination of the driving forces which shape business conditions and on the objectives set for cyclical policy. Whether the right moment for action is seized can never be decided except on the basis of a careful observation of all market phenomena. Moreover, it has never been possible to answer this question in any other way. The fact that we now know how to classify and describe the various market data more clearly than before does not make the task essentially any easier.

A glance at the continuous reports on the economy and the stock market in the large daily newspapers and in the economic weeklies, which appeared from 1840 to 1910, shows that attempts have been made for decades to draw conclusions from events of the most recent past, on the basis of empirical rules, as to the shape of the immediate future. If we compare the statistical groundwork used in these attempts with those now at our disposal, then it is obvious that we have recourse to more data today. We also understand better how to organize this material, how to arrange it clearly and interpret it for graphic presentation. However, we can by no means claim, with the modern methods of studying business conditions, to have embarked on some new principle.

2. Difficulties of Precise Prediction

No businessman may safely neglect any available source of information. Thus no businessman can refuse to pay close attention to newspaper reports. Still diligent newspaper reading is no guarantee of business success. If success were that easy, what wealth would the journalists have already amassed! In the business world, success depends on comprehending the situation sooner than others do – and acting accordingly. What is recognized as 'fact' must first be evaluated correctly to make it useful for an undertaking. Precisely this is the problem of putting theory into practice.

A prediction, which makes judgments which are *qualitative* only and not *quantitative*, is practically useless even if it is eventually proved right by the later course of events. There is also the crucial question of timing. Decades ago, Herbert Spencer recognized, with brilliant perception, that militarism, imperialism, socialism and interventionism must lead to great wars, severe wars. However, anyone who had started about 1890, to speculate on the strength of that insight on a depreciation of the bonds of the Three Empires[71] would have sustained heavy losses. Large historical perspectives furnish no basis for stock market speculations which must be reviewed daily, weekly, or monthly at least.

It is well known that every boom must one day come to an end. The businessman's situation, however, depends on knowing exactly when and where the break will first appear. No economic barometer can answer these questions. An economic barometer only furnishes data from which conclusions may be drawn. Since it is still possible for the central bank of issue to delay the start of the catastrophe with its discount policy, the situation depends chiefly on making judgments as to the conduct of these authorities. Obviously, all available data fail at this point.

But once public opinion is completely dominated by the view that the crisis is imminent and businessmen act on this basis, then it is already too late to derive business profit from this knowledge. Or even merely to avoid losses. For then the panic breaks out. The crisis has come.

VIII. *The Aims and Method of Cyclical Policy*

1. *Revised Currency School Theory*

Without doubt, expanding the sphere of scientific investigation from the narrow problem of the crisis into the broader problem of the cycle represents progress.[72] However, it was certainly not equally advantageous for political policies. Their scope was broadened. They began to aspire to more than was feasible.

The economy could be organized so as to eliminate cyclical changes only if (1) there were something more than muddled thinking behind the concept that changes in the value of the monetary unit can be measured, and (2) it were possible to determine in advance the extent of the effect which accompanies a definite change in the quantity of money and fiduciary media. As these conditions do not prevail, the goals of cyclical policy must be more limited. However, even if only such severe shocks as those experienced in 1857, 1873, 1900/01 and 1907, could be avoided in the future, a great deal would have been accomplished.

The most important prerequisite of any cyclical policy, no matter how modest its goal may be, is to renounce every attempt to reduce the interest rate, by means of banking policy, below the rate which develops on the market. That means a return to the theory of the Currency School, which sought to suppress all future expansion of circulation credit and thus all further creation of fiduciary media. However, this does not mean a return to the old Currency School programme, the application of which was limited to banknotes. Rather it means the introduction of a new programme based on the old Currency School theory, but expanded in the light of the present state of knowledge to include fiduciary media issued in the form of bank deposits.

The banks would be obliged at all times to maintain metallic backing for all notes – except for the sum of those outstanding which are not now covered by metal – equal to the total sum of the notes issued and bank deposits opened. That would mean a complete reorganization of central bank legislation. The banks of issue would have to return to the principles of Peel's Bank Act, but with the provisions expanded to cover also bank balances subject to check. The same stipulations with respect to reserves must also be applied to the large national deposit institutions, especially the postal savings.[73] Of course, for these secondary banks of issue, the central bank reserves for their notes and deposits would be the equivalent of gold reserves. In those countries where checking accounts at private commercial banks play an important role in trade – notably the United States and England – the same obligation must be exacted from those banks also.

By this act alone, cyclical policy would be directed in earnest toward the elimination of crises.

2. 'Price Level' Stabilization

Under present circumstances, it is out of the question, in the foreseeable future, to establish complete 'free banking' and place all banking transactions, including the granting of credit, under ordinary commercial law. Those who speak and write today on behalf of 'stabilization,' 'maintenance of purchasing power' and 'elimination of the trade cycle,' can certainly not call this more limited approach 'extreme.' On the contrary! They will reject this suggestion as not going far enough. They are demanding much more. In their view, the 'price level' should be maintained by countering rising prices with a restriction in the circulation of fiduciary media and, similarly, countering falling prices by the expansion of fiduciary media.

The arguments that may be advanced in *favour* of this modest programme have already been set forth above in the first part of this work. In our judgment, the arguments which militate *against* all monetary manipulation are so great that placing decisions as to the formation of purchasing power in the hands of banking officials, parliaments and governments, thus making it subject to shifting political influences, must be avoided. The methods available for measuring changes in purchasing power are necessarily defective. The effect of the various manoeuvres, intended to influence purchasing power, cannot be quantitatively established – neither in advance nor even after they have taken place. Thus proposals which amount only to making approximate adjustments in purchasing power must be considered completely impractical.

Nothing more will be said here concerning the fundamental absurdity of the concept of 'stable purchasing power' in a changing economy. This has already been discussed at some length. For practical economic policy, the only problem is what inflationist or restrictionist measures to consider for the partial adjustment of severe price declines or increases. Such measures, carried out in stages, step by step, through piecemeal international agreements, would benefit either creditors or debtors. However, one question remains: Whether, in view of the conflicts among interests, agreements on this issue could be reached among nations. The viewpoints of creditors and debtors will no doubt differ widely, and these conflicts of interest will complicate still more the manipulation of money internationally, than on the national level.

3. International Complications

It is also possible to consider monetary manipulation as an aspect of national economic policy, and take steps to regulate the value of money independently, without reference to the international situation. According to Keynes,[74] if there is a choice between stabilization of prices and stabilization of the foreign exchange rate, the decision should be in favour of price stabilization and against stabilization of the rate of exchange. However, a nation which chose to proceed in this way would create international complications because of the repercussions its policy would have on the content of contractual obligations.

For example, if the United States were to raise the purchasing power of the dollar over that of its present gold parity, the interests of foreigners who owed dollars would be very definitely affected as a result. Then again, if debtor nations were to try to depress the purchasing power of their monetary unit, the interests of creditors would be impaired. Irrespective of this, every change in value of a monetary unit would unleash influences on foreign trade. A rise in its value would foster increased imports, while a fall in its value would be recognized as the power to increase exports.

In recent generations, consideration of these factors has led to pressure for a single monetary standard based on gold. If this situation is ignored, then it will certainly not be possible to fashion monetary value so that it will generally be considered satisfactory. In view of the ideas prevailing today with respect to trade policy, especially in connection with foreign relations, a rising value for money is not considered desirable, because of its power to promote imports and to hamper exports.

Attempts to introduce a national policy, so as to influence prices independently of what is happening abroad, while still clinging to the gold standard and the corresponding rates of exchange, would be completely unworkable. There is no need to say any more about this.

4. The Future

The obstacles, which militate against a policy aimed at the complete elimination of cyclical changes, are truly considerable. For that reason, it is not very likely that such new approaches to monetary and banking policy, that limit the creation of fiduciary media, will be followed. It will probably not be resolved to prohibit entirely the expansion of fiduciary media. Nor is it likely that expansion will be limited to only the quantities sufficient to counteract a definite and pronounced trend toward generally declining prices. Perplexed as to how to evaluate the serious political and economic doubts which are raised in opposition to every kind of manipulation of the value of money, the people will probably forego decisive action and leave it to the central bank managers to proceed, case by case, at their own discretion. Just as in the past, cyclical policy of the near future will be surrendered into the hands of the men who control the conduct of the great central banks and those who influence their ideas, i.e., the moulders of public opinion.

Nevertheless, the cyclical policy of the future will differ appreciably from its predecessor. It will be knowingly based on the Circulation Credit Theory of the Trade Cycle. The hopeless attempt to reduce the loan rate indefinitely by continuously expanding circulation credit will not be revived in the future. It may be that the quantity of fiduciary media will be intentionally expanded or contracted in order to influence purchasing power. However, the people will no longer be under the illusion that technical banking procedures can make credit cheaper and thus create prosperity without its having repercussions.

The only way to do away with, or even to alleviate, the periodic return of the trade cycle – with its denouement, the crisis – is to reject the fallacy that prosperity can be produced by using banking procedures to make credit cheap.

NOTES

1. *MME*. 'Monetary theory of the trade cycle,' p. 91; 'Trade cycle,' p. 139.
2. *MME*. 'Classical economics,' 'Classic liberalism' and 'Classical theory of value,' pp. 20–1.
3. *MME*. 'Austrian School,' p. 6; and miscellaneous definitions under 'Subjective . . .,' pp. 133–4.
4. *MME*. 'Historicism,' p. 60; 'Nominalism,' pp. 98–9.
5. *MME*. 'Empiricism,' p. 39; 'Institutionalism,' p. 68.
6. Sixteen years ago when I presented the Circulation Credit Theory of the crisis in the first German edition of my book on *The Theory of Money and Credit* (1912), I encountered ignorance and stubborn rejection everywhere, especially in Germany. The reviewer for Schmoller's Yearbook [*Jahrbuch für Gesetzgebung, Verwaltung und Volkswirtschaft*] declared: 'The conclusions of the entire work [are] simply not discussable.' The reviewer for Conrad's Yearbook [*Jahrbuch für Nationalökonomie und Statistik*] stated: 'Hypothetically, the

author's arguments should not be described as completely wrong; they are at least coherent.' But his final judgment was 'to reject it anyhow.' Anyone who follows current developments in economic literature closely, however, knows that things have changed basically since then. The doctrine which was ridiculed once is widely accepted today. LvM.

7. *Zeitschrift für Volkswirtschaft, Sozialpolitik und Verwaltung*, vol. vii, p. 132. LvM.

8. In the German text Mises uses the English term, 'Standard of deferred payments,' commenting in a footnote: 'Standard of deferred payments is "Zahlungsmittel" in German. Unfortunately this German expression must be avoided nowadays. Its meaning has been so compromised through its use by Nominalists and Chartists that it brings to mind the recently exploded errors of the State Theory of Money.' See above for comments on 'State Theory of Money,' p. 14n., and 'Chartism,' p. 24n.

9. Jevons, Wm Stanley, *Money and the Mechanisms of Exchange*, 13th edn (London, 1902), pp. 328ff. LvM.

10. Keynes, John Maynard, *A Tract on Monetary Reform* (London, 1923; New York, 1924), pp. 177ff. LvM.

11. Fisher, Irving, *Stabilizing the Dollar* (New York, 1925), pp. 79ff. LvM.

12. This is not the place to examine further the theory of the formation of the purchasing power of the monetary unit. In this connection, see pp. 97–165 in *The Theory of Money and Credit*. LvM.

13. The quantity of 'money in the broader sense' is equal to the quantity of money proper [i.e., commodity money] plus the quantity of fiduciary media [i.e., notes, bank deposits not backed by metal, and subsidiary coins.] LvM. [See also *MME* , 'Commodity money,' p. 22, 'Fiduciary media,' p. 48 and 'Money in the broader sense,' p. 92.]

14. Machlup, Fritz, *Die Goldkernwährung* (Halberstadt, 1925), p. xi. LvM.

15. A monetary standard based on a unit with a flexible gold parity; 'Golddevisenkernwährung,' literally a standard based on convertibility into a foreign monetary unit, in effect a 'flexible gold exchange standard.' In later writings, Professor Mises shortened this to 'flexible standard' and this term will be used henceforth in this translation. See *Human Action* (ch. xxxi, sect. 3). See also *MME*, 'Flexible standard,' p. 49, and 'Gold exchange standard,' pp. 53–4.

16. Mises used 'liberal' in its original sense and not in the currently popular sense. Thus 'liberalism' means 'classical liberalism,' which stood for limited government, protection of private property, freedom

for the individual and the market. For Mises' definition, see *Human Action*, 2nd edn (1963), p. v. Also *MME*, 'Liberal,' pp. 79–80.

17. Cassell, Gustav, *Währungsstabilisierung als Weltproblem* (Leipzig, 1928), p. 12. LvM.

18. Eduard Suess (1831–1914) published a study in German (1877) on 'The Future of Gold.'

19. *The Theory of Money and Credit*, pp. 116ff. LvM.

20. Hans Vaihinger (1852–1933), author of *The Philosophy of As If* (German, 1911; English translation, 1924).

21. *The Theory of Money and Credit*. pp. 239ff. LvM.

22. At this point, in a footnote, Professor Mises commented on a controversy he had had with a student over terminology. He again recommended, as he had in 1923 (see above, p. 3n.), continuing to use Menger's terms which enjoyed general acceptance. The simpler English terms, which Mises developed and adopted later – notably in *Human Action*, pp. 419–24, where he describes 'goods-induced' or 'cash-induced' changes in the value of the monetary unit – are used in this translation. For those who may be interested in this controversy, the original footnote follows:

Carl Menger referred to the nature and extent of the influence exerted on money/goods exchange ratios [prices] by changes from the money side as the problem of the 'internal' exchange value (innere Tauschwert) of money [translated in this volume as 'cash-induced changes']. He referred to the variations in the purchasing power of the monetary unit due to other causes as changes in the 'external' exchange value (aussere Tauschwert) of money [translated as 'goods-induced changes']. I have criticized both expressions as being rather unfortunate – because of possible confusion with the terms 'extrinsic and intrinsic value' as used in Roman canon doctrine, and by English authors of the 17th and 18th centuries. (See the German editions of my book on *The Theory of Money and Credit* (1912), p. 132; (1924), p. 104). Nevertheless, this terminology has attained scientific acceptance through its use by Menger and it will be used in this study when appropriate.

There is no need to discuss an expression which describes a useful and indispensable idea. It is the concept itself, not the term used to describe it, which is important. Serious mischief is done if an author chooses a new term unnecessarily to express a concept for which a name already exists. My student, Gottfried Haberler, has criticized me severely for taking this position, reproaching me for being a slave to semantics. (See Haberler, *Der Sinn der Indexzahlen* (Tübingen, 1927), pp. 109ff.). However, in his relevant remarks on this problem,

Haberler says nothing more than I have. He too distinguishes between price changes arising on the goods and money sides. Beginners should seek to expand knowledge and avoid spending time on useless terminological disputes. As Haberler points out, it would obviously be wasted effort to 'seek internal and external exchange values of money in the real world.' Ideas do not belong to the 'real world' at all, but to the world of thought and knowledge.

It is even more astonishing that Haberler finds my critique of attempts to measure the value of the monetary unit 'inexpedient,' especially as his analysis rests entirely on mine. LvM.

23. See *The Theory of Money and Credit*, pp. 38ff. LvM. [See also *MME*, 'Value,' p. 145.]

24. See *Socialism*, pp. 121ff. LvM.

25. Mises refers here, of course, to the 1923 breakdown of the German monetary system.

26. See *The Theory of Money and Credit*, pp. 139ff. LvM.

27. *MME*. 'Credit money,' pp. 27–8.

28. Fisher, Irving, *The Rate of Interest* (New York, 1907), pp. 77ff. LvM.

29. Gossen, Hermann Heinrich, *Entwicklung der Gesetze des menschlichen Verkehrs und der daraus fliessenden Regeln für menschliches Handeln*, New edn (Berlin, 1889), p. 206. LvM.

30. See also my critique of Fisher's proposal in *The Theory of Money and Credit*, pp. 403ff. LvM.

31. Whether this is considered a change of purchasing power from the money side or from the commodity side is purely a matter of terminology. LvM.

32. Since this was written almost every government has become the largest borrower in its respective country. Thus today's government officials are inclined to the debtor's viewpoint, favouring low interest rates to keep down government interest payments.

33. I.e. 'classical liberalism.' See note 16 above.

34. In conversation, Professor Mises explained that this is a Greek term, meaning 'shaking off of burdens.' It was used in the 7th century BC and later to describe measures enacted to cancel public and private debts, completely or in part. Creditors then had to bear the burden, except to the extent that they might be indemnified by the government.

35. Keynes' 1923 proposal, *A Tract on Monetary Reform*. See note 10 above.

36. For the imaginary 'stationary economy,' Mises later preferred the more descriptive term, 'evenly rotating economy,' which he used in *Human Action*. See *MME*, 'Evenly rotating economy,' pp. 43–4.

37. Lord Samuel Jones Loyd Overstone (1796–1883) was an early opponent of inconvertible paper money and a leading proponent of the principles of Peel's Act of 1844. See *MME*, 'Peel's Act of 1844,' pp. 104–5.
38. See Mises' *Theory and History* (New Haven: Yale, 1957; New Rochelle, N.Y.: Arlington House, 1969).
39. Regarding the theories of Wm Stanley Jevons, Henry L. Moore and Wm Beveridge, see Wesley Clair Mitchell's *Business Cycles* (New York: National Bureau of Economic Research, 1927), pp. 12ff. LvM.
40. *MME*. 'Circulation credit,' pp. 19–20.
41. As mentioned above, the most commonly used name for this theory is the 'Monetary Theory.' For a number of reasons the designation 'Circulation Credit Theory' is preferable. LvM. [See *Human Action*, ch. xx, sect. 8, where Mises refers to this theory as 'The Monetary or Circulation Credit Theory of the Trade Cycle.']
42. If expressions such as cycle, wave, etc., are used in business cycle theory, they are merely illustrations to simplify the presentation. One cannot and should not expect more from a simile which, as such, must always fall short of reality. LvM.
43. *MME*. 'Commodity credit,' pp. 21–2.
44. For further explanation of the distinction between 'commodity credit' and 'circulation credit' see Mises' essay of 1946 reprinted below, especially pp. 217–19.
45. In 1928, fiduciary media were issued only by discounting what Mises called commodity bills, or short-term (90 days or less) bills of exchange endorsed by a buyer and a seller and constituting a lien on the goods sold.
46. Albert Hahn and Joseph Schumpeter have given me credit for the expression 'forced savings' or 'compulsory savings.' See Hahn's article on 'Credit' in *Handwörterbuch der Staatswissenschaften* (4th edn, vol. v, p. 951) and Schumpeter's *The Theory of Economic Development* (2nd German language edn, 1926); [English trans., Harvard Univ. Press, 1934, p. 109n]). To be sure, I described the phenomenon in 1912 in the first German language edition of *The Theory of Money and Credit* [see pp. 208ff. and 347ff. of the English translation]. However, I do not believe the expression itself was actually used there. LvM.
47. In place of 'equilibrium,' Mises later came to prefer 'the final state of rest.' See the LvM note 48 below.
48. In the language of Knut Wicksell and the Classical economists. LvM.
49. Later Mises came to use the term 'evenly rotating economy' in lieu of

'static equilibrium.' See *MME*, 'Evenly rotating economy,' pp. 43–4, and 'Stationary economy,' p. 132.

50. This was in the days before labour unions were privileged to raise wage rates above those of the unhampered market.

51. I believe this should be pointed out here again, although I have exhausted everything to be said on the subject (pp. 71–2) and in *The Theory of Money and Credit*, pp. 361ff. Anyone who has followed the discussions of recent years will realize how important it is to stress these things again and again. LvM.

52. 'Failure monopoly' is Mises' later term for such malinvestments. See *MME*, p. 45.

53. To avoid misunderstanding, it should be pointed out that the expression 'long-waves' of the trade cycle is not to be understood here as it was used by either Wilhelm Röpke or N. D. Kondratieff. Röpke, *Die Konjunktur* (Jena, 1922), p. 21, considered 'long-wave cycles' to be those which lasted 5–10 years generally. Kondratieff ('Die langen Wellen der Konjunktur' in *Archiv für Sozialwissenschaft*, vol. 56, pp. 573ff.) tried to prove, unsuccessfully in my judgment, that, in addition to the 7–11 year cycles of business conditions which he called medium cycles, there were also regular cyclical waves averaging 50 years in length. LvM.

54. The German term, 'Sanierungskrise,' means literally 'restoration crisis,' i.e., the crisis which comes at the shift to more 'healthy' monetary relationships. In English this crisis is called the 'stabilization crisis.'

55. *MME*. 'Credit expansion,' p. 27.

56. Overstone, Samuel Jones Loyd (Lord). 'Reflections Suggested by a Perusal of Mr. J. Horsley Palmer's Pamphlet on the Causes and Consequences of the Pressure on the Money Market,' 1837. (Reprinted in *Tracts and Other Publications on Metallic and Paper Currency*, London, 1857), p. 31. LvM.

57. See *Theorie des Geldes und der Umlaufsmittel* (1912), pp. 433ff. I had been deeply impressed by the fact that Lord Overstone was also apparently inclined to this interpretation. See his *Reflections*, op. cit., pp. 32ff. LvM. [These paragraphs were deleted from the 2nd German edition (1924) from which was made the H. E. Batson English translation, *The Theory of Money and Credit*, published 1934, 1953 and 1971.]

58. William Douglass (1691–1752), a renowned physician, came to America in 1716. His 'A Discourse Concerning the Currencies of the British Plantations in America' (1739), first appeared anonymously.

59. See the examples cited in *The Theory of Money and Credit*, pp. 387ff. LvM.

60. See note 47 above.
61. Of fractional reserves against notes and demand deposit liabilities.
62. Even the countries that have followed different procedures in this respect have, for all practical purposes, placed no obstacle in the way of the development of fiduciary media in the form of bank deposits. LvM.
63. According to Professor Mises, the 'three European empires' were Austria-Hungary, Germany and Russia. This designation probably comes from the 'Three Emperors' League' (1872), an informal alliance among these governments. Its effectiveness was declining by 1890, and World War I dealt it a final blow.
64. By 'modern,' Mises means the theories of the Austrian School.
65. Mises undoubtedly refers here to the way the Federal Reserve System reacted to the post World War I boom, when it brought an end to credit expansion by raising the discount rate, thus precipitating the 1920–1 correction period, popularly called a 'recession.'
66. Frédéric Bastiat (1801–50) replied to an open letter addressed to him by an editor of *Voix du Peuple*, 22 October 1849. Then the Socialist, Pierre Jean Proudhon (1809–65), answered. Proudhon, an advocate of unlimited monetary expansion by reduction of the interest rate to zero, and Bastiat, who favoured moderate credit expansion and only a limited reduction of interest rates, carried on a lengthy exchange for several months, until 7 March 1850. (*Oeuvres Complètes de Frédéric Bastiat*, 4th edn, vol. 5 (Paris, 1878), pp. 93–336.
67. *MME*. 'Money in the narrower sense,' p. 92.
68. This Harvard barometer was developed at the University by the Committee on Economic Research from three statistical series which are presumed to reveal (1) the extent of stock speculation, (2) the condition of industry and trade and (3) the supply of funds.
69. See above, p. 46, note 4.
70. See note 16 above.
71. Austria-Hungary, Germany and Russia. See note 63 above.
72. Also, as a result of this, it became easier to distinguish crises originating from definite causes (wars and political upheavals, violent convulsions of nature, changes in the shape of supply or demand) from cyclically-recurring crises. LvM.
73. The Post Office Savings Institution, established in Austria in the 1880s and copied in several other European countries, played a significant, if limited, role in monetary affairs. See Mises' comments in *Human Action*, pp. 445–6.
74. Keynes, John Maynard, *A Tract on Monetary Reform* (London, 1923; New York, 1924), pp. 156 ff. LvM.

Ludwig von Mises, 'The Treatment of "Irrationality" in the Social Scien-ces', Philosophy and Phenomenological Research, 1944, Richard M. Ebel-ing (ed.), *Money, Method and the Market Process* (Norwell, Mass: Kluwer, 1990), pp. 16–36.

A12

This paper was first published in *Philosophy and Phenomenological Research* vol. 4, no. 4 (June 1944) pp. 527–45. It was republished in *Money, Method, and the Market Process: Essays by Ludwig von Mises*, selected by Margit von Mises, by Praxeology Press of the Ludwig von Mises Institute and Kluwer Academic Publishers.

0360
0113

24

The Treatment of 'Irrationality' in the Social Sciences

LUDWIG von MISES

I

One of the manifestations of the present-day 'revolt against reason' is the tendency to find fault with the social sciences for being purely rational. Life and reality, say the critics, are irrational; it is quite wrong to deal with them as if they were rational and open to interpretation by reasoning. Rationalism fixes its eyes upon accessory matters only; its cognition is shallow and lacks profundity; it does not penetrate to the essence of things. It is an absurdity to press into dry rational schemes and into bloodless abstractions the finite variety of life's phenomena. What is needed is a science of irrationality and an irrational science.

The main target of these attacks is the theoretical science of human action, praxeology, and especially its hitherto best-developed part, economics or catallactics. But their scope includes the historical discipline too.

It should be realized that political motives have prompted this storm. Political parties and pressure groups whose programs cannot stand criticism based on dispassionate reasoning grasp at the straw of such an evasion. But science does not have the right to dispose of any objection merely on account of the motives which instigated it; it is not entitled to assume beforehand that a disapprobation must needs be unfounded because some of its supporters are imbued by party bias. It is bound to reply to every censure without any regard to its underlying motives and its background.

The challenge to reason and rationality did not rise in Germany. Like all other social doctrines and philosophies it had its origin in Western Europe. But it has prospered better on German soil than anywhere else. It has for a long time been the official doctrine of the Prussian universities. It has fashioned present-day German mentality, and the Nazi philosophers proudly style it 'German social philosophy.' German *Staatswissenschaften* have refuted economics wholesale as a spurious product of the British and Austrian mind, and German historians have disparaged the achievements of Western historiography. However, we should not forget that a long line of German philosophers and historians have brilliantly succeeded in the elucidation of the epistemological problems of history.[1] Of course, to the men to whom we are indebted for these contributions no place is assigned in present-day Germany's Hall of Fame.

It would be logical to provide at the outset of a study devoted to the problems of 'rationality' and 'irrationality' a precise definition of the two terms. But it is impossible to conform to this legitimate requirement. It is precisely the characteristic feature of the objections with which we have to deal that they apply terms in a vague and ambiguous manner. They defy definiteness and logical strictness as inappropriate means for grasping of life and reality and cling to obscurity on purpose. They do not aim at clarity, but at depth *(Tiefe)*. They are proud of being inexact and of talking in metaphors.

The problem which we have to investigate is this. Is it true or not that the social sciences lost the right way because they apply discursive reasoning? Do we have to look for other avenues of approach than those provided by ratiocination and historical experience?

II

The scope of the social sciences is human action. History deals with past events, representing them from the viewpoint of various aspects. It embraces history proper, philology, ethnology; anthropology is a branch of history as far as it is not a part of biology, and psychology as far as it is neither physiology nor epistemology or philosophy. Economic history, descriptive economics, and economic statistics are, of course, history. The term sociology is used in two different meanings. Descriptive sociology deals with those historical phenomena of human action which are not viewed in descriptive economics; it overlaps to some extent the field claimed by ethnology and anthropology. General sociology, on the other hand, approaches historical experience from a more nearly universal viewpoint than that of the other historical branches. History proper, for instance, deals with an individual town or with towns in a definite period or with an individual people or with a certain geographical area. Max Weber in his main treatise deals with the town in general, i.e., with the whole historical experience concerning towns without any limitation to historical periods, geographical areas, or individual peoples, nations, races, and civilizations.[2] The subject-matter of all historical sciences is the past, they cannot teach us anything which would be valid for all human actions, that means for the future too.

The natural sciences too deal with past events. Of course, every experience is an experience of something passed away; there is no experience of future happenings. But the experience to which the natural sciences owe all their success is the experience of the experiment in which the various elements of change can be observed in isolation. The facts amassed in this way can be used for induction, a peculiar procedure of inference which has given evidence of its expediency, although its epistemological and logical qualification is still an unsolved problem.

The experience with which the social sciences have to deal is always the experience of complex phenomena. They are open to various interpretations. They do not provide us with facts which could be used in the manner in which the natural sciences use the results of their experiments for the forecast of future events. They cannot be used as building materials for the construction of theories.

Praxeology is a theoretical and systematic, not a historical science. Its scope is human action as such, irrespective of all environmental and incidental circumstances of the concrete acts. It aims at knowledge valid for all instances in which the conditions exactly correspond to those implied by its assumptions and inferences. Whether people exchange commodities and services directly by barter or indirectly by using a medium of exchange is a question of the particular institutional setting which can be answered by history only. But whenever and wherever a medium of exchange is in use, all the laws of monetary theory are valid with regard to the exchanges thus transacted.[3]

It is not the task of this article to enquire what makes such a science of praxeology possible, what its logical and epistemological character is and what method it applies. The study of the epistemological problems of the social sciences has been neglected for a long time. Even those authors who like David Hume, Archbishop Whately, John Stuart Mill, and Stanley Jevons were themselves eminent economists, dealt in their logical and epistemological writings only with the natural sciences, and did not bother about the peculiar character of the sciences of human action. The epistemology of the social sciences is the youngest branch of knowledge. Moreover, most of its work refers only to history; the existence of a theoretical science was long entirely ignored. The pioneer work of Senior and of Cairnes has only lately borne fruit.[4] The economists mostly lack philosophical training and the philosophers are not familiar with economics.

The importance of phenomenology for the solution of the epistemological problems of praxeology has not been noticed at all.[5]

But this article is not concerned with these tasks. We have to deal with those critics who blame the economists and the historians for having neglected the fact of 'irrationality.'

Action means conscious behaviour or purposive activity. It differs as such from the biological, physiological, and instinctive processes going on within human beings. It is behaviour open to the regulation and direction by volition and mind. Its field coincides with the sphere within which man is free to influence the course of events. As far as man has power to bring about an effect or a change, he necessarily acts, whether he does something or refrains from doing anything. Inactivity and passivity, letting things alone, are the outcome of a choice, are therefore action whenever a different form of behaviour would be possible. He who endures what he could change acts no less than he who interferes in order to attain another result. A man who abstains from influencing the operation of physiological and instinctive factors which he could influence also acts. Action is not only doing but no less omitting to do what possibly could be done.

Most of man's daily behaviour is simple routine. He performs certain acts without paying special attention to them. He does many things because he was trained in his childhood to do them, because other people behave in the same way and because it is customary in his environment. He acquires habits, he develops automatic reactions. But he indulges in these habits only because he welcomes their outcome. As soon as he discovers that the pursuit of the habitual way may hinder the attainment of ends considered as more desirable, he changes his attitude. A man brought up in an area in which the water is clean acquires the habit of heedlessly drinking, washing, and bathing. When he moves to a place in which the water is polluted by morbific germs, he will devote the most careful attention to procedures about which he never bothered before. He will watch himself permanently in order not to hurt himself by indulging unthinkingly in his automatic reactions and in his traditional routine. The abandonment of a settled practice into which a man has fallen is not an easy task. It is the main lesson to be learned by all those who aspire to achievements above the level of the masses. (To break off the consumption of habit-creating drugs often requires the employment of therapeutical procedures.) The fact that an act is in the regular course of affairs performed spontaneously, as it were, does not mean that it is not due to conscious volition. Indulgence in a routine which possibly could be changed is action.

Action is the mind's response to stimuli, i.e., to the conditions in which nature and other people's actions place a man. It differs as such from the functional reaction of the bodily organs. It is the outcome of a man's will.

Of course, we do not know what will is. We simply call *will* man's faculty to choose between different states of affairs, to prefer one and to set aside the other, and we call action behaviour aiming at one state and forsaking another. Action is the attitude of a human being aiming at some ends.

Praxeology is not concerned with the metaphysical problem of free will as opposed to determinism. Its fundamental insight is the incontestable fact that man is in a position to choose among different states of affairs with regard to which he is not neutral and which are incompatible with each other, i.e., which he cannot enjoy together. It does not assert that a man's choice is independent of antecedent conditions, physiological and pyschological. It does not enter into a discussion of the motives determining the choice. It does not ask why a customer prefers one pattern of a necktie to another or a motorcar to a horse and buggy, It deals with choosing as such, with the categorical elements of choice and action.

Neither does praxeology concern itself about the ultimate goals of human activity. We will have to deal with this problem too. For the moment we have only to emphasize that praxeology does not have to question ultimate ends, but only to study the means applied for the attainment of any ends. It is a science of means, not of ends.

The investigation of the fitness of concrete means to attain, by complying with the laws of nature, definite ends in the field of the practical arts, is the task of the various branches of technology. Praxeology does not deal with technological problems, but with the categorical essence of choice and action as such, with the pure elements of setting aims and applying means.

Praxeology is not based on psychology and is not a part of psychology. It was a bad mistake to call the modern theory of value a psychological theory and it was a confusion to link it up with the Weber-Fechner Law of Psychophysics.[6,7]

Praxeology deals with choice and action and with their outcome. Psychology deals with the internal processes determining the various choices in their concreteness. It may be left undecided whether psychology can succeed in explaining why a man in a concrete case preferred red to blue or bread to lyrics. At any rate such an explanation has nothing to do with a branch of knowledge for which the concrete choices are data not needing further explanation or analysis. Not what a man chooses, but that he chooses counts for praxeology.

The motives and springs of action are without concern for the praxeological investigation. It is immaterial for the formation of the price of silk whether people ask for silk because they want to be protected against cold weather or because they find it beautiful or because they want to get more sexual attractiveness. What matters is that there is a demand of a given intensity for silk.

Yet, modern psychology has brought about some results which may arouse the interest of praxeology. It was once usual to consider the behaviour of lunatics and neurotics as quite nonsensical and 'irrational.' It is the great merit of Breuer and Freud that they have disproved this opinion. Neurotics and lunatics differ from those whom we call sane and normal with regard to the means which they choose for the attainment of satisfaction and with regard to the means which they apply for the attainment of these means. Their 'technology' is different from that of sane people, but they do not act in a categorically different way.[8] They aim at ends and they apply means in order to attain their ends. A mentally troubled person with whom there is still left a trace of reason and who has not been literally reduced to the mental level of an animal, is still an acting being. Whoever has the remnants of a human mind cannot escape the necessity of acting.

III

Every human action aims at the substitution of more satisfactory conditions for less satisfactory. Man acts because he feels uneasy and believes that he has the power to relieve to some extent his uneasiness by influencing the course of events. A man perfectly content with the state of his affairs would not have any incentive to change things; he would have neither wishes nor desires, he would not act because he would be perfectly happy. Neither would a man act who, although not content with his condition, does not see any possibility of improving it.

Strictly speaking, only the increase of satisfaction (decrease of uneasiness) should be called *end*, and accordingly all states which bring about such an increase *means*. In daily speech people use a loose terminology. They call ends things which should be rather called means. They say: This man knows only one end, namely, to accumulate more wealth, instead of saying: He considers the accumulation of more wealth as the only means to get more satisfaction. If they were to apply this more adequate mode of expression, they would avoid some current mistakes. They would realize that nobody else than the individual himself can decide what satisfies *him* better and what less. They would conceive that judgments of value are purely subjective and that there is no such thing as an absolute state of satisfaction or happiness irrespective of the desires of the individual concerned. In fact, he who passes a judgment of an alleged end, reduces it from the rank of an end to that of a means. He values it from the viewpoint of an (higher) end and asks whether it is a suitable means to attain this (higher) end. But the highest end, the ultimate goal of human action, is always satisfaction of an individual's desire. There is no other standard of greater or lesser satisfaction than the individual judgments of value, different with various people and with the same people at various times. What makes a man feel uneasy and less uneasy is established by every individual from the standard of his own will and judgment, from his personal valuation. Nobody is in a position to decree what could make a fellow man happier. The innate spirit of intolerance and the neurotic 'dictatorship complex' instigate people to dispose blithely of other people's will and aspirations. Yet, a man who passes a judgment on another man's aims and volitions does not declare what would make this other man happier or less discontented; he only asserts what condition of this other man would better suit himself, the censor.

From this point of view we have to appreciate the statements of eudaemonism, hedonism, and utilitarianism. All the objections raised against these schools are invalid, if one attaches to the terms happiness, pain, pleasure, and utility formal meaning. Happiness and pleasure are what people consider as such; useful are things which people consider as appropriate means for the attainment of aims sought. The concept of utility as developed by modern economics means suitability to render some services which are deemed as useful from any point of view. This is the meaning of the axiological subjectivism [subjectivism in value theory] of modern economics. It is at the same time the test of its impartiality and scientific objectivity. It does not deal with the *ought*, but with the *is*. Its subject matter is, e.g., the explanation of the formation of prices as they really are, not as they should be or would be if men were to act in a way different from what they really do.

IV

Praxeology does not employ the term *rational*. It deals with purposive behaviour, i.e., human action. The opposite of action is not *irrational behaviour*, but a reactive response to stimuli on the part of the bodily organs and of the instincts, which cannot be controlled by volition. If we were to assign a definite meaning to the term *rationality* as applied to behaviour, we could not find another meaning than: the attitude of men intent on bringing about some effects.

The terms *irrational* and *irrationality* are mostly used for censuring concrete modes of action. An action is called irrational either because the censor disapproves of the end (i.e., of the way in which the acting individual wants to attain satisfaction) or because the censor believes that the means employed were not fit to produce the immediate effect aimed at.

119

But often the qualification of an action as irrational involves praise; actions aiming at altruistic ends, inspired by noble motives and executed to the detriment of the acting man's material well-being are considered as irrational.

We do not have to dwell upon the contradictions and logical inconsistencies involved in this use of words. The qualification of ends is without significance for praxeology, the science of means, not ends. That mortal men are not infallible and that they sometimes choose means which cannot bring about the ends sought is obvious.

It is the task of technology and of therapeutics to find the right means for the attainment of definite ends in the field of the practical arts. It is the task of applied economics to discover the appropriate methods for the attainment of definite ends in the realm of social cooperation. But if the scientists fail in these endeavours or if the acting men do not correctly apply the means recommended, the outcome falls short of the expectations of the acting individuals. Yet, an action unsuited to the end sought is still an action. If we call such an unsuitable and inexpedient action *irrational*, we do not deprive it of its qualification as purposive activity and we do not at all invalidate the assertion that the only way to conceive it essentially and categorically is provided by praxeology.

Economics does not deal with an imaginary *homo oeconomicus* as ineradicable fables reproach it with doing, but with *homo agens* as he really is, often weak, stupid, inconsiderate, and badly instructed. It does not matter whether his motives and emotions are to be qualified as noble or as mean. It does not contend that man strives only after more material wealth for himself and for his kin. Its theorems are neutral with regard to ultimate judgments of value, and are valid for all actions irrespective of their expediency.

It is the scope of history and not of praxeology to investigate what ends people aim at and what means they apply for the realization of their plans.

V

It is a frequent mistake to assume that the desire to procure the base necessities of life and health is more rational than the striving after other amenities. It is true that the appetite for food and warmth is common to men and other mammals and that as a rule a man who lacks food and shelter concentrates his efforts upon the satisfaction of these urgent needs and does not care for other things. The impulse to live, to preserve one's own life and to take advantage of every opportunity of strengthening one's vital force is a primal feature of life, present in every living being. However, to yield to this impulse is not – for man – an inextricable necessity.

All other animals are unconditionally driven by the impulse to preserve their own life and by the impulse of proliferation. They are, without a will of their own, bound to obey the impetus which at the instant prevails. It is different with man. Man has the faculty of mastering his instincts. He can rein both his sexual appetites and his will to live. He can give up his life when the conditions under which alone he could preserve it seem intolerable. Man is capable of dying for a cause or of committing suicide. To live is for man the outcome of a choice, of a judgment of value.

It is the same with the desire to live in affluence. The very fact of asceticism evidences that the striving after more amenities is not inextricable but rather the result of a choice. Of course, the immense majority prefer life to death and wealth to poverty.

On the other hand, it is arbitrary to consider only the satisfaction of the body's physiological needs as 'natural' and therefore as 'rational' and everything else as 'artificial' and therefore as 'irrational.' It is the characteristic feature of human nature that man seeks not only food and shelter like all other animals, but that he aims also at other kinds of satisfaction, that he has specifically human needs too. It was the fundamental error of the iron law of wages that it ignored this fact.

VI

The concrete judgments of value are not open to further analysis. We may assume that they are absolutely dependent upon and conditioned by their causes. But as long as we do not know how external (physical and physiological) facts produce in a human 'soul' definite thoughts and volitions resulting in concrete acts, we have to face an insurmountable dualism. In the present state of our knowledge, the fundamental statements of positivism and monism are mere metaphysical postulates devoid of any scientific foundation. Reason and experience show us two separate realms: the external world of physical and physiological events and the internal world of thought, feeling, and purposeful action. No bridge connects – as far as we can see today – these two spheres. Identical external events result sometimes in different human responses, and different external events produce sometimes the same human response. We do not know why.

We have not yet discovered other methods for dealing with human action than those provided by praxeology and by history. The suggestion of pan-physicalism that the methods of physics be applied to human actions is futile. The sterility of the pan-physicalist recipe is beyond doubt. In spite of the fanatical propaganda of its advocates nobody has ever made use of it. It is simply inapplicable. Positivism is the most conspicuous failure in the history of metaphysics.

The concrete judgments of value and the resulting acts are for history ultimate data. History tries to collect all relevant facts and it has, in this attempt, to make use of all knowledge provided by logic, mathematics, the natural sciences, and especially by praxeology. But it can never succeed in reducing all historical facts to external events open to an interpretation by physics and physiology. It must always reach a point beyond which all further analysis fails. Then it cannot establish anything else than that it is faced with an individual or unique case.

The mental act for dealing with such historical facts is, in the philosophy of Bergson, une intuition, namely la sympathie par laquelle on se transporte a l'intérieur d'un objet pour coincider avec ce qu'il a d'unique, et par conséquent d'inexprimable.[9] German epistemology calls the act *das spezifische Verstehen der Geisteswissenschaften,* or simply *Verstehen.* I suggest it be translated into English as 'specific understanding' or simply as 'understanding.' The *Verstehen* is not a method or a mental process which the historians should apply or which epistemology advises them to apply. It is the method which all historians and all other people always apply in commenting upon social events of the past and in forecasting future events. The discovery and the delimitation of the *Verstehen* was one of the most important contributions of epistemology. It is not a blueprint for a science which does not yet exist and is to be founded.

The uniqueness and individuality which remains at the bottom of every historical fact when all the means for its interpretation provided by logic, praxeology, and the natural sciences have been exhausted is an ultimate datum. But, whereas the natural sciences cannot say anything else about their ultimate data than that they are such, history can try to make its data intelligible. Although it is impossible to reduce them to their causes – they would not be ultimate data, if such a reduction were possible – the observer can understand them because he is himself a human being. We may call this faculty to understand congeniality and sympathetic intelligence. But we have to guard against the error to confuse the understanding with approval, be it only conditional and circumstantial. The historian, the anthropologist, and the psychologist sometimes register actions which are for their feelings simply repulsive and disgusting; they understand them only as actions, i.e., in establishing the underlying aims and the technological and praxeological methods applied. To understand an individual case does not mean to explain, still less to excuse it.

Neither must understanding be confused with the act of aesthetic empathy by virtue of which an individual aims at an aesthetic enjoyment of a phenomenon. *Einfühlung* [empathy] and *Verstehen* are two radically different attitudes. It is a different thing, on the one hand, to understand historically a work of art, to determine its place, its meaning, and its importance in the chain of events and, on the other hand, to appreciate it emotionally as a work of art. One can look at a cathedral with the eyes of an historian. But one can look at the same cathedral either as an enthusiastic admirer or as an unaffected and indifferent tourist. One can look at a mountain range with the eyes of a naturalist – a geologist, a geographer, or a zoologist – or with the eye of a beauty-seeker – with disgust as the ancients used to do, or with the modern enthusiasm for the picturesque. The same individuals are capable of different modes of reaction, of the aesthetic appreciation and of the scientific grasp either of the *Verstehen* or of the natural sciences.

The understanding establishes the fact that an individual or a group of individuals have engaged in a definite action emanating from definite judgments of value and choices and aiming at definite ends. It further tries to appreciate the effects and the intensity of the effects brought about by an action. It tries to assign to every action its relevance, i.e., its bearing upon the course of events.

The historian gives us an account of all facts and events concerning the battle of Waterloo as complete and exact as the material available allows. As far as he deals with the forces engaged and with their equipment, with the tactical operations, with the figures of soldiers killed, wounded, and made prisoners, with the temporal sequence of the various happenings, with the plans of the commanders and with their execution, he is grounded on historical experience. What he asserts is either correct or contrary to the fact, is either proved or disproved by the documents available or vague because the sources do not provide us with sufficient information. Other experts will either agree with him or will disagree, but they will agree or disagree on the ground of a reasonable interpretation of the evidence available. So far the whole discussion must be conducted with reasonable affirmations and negations. But that is not the total work to be achieved by the historian.

The battle resulted in a crushing defeat of the French army. There are many facts, indubitably established on the basis of documentary evidence, which could be taken to account for this outcome. Napoleon suffered from illness, he was nervous, he lacked self-confidence. His judgment and his comprehension of the situation were no longer what they used to be. His plans and orders were in many respects inappropriate. The French army was hastily organized, numerically too weak and its soldiers were partly veterans tired from the endless wars, partly inexperienced recruits. Its generals were not equal to their task, there was especially Grouchy's

123

serious blunder.[10] On the other hand, the British and the Prussians fought under the imminent leadership of Wellington and of Gneisenau, their morale was excellent, they were well organized, richly equipped, and strong in number. To what extent did these various circumstances and many others contribute to the outcome? This question cannot be answered from the information derived from the data of the case, it is open to various interpretations. The historian's opinions concerning them can neither be confirmed or refuted in the same way in which we can confirm or refute his statement that the vanguard of Blücher's [11] army arrived at a certain hour on the battlefield.

Let us take another example. We have plenty of figures available concerning the German inflation of the years, 1914–1923. Economic theory provides us with all the knowledge needed for a perfect grasp of the causes of price changes. But this knowledge does not give us quantitative definiteness. Economics is, as people say, qualitative and not quantitative. This is not due to an alleged backwardness of economics. There are in the sphere of human action no constant relations between magnitudes. For a long time many economists believed that there exists one relation of this character. The thorough demolition of this unfounded assumption was one of the most important achievements of modern economic research. Monetary theory has proved in an irrefutable way that the rise of prices caused by an increase of the quantity of money can never be proportional to this increase. Thus it destroyed by its process analysis the only stronghold of an inveterate error. There cannot be any such thing as measurement in the field of economics. All statistical figures available have importance only for economic history; they are data of history like the figures concerning the battle of Waterloo; they tell us what happened in a unique and non-repeatable historical case. The only way to utilize them is to interpret them by *Verstehen*.

The rise of German prices in the years of the First World War was not only due to the increase of the quantity of bank notes. Other changes contributed too. The supply of commodities went down because many millions of workers were in the army and no longer worked in the plants, because government control of business reduced productivity, because the blockade prevented imports from abroad, and because the workers suffered from malnutrition. It is impossible to establish by other methods than by *Verstehen* how much each of these factors – and of some other relevant factors – contributed to the rise of prices. Quantitative problems are in the sphere of human action not open to another solution. The historian can enumerate all the factors which cooperated in bringing about a certain effect and all the factors which worked against them and may have resulted in delaying and mitigating the final outcome. But he can never coordinate the various causes in a quantitative way to the effects produced. The *Verstehen* is in the realm of history the substitute, as it were, for quantitative analysis and measurement which are unfeasible with regard to human actions outside the field of technology.

Technology can tell us how thick a steel plate must be in order not to be pierced by a bullet fired at a distance of 300 yards from a Mauser rifle. It thus can answer the question why a man who took shelter behind a steel plate of a known thickness was hurt or not hurt by a shot fired. History is at a loss to explain with the same assurance why Louis Philippe lost his crown in 1848 or why the Reformation succeeded better in the Scandinavian countries than in France, Such problems do not allow any other treatment than that of the specific understanding.

The understanding is not a method which could be used as a substitute for the aprioristic reasoning of logic, mathematics and praxeology or the experimental methods of the natural sciences. Its field lies where these other methods fail: in the description of a unique and individual case not open to further analysis – its qualitative service – and in the appraisal of the intensity, importance, and strength of the various factors which jointly produced an effect – its service as a substitute for the unfeasible quantitative analysis.

The subject of the historical understanding is the mental grasp of phenomena which cannot be totally elucidated by logic, mathematics, praxeology, and the natural sciences and as far as they cannot be elucidated by science and reason. It establishes the fact that scientific enquiry has reached a point beyond which it cannot go further, and tries to fill the gap by *Verstehen*.[12] One may, if one likes, qualify the *Verstehen* as irrational because it involves individual judgments not amenable to criticism by purely rational methods. However, the method of understanding is not a free charter to deviate from the certified results obtained from the documentary evidence and from its interpretation through the teachings of the natural sciences and of praxeology. The *Verstehen* oversteps its due limits if it ventures to contradict physics, physiology, logic, mathematics, or economics. The abuses which many German scholars made of the *geisteswissenschaftliche Methode* and the spurious attempts of the German Historical School to substitute an imaginary *verstehende Nationalökonomie* for praxeological economics cannot be charged to the method itself.

German *Geisteswissenschaften* have preached the gospel of what should be an irrational science. They have substituted arbitrary judgments for reason and experience. They derive from intuition knowledge about historical events which the documents available do not provide or which are contrary to the facts as established by careful examination of the documents available. They do not refrain from drawing conclusions contradicting the statements of economic theory which they cannot refute on logical grounds. They are not afraid to produce absurdities. Their only justification is the reference to the irrationality of life.

Let us take an example from a serious and scholarly book available in English translation. Mr Ernst Kantorowicz, an historian of the esoteric circle of the poet and visionary Stephen George, in his biography of the German Emperor Frederick II, gives a correct account of the constitutional changes which took place in the reign of this Hohenstaufen monarch. Frederick's position in Germany was extremely precarious because his hereditary Norman kingdom of Sicily drew him into conflicts with the Pope and the Italian republican cities. He lacked the strength to preserve his royal authority in Germany and was forced to abandon most of the crown's rights, and to grant ample privileges to the princes. What followed, says Kantorowicz quite correctly, 'was the almost sovereign independence of each individual prince in his territory' which 'definitely hindered the amalgamation of the German people into one *German State*.'[13] So far, Kantorowicz is still on the basis of sound *Verstehen* and in perfect agreement with all other serious historians. But then comes the amazing interpretation of the visionary and mystic; he adds: 'Yet in a higher sense Frederick II perfected and completed the unified German Empire. He strengthened the prince's power . . . with more exalted statesmanship believing that the power and the brilliance of his own imperial sceptre would not pale in giving forth light but would gain radiance and would shine brighter the more mighty and brilliant and majestic were the princes whom Caesar Imperator beheld *as equals round his judgment seat*. The princes are no longer columns bearing as a burden the weight of the throne. . . . They become piers and pillars expressive of upward-soaring strength, preparing the glorious elevation of *the prince of princes and king of kings* who is born aloft on the shoulders of his peers, and who in turn exalts both kings and princes.'[14] It is true that some phrases used by the princes at the Diet preceding the extortion of the privilege had a similar ring. The princes were polite, they did not want to fill the emperor with too much bitterness and were anxious to gild the pill which they forced him to swallow. When Hitler reduced Czechoslavakia to vassalage status he too sugared the pill by the establishment of the protectorate. Yet, hardly any historian would dare to say that 'in a higher sense' Hitler 'perfected and completed' the country's independence by granting it the protection of the mighty Reich. Frederick II disintegrated the Holy Empire by the privileges granted to the princes. It is absurd to assert that 'in a higher sense' he perfected and completed it. No metaphorical speech and no appeal to the irrational can render such a dictum any more tenable.

Understanding entitles the historian to determine the role played by the

two privileges in question in the evolution of the Empire's political structure, to determine, as it were, the quantity of their effect. He might, for
instance, express the opinion that the role usually attributed to them has
been exaggerated and that other events were more destructive than these
privileges and he could try to prove his thesis, his mode of understanding.
But it is inadmissable to say: yes, this happened, such were its consequences; yet 'in a higher sense' it was just the contrary.

Human knowledge can never transcend the cognition conveyed by
reason and experience. If there is any 'higher sense' in the course of
events, it is inaccessible to the human mind.

VII

A school of thought teaches that there is an eternal, irreconcilable antagon-
ism between the interests of the individual and those of the collectivity. If
the individual selfishly seeks after his own happiness, society comes to
grief. Social cooperation and civilization are only possible at the cost of the
individual's well-being. The existence of society and its flowering require
sacrifices on the part of its members. Therefore, it is unthinkable to
imagine a human and purely rational origin of moral law and social
cooperation. Some supernatural being has blessed mankind with the revelation of the moral code and has entrusted great leaders with the mission
of enforcing this law. History is not the interplay of natural factors and
purposive human activity which, within certain limits, are open to an
elucidation by reason, but the result of the interference of transcendental
factors, repeated again and again. History is destiny, and reason can never
fathom its depths.

The conflict between the good and the evil, between collectivism and
individualism, is therefore eternal and insoluble. What separates social
and moral philosophies and political parties is a divergence of world views,
a disparity of ultimate judgments of value. This discord is rooted in the
deepest recesses of a man's soul and innate character; no ratiocination or
discursive reasoning can brush it away or reconcile its contrasts. Some
men are born with the divine call to leadership, others with the endow-
ment to espouse spontaneously the cause of the great whole and to subordinate themselves of their own accord to the rule of its champions; but
the many are incapable of finding the right way, they aim at the happiness
of their own wretched selves and have to be tamed and subjugated by the
conquering dictators. Social philosophy can consist in nothing else than in
the cognition of the eternal truth of collectivism and in the unmasking of
the spurious fallacies and pretensions of individualism. It is not the result

127

of a rational process, but rather an illumination with which intuition blesses the elect. It is vain to strive after genuine social and moral truth by the application of the rational methods of logic. To the chosen, God or *Weltgeist* gives the right intuition; the rest of mankind has simply to forsake thinking and to obey blindly the God-given authority. True wisdom and the counterfeit doctrines of rationalistic economics and rationalistic history can never agree in the appreciation of historical and social facts, of political measures and of an individual's actions. Human reason is not an appropriate tool to acquire true knowledge of the social totality; rationalism and its derivatives, economics and critical history, are fundamentally erroneous.[15]

The fundamental assumption of this doctrine, namely, that social cooperation is contrary to the interests of the individuals and can be achieved only at the expense of the individual's welfare, has long since been exploded. It was one of the great achievements of British social philosophy and classical economics that they developed a theory of social evolution which does not need to refer to the miraculous appearance of leaders endowed with superhuman wisdom and powers. Social cooperation and its corollary, division of labour, serve better the selfish interests of all individuals concerned than isolation and conflict. Every step toward peaceful cooperation brings all concerned an immediate and discernible advantage. Men cooperate and are eager to intensify cooperation exactly because they are anxious to pursue their selfish interests. The sacrifices which the individual makes for the maintenance of social cooperation are only temporary; if he abstains from antisocial actions which could give him small immediate gains, he profits much more by the advantages which he derives from the higher productivity of work performed in the peaceful cooperation of the division of labour. Thus, the principle of association eludicates the forces which integrated the primitive hordes and tribes and step by step widened out the social units until finally the oecumenical Great Society came into being. There is in the long run no irreconcilable conflict between the rightly understood selfish interests of the individuals and those of society. Society is not a Moloch to whom man has to sacrifice his own personality. It is, on the contrary, for every individual the foremost tool for the attainment of well-bring and happiness. It is man's most appropriate weapon in his struggle for survival and improvement. It is not an end, but a means, the most eminent means for the attainment of all human desires.

We do not have to enter into a detailed critique of the statements of the collectivist doctrine. We have only to establish the fact that the acts of the allegedly collectivist parties do not comply with the tenets of this philosophy. The political representatives of these parties occasionally in their speeches referred to collectivist slogans and connived at the propagation of party songs of the same tenor. But they do not ask their followers to sacrifice their own happiness and well-being at the altar of the Collectivity. They are anxious to demonstrate by ratiocination that the methods which they recommend will in the long run serve best the selfish interests of their followers. They do not ask any other sacrifices than temporary ones which, as they promise, will at a later time be rewarded by hundredfold booty. The Nazi professors and the Nazi rhymesters say: 'Efface yourself for Germany's splendor, give your wretched lives in order to make the German Nation live forever in glory and grandeur.' But the Nazi politicians use a different argument: 'Fight for your own preservation and for your future well-being. The enemies are firmly resolved to exterminate the noble race of Aryan heroes. If you do not resist, you all are lost. But if you take up the challenge courageously, you have a chance of defeating the onslaught. Many will be killed in action, but they would not have survived if the devilish plans of our foes were not to meet any resistance. Much more will be saved if we fight. We have the choice between two alternatives only: certain extermination of us all, if the enemies conquer, on the one hand, and the survival of the great majority in case of our victory on the other hand.'

There is no appeal to the 'irrational' in this purely rational – although not reasonable – reasoning. But even if the collectivist doctrine were correct, and people, in forsaking other advantages, aimed at the flowering of the Collective only under the persuasion or complusion exercised on the part of the superhuman leaders, all the statements of praxeology would remain unshaken and history would not have any reason to change its methods of approach.

VIII

The real reason for the popular disparagement of the social sciences is reluctance to accept the restrictions imposed by nature on human endeavours. This reluctance is potentially present in everybody and is overwhelming with the neurotic. Men feel unhappy because they cannot have two incompatible things together, because they have to pay a price for everything and can never attain full satisfaction. They blame the social sciences for demonstrating the scarcity of the factors which preserve and strengthen the vital forces and remove uneasiness. They disparage them for describing the world as it really is and not as they would like to have it, i.e., as a cosmos of unlimited opportunities. They are not judicious enough to comprehend that life is exactly an active resistance against adverse conditions and manifests itself only in this struggle, and that the notion of a life free from any limitations and restrictions is even inconceivable for a human mind. Reason is man's foremost equipment in the biological struggle for the preservation and expansion of his existence and survival. It would not have any function and would not have developed at all in a fool's paradise.[16]

It is not the fault of the social sciences that they are not in a position to transform society into a utopia. Economics is not a 'dismal science,' because it starts from the acknowledgment of the fact, that the means for the attainment of ends are scarce. (With regard to human concerns which can be fully satisfied because they do not depend on scarce factors, man does not act, and praxeology, the science of human action, does not have to deal with them.) As far as there is scarcity of means, man behaves rationally, i.e., he acts. So far there is no room left for 'irrationality.'

That man has to pay a price for the maintenance of social institutions enabling him to attain ends which he deems as more valuable than this price made, than these sacrifices brought for them, is obvious. It is futile to disguise the impotent dissatisfaction with this state of affairs as a revolt against an alleged dogmatic orthodoxy of the social sciences.

If the 'rational' methods of economic theory demonstrate that an a results in a p, no appeal to irrationality can make a result in a q. If the theory was wrong, only a correct theory can refute it and substitute a correct solution for an incorrect one.

IX

The social sciences have not neglected to give full consideration to all those phenomena which people may have in mind in alluding to irrationality. History has developed a special method for dealing with them: understanding. Praxeology has built up its system in such a way that its theorems are valid for all human action without any regard to whether the ends aimed at are qualified, from whatever point of view, as rational or irrational. It is simply not true that the social sciences are guilty of having left untouched a part of the field which they have to elucidate. The suggestions for the construction of a new science whose subject matter has to be the irrational phenomena are of no account. There is no untilled soil left for such a new science.

The social sciences are, of course, rational. All sciences are. Science is the application of reason for a systematic description and interpretation of phenomena. There is no such thing as a science not based on reason. The longing for an irrational science is self-contradictory.

History will one day have to understand historically the 'revolt against reason' as one of the factors of the history of the last generations. Some very remarkable contributions to this problem have already been published.

Economic theory is not perfect. No human work is built for eternity. New theorems may supplement or supplant the old ones. But what may be defective with present-day economics is certainly not that it failed to grasp the weight and significance of factors popularly qualified as irrational.

NOTES

1. For a critical presentation of these theories, cf. Talcott Parsons *The Structure of Social Action* (New York, Macmillan, 1937); Raymond Aron, *German Sociology* [1938] (Westport, CT: Greenwood Press, 1954).
2. [Max Weber, *The City,* Don Martindale and Gertrude Neuwirth, trans. and eds (New York: The Free Press, 1958) – Ed.]
3. The term 'praxeology' was first used by Espinas in an essay published in the *Revue Philosophique* vol. 30, pp. 114ff., and in his book *Les Origines de la Technologie* (Paris: F. Alcon, 1897), pp. 7ff. It was later applied by Slutsky in his essay 'Ein Beitrag zur formal-praxeologischen Grundlegung der Ökonomik,' Academie Oukräienne des Sciences, *Annales de la Classe des Sciences Sociales-Economiques* 4 (1926).
4. Cf. Nassau W. Senior, *Political Economy,* 6th edn (London: J. J. Griffen, 1872); John E.Cairnes, *The Character and Logical Method of Political Economy,* 2nd edn (London: Macmillan, 1875); Lionel Robbins, *An Essay on the Nature and Significance of Economic Science,* 2nd edn (London: Macmillan, 1935); Mises, *Epistemological Problems of Economics* [1933] (New York, 1981); *Human Action,* 3rd edn (Chicago: Henry Regenry, 1966); Alfred Schutz, *The Phenomenology of the Social World* [1932] (Evanston, IL: Northwestern University Press, 1967); F. A. Hayek, *The Counter-Revolution of Science* ([1952]; Indianapolis, Ind.: Liberty Press, 1979).
5. The book of Josef Back, *Die Entwicklung der reinen Ökonomie zur nationalökonomischen Wesenswissenschaft* (Jena: Gustav Fischer, 1929), is unsatisfactory because of the author's poor knowledge of economics. All the same, this book would deserve a better appreciation than it received.
6. Cf. Max Weber, 'Marginal Utility Theory and the So-Called Fundamental Law of Psychophysics' [1905], *Social Science Quarterly*

131

(1975): pp. 21–36; Mises, *Human Action,* 3rd edn (Chicago: Henry Regnery, 1966), pp. 125–7.

7. ['Ernst H Weber (1795–1878) proclaimed in his law of psyco-physics that the least noticeable increase in the intensity of a human sensation is always brought about by a constant proportional increase in the previous stimulus. Gustav T. Fechner (1801–87) developed this into the Weber-Fechner Law that said to increase the intensity of a sensation in arithmetical progression, it is necessary to increase the intensity of the stimulus in geometric progression,' *Mises Made Easier: A Glossary for Ludwig von Mises' Human Action,* Percy L. Greaves, Jr., comp. (Dobbs Ferry, N.Y.: Free Market Books, 1974), p. 147 – Ed.]

8. It may be of some interest for the history of ideas that young Sigmund Freud collaborated as a translator in the German edition of John Stuart Mill's collected works edited by Theodor Gomperz, the Austrian historian of ancient Greek philosophy. Joseph Breuer too was, as the present writer can attest, well familiar with the standard works of utilitarian philosophy.

9. Cf. Henri Bergson, *La Pensée et le mouvant,* 4th edn (Paris: F. Alcan, 1934), p. 205. [Passage translated as 'The sympathy with which one enters inside an object in order to identify thereby what it has that is unique and therefore inexpressible,' *Mises Made Easier: A Glossary for Ludwig von Mises' Human Action.* Percy L. Greaves, Jr., comp. (Dobbs Ferr, N.Y.: Free Market Books, 1974), p. 76 – Ed.]

10. [Emmanuel Grouchy, one of Napoleon's generals, through an error of judgment delayed notifying Napoleon of movements of the British forces in what would become the French army's last attempt to stave off the defeat at Waterloo – Ed.]

11. [Gebhard von Blücher was commander of the Prussian forces that aided the German, British, and Dutch armies to defeat Napoleon at Waterloo in 1815 – Ed.]

12. The important problem of various conflicting modes of *Verstehen* (for instance: the Catholic and the Protestant interpretation of the Reformation, or the various interpretations of the rise of German Nazism) must be treated in a special essay.

13. Cf. E. Kantorowicz, *Frederick the Second, 1194–1250,* E. O. Lorimer, trans. (London: Constable, 1931), pp. 381–2.

14. Cf. Ibid., pp. 386–7.

15. Such are the teachings of the German Historical School of the Social Sciences, whose latest exponents are Werner Sombart and Othmar Spann. It may be worthwhile to note that Catholic philosophy does not endorse the collectivist doctrine. According to the teachings of the Roman Church natural law is nothing but the dictates of reason

properly exercised, and man is capable of aquiring its full knowledge even if unaided by supernatural revelation. 'God so created man as to bestow on him endowments amply sufficient for him to attain his last end. Over and above this He decreed to make the attainment of beatitude yet easier for man by placing within his reach a far simpler and far more certain way of knowing the law on the observance of which his fate depended.' Cf. G. H. Joyce, article 'Revelation' in *The Catholic Encyclopedia*, vol. 13 (New York: Encyclopedia Press, 1913), pp. 1–5.

16. Cf. Benedetto Croce, *History as the Story of Liberty*, S. Sprigge, trans. (New York: W. W. Norton, 1941), p. 33.

Ludwig von Mises, 'Epistemological Relativism' eds. H. Schoeck and
J. W. Wiggins, 'Relativism and the Study of Man (1961), Richard M.
Ebeling (ed.) *Money, Method and the Market Process* (Kluwer, 1990), pp.
37–51.

This paper was first published in Helmut Schoeck and James W.
Wiggins, (eds), *Relativism and the Study of Man* (Princeton, NJ:
D. Van Nostrand, 1961); it was republished in *Money, Method,
and the Market Process: Essays by Ludwig von Mises*.

25

Epistemological Relativism in the Sciences of Human Action

LUDWIG von MISES

Up to the eighteenth century, historians paid little or no attention to the epistemological problems of their craft. In dealing with the subject of their studies, they again and again referred to some regularities that – as they themselves and their public assumed – are valid for any kind of human action irrespective of the time and the geographical scene of the action as well as of the actors' personal qualities and ideas. But they did not raise the question whether these regularities were of an extraneous character or inherent in the very nature of human action. They knew very well that man is not able to attain all that he wants to attain. But they did not ask whether the limits of a man's power are completely described by reference to the laws of nature and to the Deity's miraculous interference with them, on the one hand, and to the superior power of more puissant men, on the other hand.

Like all other people, the historians too distinguished between behaviour complying with the moral law and behaviour violating it. But, like all other people, they were fully aware of the fact that nonobservance of the laws of ethics did not necessarily – in this life – result in failure to attain the ends sought. Whatever may happen to the sinner in the life hereafter and on the day of the Last Judgment, the historian could not help realizing that on earth he could sometimes fare very well, much better than many pious fellow men.

Entirely new perspectives were opened when the economists discovered that there prevails a regularity in the sequence and interdependence of market phenomena. It was the first step to a general theory of human action, praxeology. For the first time people became aware of the fact that, in order to succeed, human action must comply not only with what are called the laws of nature, but also with specific laws of human action. There are things that even the most efficient constabulary of a formidable government cannot bring about, although they may not appear impossible from the point of view of the natural sciences.

It was obvious that the claims of this new science could not fail to give offense from three points of view. There were first of all the governments. Despots as well as democratic majorities are not pleased to learn that their might is not absolute. Again and again they embark upon policies that are doomed to failure and fail because they disregard the laws of economics. But they do not learn the lesson. Instead they employ hosts of pseudo economists to discredit the 'abstract,' i.e., in their terminology, vain teachings of sound economics.

Then there are ethical doctrines that charge economics with ethical materialism. As they see it, economics teaches that man ought to aim exclusively or first of all at satisfying the appetites of the senses. They stubbornly refuse to learn that economics is neutral with regard to the choice of ultimate ends as it deals only with the methods for the attainment of ends chosen, whatever these ends may be.

There are, finally, authors who reject economics on account of its alleged 'unhistorical approach.' The economists claim absolute validity for what they call the laws of economics; they assert that in the course of human affairs something is at work that remains unchanged in the flux of historical events. In the opinion of many authors this is an unwarranted thesis, the acceptance of which must hopelessly muddle the work of historians.

In dealing with this brand of relativism, we must take into account that its popularity was not due to epistemological, but to practical considerations. Economics pointed out that many cherished policies cannot result in the effects aimed at by the governments that resorted to them, but bring about other effects – from the point of view of those who advocated and applied those policies – were even more unsatisfactory than the conditions that they were designed to alter. No other conclusion could be inferred from these teachings than that these measures were contrary to purpose and that their repeal would benefit the rightly understood or long-run interests of all the people. This explains why all those whose short-run interests were favoured by these measures bitterly criticized the 'dismal science.' The epistemological qualms of some philosophers and historians met with an enthusiastic response on the part of aristocrats and landowners who wanted to preserve their old privileges and on the part of small business and employees who were intent upon acquiring new privileges. The European 'historical schools' and American Institutionalism won political and popular support, which is, in general, denied to theoretical doctrines.

However, the establishment of this fact must not induce us to belittle the seriousness and importance of the problems involved. Epistemological relativism as expressed in the writings of some of the historicists, e.g., Karl Knies and Max Weber, was not motivated by political zeal. These two outstanding representatives of historicism were, as far as this was humanly possible in the milieu of the German universities of their age, free from an emotional predilection in favour of interventionist policies and from chauvinistic prejudice against the foreign, i.e., British, French, and Austrian science of economics. Besides, Knies[1] wrote a remarkable book on money and credit, and Weber[2] gave the deathblow to the methods applied by the schools of Schmoller and Brentano[3] by demonstrating the unscientific character of judgments of value. There were certainly in the argumentation of the champions of historical relativism points that call for an elucidation.

II

Before entering into an analysis of the objections raised against the 'absolutism' of economics, it is necessary to point out that the rejection of economics by epistemological relativism has nothing to do with the positivist rejection of the methods actually used by historians.

In the opinion of positivism, the work of the historians is mere gossip or, at best, the accumulation of a vast amount of material that they do not know how to use. What is needed is a science of the laws that determine what happens in history. Such a science has to be developed by the same methods of research that made it possible to develop out of experience the science of physics.

The refutation of the positivistic doctrine concerning history is an achievement of several German philosophers, first of all of Wilhelm Windelband and of Heinrich Rickert. They pointed out in what the fundamental difference between history, the record of human action, and the natural sciences consists. Human action is purposive, it aims at the attainment of definite ends chosen, it cannot be treated without reference to these ends, and history is in this sense – we must emphasize, *only* in this sense – finalistic. But to the natural sciences the concept of ends and final causes is foreign.

Then there is a second fundamental difference. In the natural sciences man is able to observe in the laboratory experiment the effects brought about by a change in one factor only, all other factors the alteration of which could possibly produce effects remaining unchanged. This makes it possible to find what the natural sciences call experimentally established facts of experience. No such technique of research is available in the field of human action. Every experience concerning human action is historical, i.e., an experience of complex phenomena, of changes produced by the joint operation of a multitude of factors. Such an experience cannot produce 'facts' in the sense in which this term is employed in the natural sciences. It can neither verify nor falsify any theorem. It would remain an inexplicable puzzle if it could not be interpreted by dint of a theory that had been derived from other sources than historical experience.

Now, of course, neither Rickert and the other authors of the group to which he belonged, the 'Southwestern German philosophers,' nor the historians who shared their conception went as far as this last conclusion. To them, professors of German universities at the end of the nineteenth and the beginning of the twentieth century, the very idea that there could be any science claiming for its theses universal validity for all human action irrespective of time, geography, and the racial and national characteristics of people remained unknown. For men living in the spiritual climate of the second German Reich, it was an understood thing that the pretensions of 'abstract' economic theory were vain and that German *wirtschaftliche Staatswissenschaften* (the economic aspects of political science), an entirely historical discipline, had replaced the inane generalization of the school of Hume, Adam Smith, and Ricardo. As they saw it, human action – apart from theology, ethics, and jurisprudence – could be dealt with scientifically only by history. Their radical empiricism prevented them from paying any attention to the possibility of an a priori science of human action.

The positivist dogma that Dilthey, Windelband, Rickert, and their followers demolished was not relativistic. It postulated a science – sociology – that would derive from the treatment of the empirical data provided by history a body of knowledge that would render to the mind the same services with regard to human action that phsyics renders with regard to events in the sphere of nature. These German philosophers demonstrated that such a general science of action could not be elaborated by a posteriori reasoning. The idea that it could be the product of a priori reasoning did not occur to them.

III

The deficiency of the work of the classical economists consisted in their attempt to draw a sharp line of demarcation between 'purely economic activities' and all other human concerns and actions. Their great feat was the discovery that there prevails in the concatenation and sequence of market phenomena a regularity that can be compared to the regularity in the concatenation and sequence of natural events. Yet, in dealing with the market and its exchange ratios, they were baffled by their failure to solve the problem of valuation. In interpersonal exchange transactions objects are not valued according to their utility, they thought, because otherwise 'iron' would be valued more highly than 'gold.' They did not see that the apparent paradox was due only to the vicious way they formulated the question. Value judgments of acting men do not refer to 'iron' or to 'gold' as such, but always to definite quantities of each of these metals between which the actor is forced to choose because he cannot have both of them. The classical economists failed to find the law of marginal utility. This shortcoming prevented them from tracing market phenomena back to the decisions of the consumers. They could deal only with the actions of the businessmen, for whom the valuation of the consumers are merely data. The famous formula 'to buy on the cheapest and to sell on the dearest market' makes sense only for the businessman. It is meaningless for the consumer.

Thus forced to restrict their analysis to business activities, the classical economists constructed the concept of a science of wealth or the production and distribution of wealth. Wealth, according to this definition meant all that could be bought or sold. The endeavours to get wealth were seen as a separate sphere of activities. All other human concerns appeared from the vantage point of this science merely as disturbing elements.

Actually, few classical economists were content with this circumscription of the scope of economists. But their search for a more satisfactory concept could not succeed before the marginalists substituted the theory of subjective value from the various abortive attempts of the classical economists and their epigones. As long as the study of the production and distribution of wealth was considered as the subject matter of economic analysis, one had to distinguish between the economic and the noneconomic actions of men. Then economics appeared as a branch of knowledge that dealt with only one segment of human action. There were, outside of this field, actions about which the economists had nothing to say. It was precisely the fact that the adepts of the new science did not deal with all those concerns of man which in their eyes were qualified as extraeconomic that appeared to many outsiders as a depreciation of these matters dictated by an insolent materialistic bias.

Things are different for modern economics, with its doctrine of the subjective interpretation of valuation. In its context the distinction between economic and allegedly noneconomic ends becomes meaningless. The value judgments of the ultimate consumers express not only the striving after more tangible material goods, but no less the striving after all other human concerns. The narrow viewpoint of a science of – material – wealth is surpassed. Out of the discipline of wealth evolves a general theory of all choices made by acting men, a general theory of every kind of human action, praxeology. In their behaviour on the market people evidence not only their wishes to acquire more material goods, but no less all their other preferences. Market prices reflect not only the 'materialistic side' of man, but his philosophical, ethical, and religious ideas as well. The observance of religious commandments – to build and maintain houses of worship, to cease working on holidays, to avoid certain foods either always or on specific days and weeks, to abstain from intoxicating beverages and tobacco, to assist those in need, and many others – is one of the factors that determines the supply of and the demand for consumers' goods and thereby the conduct of business. Praxeology is neutral with regard to the ultimate ends that the individuals want to attain. It does not deal with ultimate ends, but with the means chosen for their attainment. It is merely interested in the question whether or not the means resorted to are fitted to attain the ends sought.

The enormous quantity of antieconomic literature published in the last hundred and fifty years turns round one argument only. Its authors repeat again and again that man as he really is and acts strives not only after more material amenities, but also after some other – higher or loftier or ideal – aims. From this point of view the self-styled Historical School attacked what they called the absolutism of the economic doctrine and advocated a relativistic approach. It is not the theme of this paper to investigate whether the economists of the classical school and their epigones were really guilty of having neglected to pay due attention to the nonmaterialistic concerns of man. But it is to be emphasized that all the objections raised by the Historical School, e.g., by Knies in his famous book,[4] are futile and invalid with regard to the teachings of modern economics.

It is customary in German political literature to distinguish between an older and a later Historical School.[5] As the champions of the older school, Roscher, Bruno Hildebrand, and Knies are named. The younger school consists of the followers of Schmoller who after the establishment of the Reich in 1870 held the chairs of economics at the German universities. This way of subdividing into periods the history of ideas is an outcome of the parochialism that induced German authors to slight all that was accomplished abroad. They failed to realize that the 'historical' opposition against what was called the absolutism of economics was inaugurated outside of Germany. Its outstanding representative was Sismondi[6] rather than Roscher and Hildebrand. But it is much more important to realize the fact that all those who in Germany as well as in other countries after the publication of the books of Jevons, Menger, and Walras criticized economic doctrine on account of its alleged materialism were fighting against windmills.

IV

Max Weber's concept of a general science of human action – to which he applied the name sociology – no longer refers to the distinction between economic action and other activities. But Weber virtually endorsed the objections raised by historicism against economics by distinguishing between genuinely rational action, on the one hand, and other kinds of action. His doctrine is so closely connected with some untranslatable peculiarities of the German language that it is rather difficult to expound it in English.

The distinction that Weber makes between 'social action' and other action is, from the point of view of our problem, of little importance. The main thing is that Weber quite correctly distinguishes between *sinnhaftes Handeln* and the merely physiologically determined reactions of the human body. *Sinnhaftes Handeln* is directed by the *Sinn* the acting individual attaches to it; we would have to translate: by the meaning the actor attaches to it and by the end he wants to attain by it. This definition would appear as a clear distinction between human action, the striving after a definite end, on the one hand, and the physiological – quasi-automatic – reactions of the nerves and cells of the human body, on the other hand. But then Weber goes on to distinguish within the class of *sinnhaftes Handeln* four different subclasses. The first of these subclasses is called *zweckrationales Handeln* and is defined as action aiming at a definite end. The second subclass is called *wertrationales Handeln* and is defined as action determined by the belief in the unconditional intrinsic value (*unbedingter Eigenwert*) of a certain way of conduct as such, without regard to its success, from the point of view of ethics, aesthetics, religion, or other principles. What Weber failed to see is the fact that also the striving after compliance with definite ethical, aesthetical, and religious ideas is no less an end than any other end that men may try to attain. A Catholic who crosses himself, a Jew who abstains from food and drink on the Day of Atonement, a lover of music who forgoes dinner in order to listen to a Beethoven symphony, all aim at ends that from their point of view are more desirable than what they have to renounce in order to get what they want. Only a personal judgment of value can deny to their actions the qualification *zweckrational*, i.e., aiming at a definite end. And what in Weber's definition do the words 'without regard to its success' mean? The Catholic crosses himself because he considers such behaviour as

141

one link in a chain of conduct that will lead him to what for him is the most important success of man's earthly pilgrimage. It is tragic that Max Weber, the eminent historian of religion, the man who tried to free German sociological thought from its naive commitment to judgments of value, failed to see the contradictions of his doctrine.[7]

Other attempts to distinguish between rational action and nonrational or irrational action were likewise based on crass misconstructions and failed. Most of them called 'irrational' conduct directed by mistaken ideas and expectations concerning the effects of definite methods of procedure. Thus, magic practices are today styled as irrational. They were certainly not fitted to attain the ends sought. However, the people who resorted to them believed that they were the right technique in the same way in which physicians up to the middle of the past century believed that bleeding is a method of preventing and curing various diseases. In speaking of human action, we have in mind conduct that, in the opinion of the actor, is best fitted to attain an end he wants to attain, whether or not this opinion is also held by a better informed spectator or historian. The way in which contemporary physicians deal with cancer is not irrational, although we hope that one day more efficacious therapeutic and prophylactic methods will be discovered. A report concerning other people's actions is confusing if it applies the term irrational to the activities of people whose knowledge was less perfect than that of the reporter. As no reporter can claim for himself omniscience, he would at least have to add to his qualification of an action as irrational the proviso 'from my personal point of view.'

Another way in which the epithet 'irrational' is often employed refers, not to the means, but to the ends of definite modes of conduct. Thus, some authors call, either approvingly or disapprovingly, 'irrational' the behaviour of people who prefer religious concerns, national independence, or other goals commonly called noneconomic to a more abundant supply of material satisfactions. Against this highly inexpedient and confusing terminology there is need to emphasize again and again the fact that no man is called to sit in judgment on other people's judgments of value concerning ultimate ends. When the Huguenots preferred the loss of all their earthly possessions, the most cruel punishments, and exile to the adoption of a creed that in their opinion was idolatrous, their behaviour was not 'irrational.' Neither was Louis XIV 'irrational' when he deprived his realm of many of its most worthy citizens in order to comply with the precepts of his conscience. The historian may disagree with the ultimate ends that the persecutors and their victims were aiming at. But this does not entitle him to call the means to which they resorted in order to attain their ends irrational. The terms 'rational' and 'irrational' are just as much out of place when applied to ends as when applied to means. With regard to ultimate ends, all that a mortal man can assert is approval or disapproval from the point of view of his own judgments of value. With regard to means there is only one question, viz., whether or not they are fitted to attain the ends sought.

Most of our contemporaries are guided by the idea that it is the worst of all crimes to force a man, by recourse to violence, to behave according to the commandments of a religious or political doctrine that he despises. But the historian has to record the fact that there were ages in which only a minority shared this conviction, and unspeakable horrors were committed by fanatical princes and majorities. He is right in pointing out that Louis XIV, in outlawing Protestantism, inflicted irreparable evils on the French nation. But he must not forget to add that the King was not aware of these consequences of his policy and that, even if he had anticipated them, he would perhaps nonetheless have considered the attainment of religious uniformity as a good for which the price paid was not too high.

The surgeons who accompanied the armies of ages past did their best to save the lives of the wounded warriors. But their therapeutic knowledge was pitifully inadequate. They bled the injured man whom only a transfusion of blood could have saved and thus virtually killed him. Because of their ignorance, their treatment was contrary to purpose. It would be misleading and inexpedient to call it irrational. Present-day doctors are not irrational, although probably better informed physicians of the future will qualify some of the therapeutical techniques as detrimental and contrary to purpose.

V

Whenever the distinction between rational and irrational is applied to ultimate ends, the meaning is that the judgments of value underlying the choice of the end in question meet with approval or disapproval on the part of the speaker or writer. Now the promulgation of judgments of value is not the business of a man in his capacity as a praxeologist, economist, or historian. It is rather the task of religion, metaphysics, or ethics. History of religion is not theology, and theology is not the history of religion.

When the distinction between rational and irrational is applied to means, the meaning is that the speaker or writer asserts that the means in question are not serving the purpose, i.e., that they are not fit to attain the ends sought by the people who resort to such means. It is certainly one of the main tasks of history to deal with the serviceableness of the means people employed in their endeavours to attain the ends sought. It is also certain that the main practical goal of praxeology and its hitherto best developed part, economics, is to distinguish between means that are fit to attain the ends sought and those that are not. But it is, as has been pointed out, not expedient and rather confusing to use for this distinction the terms 'rational' and 'irrational.' It is more appropriate to speak of means answering the intended purpose and those not answering it.

This holds true also with regard to the way in which the terms 'rational' and 'irrational' are employed by psychoanalysts. They 'call behaviour irrational that is predominately emotional or instinctual,' and furthermore 'all unconscious functions' and in this sense distinguish between 'irrational (instinctual or emotional) action as opposed to rational action, and irrational as opposed to rational thinking.'[8] Whether this terminology is expedient for the treatment of the therapeutic problems of psychoanalysis may be left to the psychoanalysts. From the praxeological point of view, the spontaneous reactions of the human body's organs and the activity of instinctual drives are not action. On the other hand, it is manifestly the outcome of a personal judgment of value to call emotional actions – e.g., the action with which a man may react to the awareness of his fellowmen's distress – irrational. It is further obvious that no other meaning can be ascribed to the term 'irrational thinking' than that it is logically invalid thinking and leads to erroneous conclusions.

VI

The philosophy of historical relativism – historicism – fails to see the fact that there is something unchanging that, on the one hand, constitutes the sphere of history or historical events as distinct from the spheres of other events and, on the other hand, enables man to deal with these events, i.e., to record their succession and to try to find out their concatenation, in other words, to understand them. This unchanging phenomenon is the fact that man is not indifferent to the state of his environment (including the conditions of his own body) and that he tries, as far as it is possible for him to do so, to substitute by purposive action a state that he likes better for a state he likes less. In a word: man acts. This alone distinguishes human history from the history of changes going on outside the field of human action, from the study of 'natural history' and its various subdivisions as, e.g., geology or the evolution of various species of living beings. In human history we are dealing with the ends aimed at by the actors, that is, with final causes.[9] In natural history, as in the other branches of the natural sciences, we do not know anything about final causes.

All human wisdom, science, and knowledge deal only with the segment of the universe that can be perceived and studied by the human mind. In speaking of human action as something unchanging, we refer to the conditions of this segment only. There are authors who assume that the state of the universe – the cosmos – could change in a way about which we simply do not know anything and that all that our natural sciences say about the behaviour of sodium and levers, for example, may be invalid under this new state. In this sense they deny 'any kind of universality to chemical and mechanical statements' and suggest that they be treated 'as historical ones.'[10] With this brand of agnostic hyperhistoricism that deals in its statements with visionary conditions about which – as they freely admit – we do not know and cannot know anything, reason and science have no quarrel.

Thinking man does not look upon the world with a mind that is, as it were, a Lockian paper upon which reality writes its own story. The paper of his mind is of a special quality that enables man to transform the raw material of sensation into perception and the perceptual data into an image of reality. It is precisely this specific quality or power of his intellect – the logical structure of his mind – that provides man with the faculty of seeing more in the world than nonhuman beings see. This power is instrumental in the development of the natural sciences. But it alone would not enable man to discover in the behaviour of his fellow men more than he can see in the behaviour of stars or of stones, in that of amoebae or in that of elephants.

In dealing with his fellow men, the individual resorts not only to the a priori of logic, but besides to the praxeological a priori. Himself an acting being, he knows what it means to strive after ends chosen. He see more in the agitation and the stir of his fellow men than in the changes occurring in his nonhuman environment. He can search for the ends their conduct is aiming at. There is something that distinguishes in his eyes the movements of germs in a liquid as observed in the microscope from the movements of the individuals in the crowd he may observe in the rush hour at New York's Grand Central Terminal. He knows that there is some 'sense' in a man's running around or sitting still. He looks upon his human environment with a mental equipment that is not required or, to say it more precisely, is downright obstructive in endeavours to explore the state of his nonhuman environment. This specific mental equipment is the praxeological a priori.

The radical empiricism of the historicists went astray in ignoring this fact. No report about any man's conduct can do without reference to the praxeological a priori. There is something that is absolutely valid for all human action irrespective of time, geography, and the racial, national, and cultural characteristics of the actors. There is no human action that can be dealt with without reference to the categorical concepts of ends and means of success and failure, of costs, of profit or loss. What the Ricardian law of association, better known as the law of comparative cost, describes is absolutely valid for any kind of voluntary human cooperation under the division of labour. What the much derided economic laws describe is precisely what must always and everywhere happen provided the special conditions presupposed by them are present.

Willy nilly, people realize that there are things they cannot achieve because they are contrary to the laws of nature. But they are loath to admit that there are things that even the most powerful government cannot achieve because they are contrary to praxeological law.

VII

Different from the case of the historians who are loath to take cognizance of the praxeological a priori is the case of the authors who belong to the various historical, 'realistic,' and institutional schools of economics. If these scholars were consistent, they would limit their studies to what is called economic history; they would deal exclusively with the past and would carefully abstain from asserting anything about the future. Prediction about events to come can be made only on the ground of knowledge of a regularity in the succession of events that is valid for every action irrespective of the time and the geographical and cultural conditions of its occurrence. Whatever economists committed to historicism or institutionalism do, whether they advise their own governments or those backward foreign countries, is self-contradictory. If there is no universal law that describes the necessary effects of definite ways of acting, nothing can be predicted and no measure to bring about any definite results can be recommended or rejected.

It is the same with those authors who, while rejecting the idea that there are economic laws valid for all times, everywhere, and for all people, assume that every period of history has its own economic laws that have to be found a posteriori by studying the history of the period concerned. These authors may tell us that they have succeeded in discovering the laws governing events up to yesterday. But – from the point of view of their own epistemological doctrine – they are not free to assume that the same laws will also determine what will happen tomorrow. All that they are entitled to affirm is: experience of the past shows that A brought about B; but we do not know whether tomorrow A will not bring about some other effects than B.

Another variety of the denial of economics is the trend doctrine. Its supporters blithely assume that trends of evolution as manifested in the past will go on. However, they cannot deny that in the past trends did change and that there is no reason whatever to assume that present trends will not one day change too. Thus, this becomes especially manifest when businessmen, concerned about the continuation of prevailing trends, consult economists and statisticians. The answer they get is invariably this: statistics show us that the trend you are interested in was still continuing on the day to which our most recent statistical data refer; if no disturbing factors turn up, there is no reason why the trend should change; however, we do not know anything about the question whether or not such new factors will present themselves.

VIII

Epistemological relativism, the essential doctrine of historicism, must be clearly distinguished from the ethical relativism of other schools of thought. There are authors who combine praxeological relativism with ethical relativism. But there are also authors who display ethical absolutism while rejecting the concept of universally valid praxeological laws. Thus, many adepts of the Historical School of economics and of institutionalism judge the historical past from the point of view of what they consider as indisputable, never-changing moral precepts, e.g., equality of wealth and incomes. In the eyes of some of them private property is as such morally objectionable. They blame the economists for an alleged praise of material wealth and disparagement of more noble concerns. They condemn the system of private enterprise as immoral and advocate socialism on account of its presumed higher moral worth. As they see it, Soviet Russia complies better with the immutable principles of ethics than the nations of the West committed to the cult of Mammon.

As against all this emotional talk there is need to point out again: praxeology and economics, its up to now best developed branch, are neutral with regard to any moral precepts. They deal with the striving after ends chosen by acting men without any regard whether these ends are approved or disapproved from any point of view. The fact that the immense majority of men prefer a richer supply of material goods to a less ample supply is a datum of history; it does not have any place in economic theory. Economics neither advocates capitalism nor rejects socialism. It merely tries to show what the necessary effects of each of these two systems are. He who disagrees with the teachings of economics ought to try to refute them by discursive reasoning, not by abuse, insinuations, and the appeal to arbitrary, allegedly ethical standards.

147

NOTES

1. [Karl Knies, *Geld und Kredit*, 3 vols (Berlin: Weidmann, 1873–9) – Ed.]
2. [Max Weber, *Wirtschaft und Gesellschaft* vol. 1 of *Grundriss der Sozialökonomik* (Tübingen, 1922). English language edition *The Theory of Social and Economic Organization*, A. M. Henderson and Talcott Parsons, trans. (Glencoe, IL.: Free Press, 1947) – Ed.]
3. [Gustav Schmoller was the founder of the 'Younger' German Historical or 'Historicoethical' School. Its program combined an historical approach to economic phenomena with the pursuit of economic and social politics grounded in 'moral principles.' Lujo Brentano was a prominent proponent and follower of Schmoller but disagreed on matters of methodology – Ed.]
4. The first edition was published in 1853 under the title *Die politische Ökonomie vom Standpunkte der geschichtlichen Methode*. The second edition was published in 1883 under the title *Die politische Ökonomie vom geschichtlichen Standpunkte*. It is by and large a reprint of the earlier edition enlarged by many additions.
5. [The 'older' Historical School proponents did not advocate politics as a means of intervention, nor a basis for economic reasoning as did the 'younger' Historical School advocates – Ed.]
6. [Jean Charles Leonard Sismondi was a Swiss economist and historian. He thought that the focus of economics should be man and social reform not wealth and laissez faire. Sismondi was the first to practice modern period analysis in 1819 – Ed.]
7. There is no need to enter into an analysis of the two other subclasses enumerated by Weber. For a detailed critique of Weber's doctrine, see my essay 'Sociologie und Geschichte,' in *Archiv für Sozialwissenschaft* vol. 61 [1929], reprinted in my book *Grundprobleme der National-ökonomie* (Jena: Gustav Fischer, 1933), pp. 64–121. In the English-language translation of this book, *Epistemological Problems of Economics*, George Reisman, trans. and Arthur Goddard, ed. (Princeton: D. Van Nostrand, 1960), this essay appears on pp. 68–129.
8. H. Hartmann, 'On Rational and Irrational Action', *Psychoanalysis and the Social Sciences*, vol. 1 (1947), p. 371.
9. When the sciences of human action refer to ends, they always mean the ends that acting men are aiming at. This distinguishes these sciences from the metaphysical doctrines known under the name of 'philosophy of history' that pretend to know the ends toward which a superhuman entity – for instance, in the context of Marxism, the

'material productive forces' – directs the course of affairs independently of the ends the acting men want to attain.

10. Otto Neurath, 'Foundations of the Social Sciences,' *International Encyclopedia of Unified Science,* vol. 2, no. 1 (Chicago: University of Chicago Press, 1956), p. 9.

150-58

D40

[1961]

Ludwig von Mises, 'Markt', *Handwörterbuch der Sozialwissenschaften*
(Stuttgart: Gustav Fischer, 1961), vol. 7, pp. 131–6.

D41

This paper is a specially translated version of an encyclopedia
article which Mises contributed (at the age of eighty) to the *Handwörterbuch der Sozialwissenschaften*, under the title 'Markt'. The
paper expresses Mises's mature summing up of his understanding
of the market process. It has been translated especially for this
volume.

*not an
E text*

26

Market

LUDWIG von MISES

Translated by

WILLIAM KIRBY

1. The market process
2. Monopoly and competition
3. Speculation
4. Partial markets
5. Profit and loss
6. Inequality of income and property

1. *The Market Process*

'Market' is what economics calls the process whereby, in an economy based on division of labour and private ownership of the means of production (market economy), production is steered into paths where it best serves to satisfy the most pressing needs of consumers.

The consumers are sovereign. By purchasing or refraining from purchases, they decide the profit or loss of entrepreneurs. Profit and loss guide the command over the means of production into the hands of those who know how to use them most effectively in the service of consumers. In a market economy ownership of the means of production is a social mandate, as it were, which is withdrawn from the mandatary if he does not carry out the instructions of his customers, the consumers.

A business is profitable if it serves to supply consumers as well as possible. It is unprofitable if consumers prefer a different use of the relevant means of production. To construct an opposition between *profitability* and *productivity* is meaningless, so long as one remains within the

151

framework of market economy and does not place consumer sovereignty in question. Whoever describes a profitable business as unproductive sets his own opinion about what should be produced and consumed above the opinion of the market parties. He presumes to know better than the consumers themselves what is of use to them. He thus gives his personal judgement a capacity which makes it appear as a universal truth and rule of life. If he calls for the state to take compulsory measures to affirm productivity against mere profitability, he tacitly assumes that everyone's judgements concur about what is and what is not productive, and that his own opinion will also be that of the authorities.

In describing the market process, one usually speaks of the free play of economic forces. Another image which is often used to characterize the market is that of an *automatic mechanism*. The supposedly blind rule of a mechanism is contrasted to the conscious intervention of the wise planning authorities. Such metaphorical expressions obscure the real facts of the matter. All market phenomena result from attempts by everyone seeking to buy or sell on the market to secure the best possible covering of their requirements. It is wrong to describe such individual actions as unconscious behaviour by contrasting them to conscious intervention by the authorities.

People are not infallible, including in their economic activities. Everyone is free to criticize the behaviour of their fellow humans – for example, their predilection for alcoholic drinks, dubious spectacles, boxing or wrestling matches, and so on – and to make an attempt to talk them into more prudent use of their resources. However, by replacing the market with a planned economy and placing individuals under government tutelage, one does not solve the problems stemming from the inadequacy of the human spirit. Kings, leaders and officials are also human beings who can make mistakes. The freedom which the market gives to individuals may be questioned by metaphysical thinking. But it embodies, in respect of the satisfaction of wants, the ideal of freedom which is the essence of Western culture and differentiates it from the oriental way of life. In this sense, a market which is ultimately governed by consumers is an essential element in the modern social order and culture.

State-owned and municipal enterprises, operating in the framework of a social order which otherwise rests on private ownership of the means of production, are as dependent as private businesses on the market. They must fit in with market commerce as buyers (of raw materials, semi-finished goods, tools and labour) and as sellers (of goods or services), and to hold their own they must strive to make profits and to avoid losses. If attempts are made to reduce or eliminate this dependence by covering business and capital losses through subsidies out of tax revenue, this will merely postpone the onset of the market reaction. For it is not the tax-collecting state but the workings of the market which ultimately decide who is a burden on fiscal revenue and what effect it has upon production, the supply of goods, the management of capital and the formation of income. Here too buyers' sovereignty and the inexorability of market laws show to advantage. When one speaks of a private capitalist sector and a state sector of the national economy, it should not be forgotten that the state sector too is dependent upon the market.

2. *Monopoly and Competition*

The dominant market tendency to adapt production as closely as possible to consumer wishes does not fully take effect only in the case of monopoly prices. For monopoly pricing to be possible, it is not enough that the supply of a good or a service is monopolized. There must also supervene a particular structure of demand. Consumers must value the monopoly good so highly that, if its price rises above the potential competitive price, they do not so limit their purchases that the seller fares worse than by selling at the competitive price.

An example may clarify the effect of monopoly prices. If the prices for copper are competitive, there is a tendency to exploit the mines to a point where further exploitation no longer covers additional expenditures of complementary material and human means of production. If there are monopoly prices for copper, the exploitation of the mines will be inter-rupted at an earlier point. The non-specific complementary means of production which are saved as a result will be employed in other ways to produce articles that consumers would otherwise lack. Yet the consumers would have preferred a better copper supply than to be supplied with these other articles.

At any given time, market prices tend towards a situation in which supply and demand coincide. At that price – which classical economists called the natural price and the older subjectivists the equilibrium price but for which we shall use the better term *final price* – everyone who wants to buy can buy and everyone who wants to sell can sell. But since the factors determining price are subject to constant change, the final price in reality – contrary to the image of the regular economy of static equilibrium – changes again and again before the market price has caught up with it.

Interventionist and socialist writers maintain that the theory of market and price developed by economists is valid only for the conditions of an economy made up of small and medium-sized businesses. The large enter-prises characteristic of 'late capitalism' are supposed to be so powerful that

153

they can impose their will on consumers. There can be no competition in the face of these mammoth corporations. So long as they hold sway, there can no longer be that which corresponded to market in the terminology of political economy.

Around the turn of the twentieth century the railway companies were put forward as a typical example of such huge enterprises against which competition can never prevail. But that allegedly irresistible power of the railways has not been able to prevent or even to slow down the emergence of extremely dangerous competitors in the shape of motor vehicles and aircraft. As soon as something comes onto the market which appeals more to consumers than what the big corporations of today turn out, the same process will be repeated. For the larger an enterprise is, the greater is its dependence on the market – that is, on consumers. Large corporations have therefore developed methods of market analysis and systematic research into consumer preferences. The growing sums spent on advertising to attract customers is further evidence of the buyer's surpassing power.

Competition does not take place only among those who offer the same item for sale, but also among those who wish to sell different articles. The sums which a consumer spends on buying any commodity reduce the sums which he can put up to buy other commodities. All entrepreneurs try hard to draw into their coffers as much as possible of the cash at the public's disposal. All goods and services are in competition with all other goods and services. One mistakes the nature of competition if one thinks that the manufacturer's efforts to 'distinguish' his products – i.e., to give them properties which should make them more desirable to consumers than those of other manufacturers – are measures which give competition a 'monopolistic' structure. The drive to supplant competitors by means of such product differentiation is one of the most important methods of competition. It is precisely such efforts which arouse and keep awake the intrinsic power of the capitalist market to work towards constant improvement in the provision of people's requirements.

3. Speculation

Business activity [*Wirtschaften*] serves the satisfaction of future wants. Since nothing can be predicted with any degree of certainty about the shape of the future, any activity directed to the supply of wants is based upon suppositions and expectations. The behaviour not only of producers but also of consumers is speculative. The consumer who makes a purchase calculates that his future wants will be better met by the good in question than by other goods whose acquisition he has deferred so that he can buy precisely this good. All business, including that of self-sufficient people and of the leader of a socialist organization, is speculation. Whoever spends time, money and effort on training for a particular occupation is also speculating. Only the future will decide whether he has acted rightly.

By the term *market situation* we mean the sum of expectations regarding the shape of prices in the future, both the future of the next moment and the more distant future. The market parties form these expectations from their knowledge of the prices paid in the most recently concluded business, and from their assessment of the changes which new facts – whether they have already occurred or are expected to occur – will make to those prices. Every individual is delighted if the expectations which have determined his behaviour prove to be correct or if conditions turn out better than he expected. But if it transpires that another preference would have been more judicious, then those who have suffered harm by misjudging the future situation (bad speculation) are apt to demand that the state should come to their rescue. The only source for the provision of such aid is a cut in the profits of those who have speculated well. The further this policy of equalizing profits and losses makes headway, the more will the market be obstructed in carrying out its function. The task of pointing production in a particular direction must then be assumed by the state.

4. Partial Markets

The market is one and indivisible. All prices are interconnected and determine one another. Each part of the market is dependent upon all others and influences them in turn. There have been and still are today groups of people who live in complete autarky, outside the exchange society encompassing the rest of the world. Within a system of market economy, however, all actions are potentially bound up with the market. Anyone who is self-sufficient in certain requirements will influence the market price of the articles in question and will be influenced by it in turn.

The partial markets on which means of production are sold are as dependent upon final consumers as the various markets for ready-to-use goods. The same is true of stock exchanges. Stock exchanges determine how capital goods available for additional investment are divided between various investment opportunities. Newly formed capital, as well as reserve and depreciation funds available for new investment which were constituted for the replacement of capital goods used up in past production, are steered by the stock market into lines of production which, in the opinion of speculators, appear to offer the most favourable prospects. At the stock exchange itself there are neither profits nor losses. Profits and losses in

155

stock-market business are the result of correct or incorrect investment anticipation of the future behaviour of consumers.

The formation of prices on the labour market is as dependent on final consumer demand as it is on the market for material means of production. That was never in doubt in the case of the earnings of stage personalities or professional sportsmen. But it is on the market and nowhere else that the wages for all other duties and labour are formed. On the free labour market (i.e. one unimpeded by any compulsion), the prevailing tendency is for the wage of every kind of labour to be established in such a way that everyone who wants to work for that wage will find work and everyone who wants to employ workers at that rate will find them. The free labour market tends towards full employment. If government decree or trade union compulsion stipulates minimum wages which exceed the potential market rates, then permanent unemployment of a section of job-seekers will be the result (*institutional unemployment*).

John Maynard Keynes has also recognized this. The peculiarity of his recommended full-employment policy is that it strives to eliminate institutional unemployment not by re-establishing a free labour market but by increasing the money supply. Keynes started from the expectation that, while nominal money-wages were maintained, a gradual, 'automatic' lowering of real wages through inflationary price rises would run into less resistance on the part of wage-earners than would undisguised attempts to adjust money-wages to the market. Given the popularity which the indexation method has acquired, it is to be doubted whether Keynes's expectation has come true.

5. *Profit and Loss*

In the scenario of a regular or stationary economy, the price of each product equals the sum of the prices paid for the complementary means of production, including the interest corresponding to the necessary production time. Hence there are neither profits nor losses. In the constantly changing real economy, a mismatch arises again and again between supply and demand. To overcome this mismatch, production has to be readjusted to the changed conditions. From this adjustment process come the entrepreneur's profits or losses.

Profits or losses result from the fact that the adjustment of output to the new situation is not completed at one stroke throughout the market system. Entrepreneurs who correctly predicted the change and acted accordingly receive surpluses because, on the one hand, they realize higher prices for the product, and on the other hand, because they can still buy means of production at the lower prices corresponding to the earlier situation. Both sources of their profit dry up in the further course of events. Increased output of the profit-earning article lowers its price, and at the same time the prices of the complementary means of production increase. If no further changes were to occur, stationary equilibrium would be established in which there were neither profits nor losses. The tendency on the market is for profits and losses to disappear. Profit and loss are permanent features only because the economic data are continually changing and a regular economy is no more than a mental construct to which real life never corresponds. Profit and loss are, so to speak, reward and punishment which consumers mete out for faster or slower fulfilment of their wishes.

It would be inapt to describe the appearance of entrepreneurial profits and losses as a transitional phenomenon or a frictional phenomenon and their absence as the ideal state of affairs in the economy. Uninterrupted striving to improve the satisfaction of wants is a characteristic human feature. The state of equilibrium discussed in economics is not a goal whose achievement appears desirable from some points of view. It is a conceptual aid which should impart knowledge of a differently constructed reality. Political bias is in operation when one calls imperfect a market on which there is no stationary equilibrium, and imperfect or incomplete the competition which takes place on that market.

6. Inequality of Income and Property

In the society based upon conquest and forcible appropriation of the land – a society which Adam Ferguson, Claude Henri de Rouvroy de Saint-Simon and Herbert Spencer termed militarism and which contemporary Anglo-Saxon writings describe as feudalism – unequal distribution of landed property is political in origin. One is rich or poor according to how much one is allocated by the conqueror or his descendants. A change in the distribution of property can only be achieved by political means.

In a market economy, the prevailing tendency is to make the means of production available to those who know how best to employ them in accordance with consumer wishes. Inequality in the size of income and property is the result of the behaviour of consumers. It is they who make some people rich and others poor. If one is fully to master the expression distribution of income and property – which gives a wrong idea of the facts of market economy – one must be clear that the distribution is carried out by the consumers, whose only concern is that their interests are looked after in the best possible way. In the militarist social order, it may be the

157

case that the poor man's indigence is the other side of the rich man's affluence. In market economy, the growing property of the rich and the shrinking property of others are the result of improving satisfaction of wants for the remaining members of society. The processes which raise the average standard of living are what make large fortunes appear and disappear. The view which sees the amassing of large fortunes as a detraction from the welfare of other compatriots is a mistaken view of the nature of market economy. The source of market wealth is the raising of consumers' living standards, and vice versa. Measures aimed at levelling out inequality in income and wealth are at the expense of consumers' living standards. From the standpoint of consumers' interests, taxation of company losses would be more justifiable than taxation of company profits. Inequality of wealth and income is an essential element of market economy. Karl Marx and Friedrich Engels correctly recognized in the *Communist Manifesto* that 'sharply progressive taxes' and 'abolition of the right of inheritance' would lead to the destruction of market economy.

The interventionist policy of the present day is bent on counteracting the decisions which consumers make in the marketplace. It seeks to eliminate the market. It is not always realized that in that case the government must eventually take on the running of the production process and thus put socialism in the place of market economy.[1]

NOTES

1. The text of the German original here includes a bibliography of sources in German, English and French.

Frederick Hayek, 'Das intertemporale Gleichgewichtssystem der Preise und die Bewegungen des Geld wertes', *Weltwirtschaftliches Archiv* (1928), pp. 33–76.

This paper by Friedrich Hayek (1899–1992) is widely cited as a pioneering contribution to the theory of intertemporal equilibrium. It is perhaps the most important – if not necessarily the most 'Austrian' – of Hayek's early contributions. It has been translated especially for this volume.

27

The System of Intertemporal Price Equilibrium and Movements in the 'Value of Money'

FREDERICK HAYEK

Translated by

WILLIAM KIRBY

Contents:[1] 1. Consequences of the customary abstraction from time in economic theory. – 2. The lack of a theoretical basis for judging the significance of different prices for the same goods at different points in time. – 3. This basis can be created only if the question is treated as a problem of equilibrium. – 4. The temporally determined difference in value of identical goods. – 5. Intertemporal exchange. – 6. Differences in the supply of certain goods at two points in time must affect the intertemporal exchange ratios of all goods. – 7. Intertemporal exchange ratios and successive money prices. – 8. The system of price equilibrium with periodically recurring changes in the conditions of production; 9. with single but persisting changes in the conditions of production. – 10. The influence of automatic changes in the money supply of a controlled currency on the 'natural' level of prices. – 11. The parallel movement of output and prices in empirical reality. – 12. On the origin of the theory that the money supply necessarily adjusts to the 'demand for money'. – Appendix: Necessary price movements and the rate of interest.

1. Every economic activity stretches out in time. All economic processes last a certain time, and all connections between them necessarily extend over longer or shorter periods. Theoretical research does employ, at least initially, the methodologically valuable fiction of abstracting from the flow of time and postulating an economic system in which all individual

161

processes work themselves out simultaneously and thus form the prices of all commodities of one kind under the same conditions. However, the results achieved in that stage of research can offer only an incomplete explanatory schema for processes in the actually existing economy. In reality, a large part of all economic activity is directed at balancing the supply of wants at various points in time – so large that common usage tends to describe as economic this part of human behaviour in particular.

Now, prices also serve a major function in guiding and regulating all economic activity in a commercial economy with regard to the temporal distribution of individual processes. But precisely that function has so far been given very scant treatment in economic science. In the main, the results obtained in the first stage of theoretical research are considered sufficient for the tackling of all concrete problems, and no effort is made to supplement them with a fundamental investigation into the significance of the time factor for the structure of the price system.

As soon as we adopt more realistic premises, however, instead of those oversimplified ones which all too often fly in the face of reality, we find that to abstract from the flow of time does such violence to the facts that the results thereby obtained are dubious to say the least. At the moment when – unlike in the elementary accounts of pure theory – we are no longer dealing only with simultaneously constituted prices but have to consider a money economy with its necessarily successive formation of prices, we are faced with a problem for which we would search in vain within the existing systems of economic theory. For then the task is no longer just to explain the necessity and function of a certain gradation within simultaneously existing prices, but to investigate the necessity and significance of the relative level of prices at successive points in time.

2. There can be no doubt, then, that even in a static economy where the same processes repeat themselves in an unchanging sequence, the same goods do not necessarily fetch the same prices at each point in time; rather, under certain conditions they fetch different prices at different points in time, and these price changes *must* repeat themselves if the economy is to proceed on a steady course. The reason for this is that a steady course of the economy is not at all synonymous with continual unwinding of all the individual processes that it involves – indeed, with the given external conditions this will never be the case. The approach which abstracts from time, driven by the (for it) necessary assumption that the successive economic periods are completely identical, overcomes such difficulties by making these periods so long that even the wants and production processes repeated at the longest intervals are included within them. Thus the economic period covered by the equilibrium system of elementary theory is at first so extended that it encompasses even the

longest-wave price variations determined by the discontinuity of individual economic processes, and these price variations are then made to disappear through the mental shifting of all exchange-acts to one point in time. Seasonally related changes in individual economic processes would already entail periods of at least one year, and these become much longer as a result of once-only production processes of far greater duration. But this simplification, permissible only as a first step, has also obscured the fact that there must be different prices at successive points in time.[2] Now, in fact, it is not at all an exception but rather the rule that, in exchange processes which repeatedly take place at various points in time over those longer periods, and even at certain times within a static economy, different conditions ensue and hence different prices are formed. Not only external circumstances such as the changing season or time of day and the technical specificity of many production processes, but also natural variations in human needs determine that even a regularly unfolding economy cannot present the same picture at every moment, and that the same processes can only periodically recur within it. But this entails that – since the available goods cannot usually be transferred across time simply at discretion and without special expenditure – even in such an economy the influences affecting the prices of similar goods at different times, and hence those prices themselves, will be different.

This price differentiation for the same goods at different times within a regularly unfolding economy is thus also a necessary precondition of its regular unfolding, rather as the price differentiation of one good at different places resulting from transport costs and the like must be regarded in static theory as the precondition of equilibrium.[3] Still less than the determinants and function of this interlocal price system, however, have those of the *intertemporal price system* yet been adequately investigated. We may even say that existing theory usually deals only with the command over goods given at one time and one place, and with very few exceptions completely ignores differences that do not fit its schema.

Almost all the exceptions are taken up in the well-known work of *E. von Böhm-Bawerk*, which is exceedingly rich in ideas but offers little in the way of positive results for the questions that we are addressing. The most important further step has been taken by *F. A. Fetter*, with his remarks on the influence which the temporally determinate character of the enjoyment of goods has upon their valuation. His concept of *time value* has a bearing upon at least the most significant of the problems at issue here. To my knowledge, however, Fetter has also not taken up the decisive question in this context – namely, the importance of the temporal gradation of the prices of a good for the undisturbed course of the economy.[4] Very occasionally, in connection with the theory of interest (K. Wicksell, I. Fisher,

L. Mises), brief consideration has been given to the importance of price differentiation across time and to the effect of disturbances to the normal gradation of prices. But as far as I am aware, these problems have never been tackled in their full scope.

For the handling of a problem such as this in economic theory there should only be one method: to ask what are the conditions with which any structure of prices must comply if the corresponding structure of the economy is to remain in existence – or, what are the consequences which must follow if the actual price gradation deviates from those conditions in any way. As in any other price problem, the task here is also to establish what circumstances determine the exchange ratio between two goods, except that in this case we are dealing with goods which, even if identical from a technical point of view, are given at different points in time.

Now, knowledge that there must be an intertemporal price system is not only hard to square with the widespread view that temporally constant prices are a precondition of the undisturbed flow of the economy; it stands in the sharpest contradiction with that view. Further investigation will show that if there is a general rise in production, a state of equilibrium can exist only with a corresponding decrease in prices – so that the continuing stability of prices must in that case lead to temporary disturbances in the correspondence between supply and demand. Before this can be demonstrated in greater detail, however, we have to analyse more precisely the necessity and the preconditions of a temporal state of equilibrium and to establish the criteria for its presence or absence. This is especially necessary because it has been argued that the concept of equilibrium, or the static approach which its use involves, is applicable only to an economy without a time dimension,[5] and because it is at least unusual to treat price changes – or, more accurately, the price differentiation of technically identical goods at different points in time – within the framework of an equilibrium system.

3. Nevertheless, the concept of equilibrium is as indispensable a tool for the understanding of temporal price differentiation as it is for any other investigation in economic theory. Strictly speaking, its area of application is even identical with that of economic theory, because only with its help can one synthetically represent the large number of different tendencies operating at each moment in any economic system. In essence it contains nothing other than the assumption that the interconnections between economic phenomena obey a particular law, which manifests itself in the fact that in any given constellation of circumstances (or 'data') affecting it the whole economy tends towards a quite definite organization of its parts. Attempts to explain economic processes can only start from the fact that in each constellation of such circumstances there is only one definite course

of action which corresponds to the interests of each economic subject, and that he will therefore keep changing his dispositions until he arrives at the most favourable uses of the means available to him.

Even in the case of some change in the external circumstances, it is in the nature of things that for the whole period in which it applies, only one way of disposing of the goods accessible to each subject will offer him the maximum satisfaction. If the individual is from the outset able to predict the change in question, he will make his dispositions accordingly; if he is not able to do this, he will probably have to conclude later that he would have obtained a greater return with a different way of arranging things as a whole and that he has actually incurred a loss in relation to that other possibility. Only in the first of these two cases will the return from the particular dispositions live up to the expectations to which they gave rise; only then will there be no incentive to change them. Assuming that when a person opts for a certain distribution of the available means among the different uses, he clearly sees all the conditions which will exist when the action is undertaken, we can say that only one definite structure of those dispositions will correspond to equilibrium. Thus, if we know the variations in those conditions for each point in a forthcoming period of time, then it does not matter how long that period is or how great the differences between the actual conditions at each moment: the same relations must always obtain among the particular dispositions of the economic subjects, and hence among all economic processes in that segment of time, as those which are derived from the postulated timeless system of equilibrium.

It is thus by no means a precondition of a static economic state that wants and potential production should be the same at every point in the relevant period. Rather, the precondition for equilibrium to appear is that the wants and means of production existing at each moment should be known to the economic subjects when they are drawing up their economic plans for the whole period.[6] No doubt this condition is never present in reality, but numerous changes are known beforehand and in order to judge their effects it is necessary to investigate the fundamental ways in which such cases are related to the ideal case of equilibrium.

An economic system extended in time must therefore, even if statically considered, take into account the temporal determinateness of the various data; or – to say the same thing more understandably, though at the risk of misunderstandings – it must allow for temporal changes in the data which can be foreseen and which, as in the case of changes linked to the seasons, would be present in any temporally extended system. The purpose of studying such an economic system is to establish the price gradations of technically identical goods at different moments of the period in question – gradations which, because of the difficulties hindering the transfer of goods from one time to another, must be present, just as such goods will, for similar reasons, fetch different prices at different places. In accordance with the fundamental idea of modern price theory, this investigation must be preceded by a brief look at the laws of subjective valuation of goods at different moments, as the basis for an explanation of exchange relations.

4. So, let us for the time being consider the valuing activity of an isolated individual and ask how his provision with, and hence valuation of, a good is structured at different points within a time period. Let us then assume that – for example, because of known differences in the technical conditions of production (influence of the seasons on agriculture!) – it is predictably more difficult to obtain the good at some times than it is at others. (It is already contained in this assumption that one cannot transfer from the former times to the latter without special expenditure.) The answer will then in every case be that goods available at a time when they can be obtained only with greater difficulty or – which comes to the same thing economically – in a smaller quantity will be valued more highly than technically identical goods available in, for example, a more favourable season. It would evidently be inappropriate if, despite the greater expenditure required at one time for the same satisfaction of a want, the economic subject were to set his sights on obtaining it at that time – for the return would necessarily be greater if the same outlay were made for the satisfaction of a different want for which conditions were not particularly unfavourable at that point in time.[7] If an attempt is made even under such conditions to arrange supply of the good at the two times in such a way that its marginal utility, and hence its (subjective) value, is always the same, the inevitable result will be that, in relation to other supply, the outlay will at one time be too large or at the other time too small for the satisfaction of that want – or both. It will be possible to end the well-known displacements which this must entail only if this good, in relation to others, is valued more highly at the second point in time than it is at the first, so that at the second time either it has a higher value or all other goods have a lower value than at the first time (or – which actually must be the case – both are true). Under these conditions, therefore, a state of equilibrium presupposes differential valuation of the particular goods at different moments in the period over which it extends.

5. To pass from derivation of the necessary gradation of a good's subjective value to the determinants of the temporal gradation of prices, the possibility for two individuals to exchange technically identical goods available at different points in time must now be included among the premises. In view of the point in the general enquiry at which we now find ourselves, this will at first have to be done on the assumption that this exchange is effected directly – that is, without the use of a means of

exchange. Here as everywhere, of course, a prerequisite for exchange to take place is that the parties to the exchange should have a relatively different valuation of the good in question.[8] This is possible because the reasons for the just-described temporal gradation in the subjective valuations may naturally be of a quite individual character and operate in opposite ways for different people. Some persons will therefore be prepared to exchange goods available at one time for similar goods available at another time, and as a rule they will find other persons who are willing to undertake this exchange with them. Does such exchange usually or only ever take place in such a way that like quantities of the good available at one time are exchanged for the same quantities of the same good available at another time?[9] Or are there circumstances under which this exchange ratio cannot persist but, so long as it does, supply and demand do not coincide and it even gives rise to further shifts in supply and demand which continue until another exchange ratio has established itself on the market? The analogy between this and any other price problem is no doubt sufficient for the question to be answered in the affirmative.[10]

Since the potential variations in the participants' relative valuation of the exchange good are exactly the same as in any other formation of prices, it is certain that the exchange ratio between good x at time 1 (henceforth x_1, where x represents a *quantitative* unit) and good x at time 2 (henceforth x_2) may just as easily take the form $x_1 : 2x_2$ or $2x_1 : x_2$ or any other form as the form $x_1 : x_2$. And it is equally certain that if the exchange ratio between quantities of a good available at different times does not correspond to the market situation, the consequences will be the same as in other cases where the established price does not correspond to the market situation. If, for example, an exchange ratio $x_1 : x_2$ is arbitrarily fixed on the market when supply and demand would only balance at a ratio of $2x_1 : x_2$ for such an intertemporal exchange, so that there is an excess supply of x_1 and an uncovered demand for x_2 at the current price, this will have the consequence – unless for some reason an immediate change can occur in the market price – that so long as this price holds, production is less advantageous at the second time than it would be with a 'correct' price, since x_2 could then be obtained more cheaply by exchange for x_1 than by separate measures to produce the good at time 2. This must also entail that, comparatively speaking, the supply of this good shifts further to the disadvantage of the second point in time. Thus, on the one hand, the imbalance between supply and demand is reinforced on the market for intertemporal exchange and the pressure mounts accordingly on the existing price of x_1; but on the other hand, the 'false' price induces individuals to provide goods for the first point in time in an amount which conflicts with a rational distribution of supply over the whole time period.

Even if the 'false' price were to be artificially maintained, it would still be the case – since the supply of x_1 would then exceed that of x_2 – that a number of people who decided to make available greater quantities of x_1 only on the understanding that x_1 could be exchanged for x_2 at a ratio of $x_1 : x_2$ would be disappointed in their expectation of improving their supply at time 2 through such exchange, and would have to conclude that they would have done better to direct their outlay straight to the procurement of x_2.

6. It should now be sufficiently clear that, on the assumption of pure barter, the exchange between goods of the same kind available at different times will normally take place not in a ratio of $1:1$ but in some other ratio depending upon circumstances and in accordance with the same laws that govern the formation of other prices. Strictly speaking, technically identical goods available at different times should be regarded in economic terms as different goods, in the same way that this is necessary in the case of technically identical goods located at different places.[11] As soon as this is realized, it no longer appears strange but actually self-evident that in a static system, too, goods available at different times but otherwise the same should fetch different prices. But before the necessity of a definite gradation of money prices for technically identical goods at different points in time can be exactly derived from the known necessity of certain ratios in intertemporal exchange, we must carry a step further our investigation into the effects of intertemporal exchange in kind: that is, we have to show to what extent the influences determining the exchange ratio between goods of one type but at two times also affects the exchange relations between all other goods available at the two points in time.

The effects of the differential difficulty in supplying a particular good at different times, combined with the impossibility of transferring it from one time to another without extra expenditure, are by no means limited to the fact that a ratio other than $1:1$ must obtain in the exchange of quantities of this good available at different times; they must also extend to the exchange ratio between quantities of all other goods available at the two times. The different potential supply of a good at two times thus first of all implies that that good's ratio of exchange with the other goods must necessarily be different at the two times. If, for instance, good x can be exchanged for good y at the first time in a ratio of $2x_1 : 3y_1$, then at the second time, when x is more difficult to obtain, an exchange relation of, say, $2x_2 : 4y_2$ will firstly take shape. Nevertheless, at the second time as opposed to the first, the price of x in terms of y will not normally be higher by the full amount by which x is more difficult to obtain, since now proportionally more labour and other productive forces must be expended on the production of x and less on the production of y. The value of x will

168

thus increase by less, but the value of y will also increase in comparison with the first point in time and the exchange ratio of $x_2 : y_2$ will only partially express the higher outlay required to produce x_2. In this way, however, y_2 would reach a higher value than y_1, both in its direct uses and as a means of acquiring x_2, so that there would be a tendency for y_1 to be exchanged for y_2. If we further assume that, as will usually be the case, a transfer of y from the first to the second point in time is not possible without special expenditure, then the exchange ratio between y_1 and y_2 cannot be $y_1 : y_2$ but must shift quite definitely to the advantage of y_2 – it being understood that this does not depend upon any circumstance directly affecting the supply of y or the demand for it. In order to restore the equilibrium disturbed by changes affecting one good, there must also be changes in the intertemporal exchange ratios of other goods; these must be such that quantities of other goods for which the good in question can be exchanged at the future time may also not be obtained in the intertemporal exchange more cheaply than that good itself. The difference in exchange ratios between different commodities at different times therefore makes it advantageous to speculate on premiums – and so necessary to alter the exchange ratio – even when there is no intrinsic reason why the commodities should exchange at an intertemporal ratio other than 1:1.

In summary, we can say that the difference in conditions which will always occur at different times for at least the supply of a certain number of goods, together with the restricted possibility of transferring goods from one time to another, must entail that between the goods of all kinds available at different points in time there are definite intertemporal exchange ratios similar to those which take shape between goods available at the same time. In fact, neither of these groups of exchange ratios can be explained in isolation; both can be understood only as component parts of a single system which must include the intertemporal exchange ratios. The exchange ratios for simultaneously available goods thus constitute at most a sub-system with limited autonomy, in the same sense in which this can be said, for example, of the prices prevailing at one place in comparison with the price system for the whole country or with international prices.[12]

As is so often the case with problems in economics, the main difficulty here in grasping these temporal exchange ratios is the fact that the technical indicators which dominate our mental image of the sameness of goods make it very difficult for us to regard goods that are technically the same as not also economically the same. That this must happen for goods available at different times also follows from the fact that commodities which are technically the same but have different time qualities cannot be as easily used for the same purpose, and some of them perhaps not at all. From the

169

point of view of economics, such technically identical but not simultaneously present goods – and therefore the conditions to which their value and price are subject – cannot differ in position from some other goods which, though mostly of the same origin, are ultimately subject to different production processes (in the broadest sense of the term) which mean that they can only be directly used for different purposes. These goods too – like the technically identical goods located at different places that we have repeatedly used for comparison – may best be described as goods closely related in production, between whose value and price there is an especially close connection which does not always have to be one of identity.

7. So far, the argument has been based on the assumption that all exchange acts in the economic system are effected without the use of a means of exchange. We have thus been able to talk of prices not in the strict sense of the term but only in that of exchange ratios between any goods, so that the intertemporal relations of magnitude have been discussed not in the gradation of money prices obtained at different times, but only in the case of direct exchange of two goods available at different times. Now, however, we must investigate whether the same necessity of a definite exchange ratio between two goods given at different times also holds when, instead of taking place directly, the exchange breaks down into, first, the giving up of one good to acquire means of exchange, and then later, the giving up of the means of exchange to acquire another good. This is the general question posed at the beginning of our investigation, which here takes a more specific form. Does the temporal gradation of most money prices have a definite and necessary function, and if it does, what are the consequences of an externally determined deviation of the temporal price gradation from this 'natural' level?

The considerations set out in the last section have already afforded an essentially positive answer to this question. Once it is recognized that the possibility of transferring certain goods from one time to another joins together all exchange ratios within and between the two times into a system in which they all tend toward equilibrium, it is clear that the same law must apply to the relative magnitude of the quantities of goods obtainable at different times for a certain quantity of the means of exchange. The only difference between this case and the one set out in greater detail in the previous section is that here the same result is not obtained indirectly by an interpolated exchange of two other goods; rather, because the means of exchange allows more completely than most other goods a cost-free (or even lucrative) store to be held for the future, it is itself set aside and used to acquire the desired good at a second point in time.

It would thus appear to have been demonstrated that, in a temporally extended economic system which is at equilibrium, the relative level of the money price of any good must vary according to the given conditions at each moment; and that all that remains is to show by concrete examples what must be the consequences for proportional development whenever this price system is disturbed by influences which have nothing to do with the original impetus of the economy.

It may nevertheless be necessary to explain the connections in a little more detail, as it is perhaps not immediately obvious, for example, that the existence of the same money prices in any relationship at two different times is synonymous with the existence of an intertemporal exchange ratio of 1:1, and that all other relationships of two prices at different times correspond to one and the same intertemporal exchange ratio. The differences in the marginal utility of the means of exchange also present absolutely nothing new which did not already have to be taken into account in analysing ratios of exchange in kind. Here too, as has already been shown, the marginal utility of most goods will be different at particular points in time and must remain so even with the attainment of equilibrium, whereas the striving to eliminate as far as possible supply differences will actually give rise instead to the undertaking of intertemporal exchange acts, and the emergence of definite exchange ratios, in which the inevitably remaining supply differences find expression. Similarly, the different marginal utility of money expresses only the necessarily unequal supply at two points in time, and cannot take the place of that necessary price gradation at the successive times. It will be shown in subsequent sections, on the basis of some rather more concrete assumptions, what must inescapably follow if monetary policies are used to keep prices unchanged.

8. Foreseeable changes in data, which as such may be built into the economic plan and whose effects are amenable to an equilibrium approach, can be essentially divided into three groups: those which recur at precise intervals; those which continue to be regular in both direction and extent; and lastly, those whose one appearance as a result of currently observable developments or of known human decisions is to be expected with certainty at a particular point in time. The effects can be most plainly seen in cases belonging to the first group. Observation of the effects of changes in external conditions which recur in accordance with the laws of nature at relatively short intervals also shows most plainly that they can become comprehensible only through being joined in thought within an equilibrium system. But this also shows how unwarranted and inappropriate are all attempts to restrict application of the concept of equilibrium to systems which only extend over periods of time in which all external conditions remain constant – instead of only assuming, as we do here, that there is no deviation from the expected course of things.

Among the cases of the first group, the temporal price gradations most familiar to us – whose necessity is immediately understandable – are the ones connected with the most short-term of such periodic changes, the times of the day. It is hardly possible to deny that the explanation for the different prices of a good or service at different times of the day still falls within the province of static theory, and scarcely anyone can doubt that from the point of view of economics the services provided one time by day and another time by night must count as different goods. One of the best-known examples of this kind is the frequently higher night-time price of a tram ticket, although the same phenomenon can be observed in the most varied cases, such as the price of theatre tickets for matinee and evening performances or the usually much-reduced night tariff for electricity. It will suffice to consider the first example more closely to show the fundamental concordance of this price differentiation of technically identical goods at different hours of the day with the price gradation of different goods sold at the same time, and that here too there is a connection which can be explained only by means of the concept of equilibrium.

It is clearly possible that a night tram service can only continue to make a profit with a relatively higher fare, and in such a case (naturally assuming free formation of prices) both the provision of night transport at a not-increased price and its complete omission would signify a loss for the entrepreneur. This means nothing other than that so long as night transport is not provided at correspondingly higher prices, the entrepreneur would gain from a change in the conditions for his service. Thus, only if night fares are set at an appropriate level will the market situation not necessarily give rise to changes and equilibrium be attained. And this price gradation too can be understood only as an equilibrium system in which each economic subject has so arranged things that he achieves the desired purpose.

Essentially the same thing can be said about price gradations which occur in the course of seasonal changes. Again it is not difficult to show that the price differentiation of technically identical goods in different seasons serves a definite function, and so long as there is no equilibrium the market participants stand to gain by continually altering their dispositions in a way that modifies the price gradation in the direction of equilibrium. An example here might be the well-known difference in the prices of such agricultural produce as cereals, shortly before and immediately after the harvest. Perhaps the analogous difference in egg prices within and outside the peak laying season would serve still better for many purposes, because with a corresponding outlay production can be increased for each season.

We are thus talking here of goods which are harder to supply during certain parts of the year – whether because climatic or other factors entail major expenses if production is to structured in such a way that goods are ready for consumption at that time, or because they cannot be finished at all at that time but have to be carried over from an earlier time at a certain cost. It is well known that these circumstances are also expressed in corresponding price differences for the various times of the year. Once again it is only a question of showing that a quite definite gradation of these prices is a necessary condition for regular repetition of existing economic processes, as is also the case with simultaneously applicable prices. This can best be seen if we look at what would necessarily follow from the establishment of two prices at the two times, with no such equilibrium relation between them. Let us assume, then, that of the two times to be considered, the good in question can be produced at the first considerably more cheaply than at the second, although the money prices they can fetch are the same at both. From what has already been said, this evidently means that the good is valued too high at the first time and too low at the second. Consequently, expenditure on future provision of the good will be less attractive, and conversely greater expenditure will be made for its provision in the present, since at current prices the most advantageous method of covering requirements at the second time is to sell the good at the first time and to use the proceeds to buy it at the second. It must be stressed, however, that at least for a certain number of individuals, the expectation which prompted their dispositions with regard to the good is not fulfilled; that is, at the given prices some of them will not be able to obtain the good at the second time, since then it would by hypothesis be more difficult to procure and at an equilibrium price would in most cases appear less plentifully on the market. In our case, however, its scarcity at the second time – and hence the disproportion between supply and demand – would increase still further because the existence of the same price at the first time would not even make it seem profitable to put up those costs for the provision of the good at the second time which the purchasers would still be willing to pay. As a result of the expectation of price constancy, therefore, the situation at the second time will be such that not even an additional price increase to the level corresponding to equilibrium would suffice to bring supply and demand into balance. Prevention of the price gradation necessary at different times will entail that tendencies to a change in prices are further strengthened and must sooner or later prevail if there is not to be a complete disorganization of the market.

Investigation of the opposite case yields similar results. Let us assume that some natural produce fetches the same prices in two different seasons, but that at the later time – because of more favourable weather conditions

– it can be produced in greater quantity with the same expenditure. It will then evidently be advantageous to expand production of the good at the more distant as opposed to the more proximate time. At the point closer in time one will acquire just these goods more cheaply by buying them than by producing them oneself, whereas later more will be obtained for goods produced by oneself than has been spent on their provision in the intervening period. This must spur a sharp cutback in production for the first time and an undue expansion for the second. But in comparison with other supply, this will lead to a situation where a shortage of the good appears at the more proximate time and a surplus at the more distant time, again because some of the purchasers at the first time will not be able to buy at the expected price and some at the second time will not be able to sell at the expected price. At both moments supply and demand will not balance, because at both the same price corresponds to the marginal cost of quite different quantities of product and to the marginal supply of a quantity of buyers that differs in the opposite direction.

What has so far been explained for the prices of separate goods at different times will, in certain circumstances, also apply to the prices of all goods in a national economy and thus to the so-called 'general price level'. Let us try to make things as clear as possible with a highly idealized example. If we assume that an isolated nation mainly feeds itself on a fruit which can be ripened in any season at very different costs but in practice will only keep for a couple of days, then not only this fruit but most other goods as well will fetch different prices at different times of the year. It is thus assumed that shortly before the point of ripening, labour necessary to provide the fruit is taken on in a commensurate amount. Consequently, at the time when production conditions are unfavourable, some of the implements and capital in use elsewhere will be made available for the cultivation of this fruit, so that at that time there will also be worse provision of all the other goods which can be kept only with a certain expenditure – and it does not thereby become possible to bring the food supply to the level of the more favourable season. Everyone will therefore be provided with most goods very differently at different times of the year: now relatively well with most goods, now relatively badly with most goods. If, in these conditions, the various goods could be obtained at any time for the same money price, everyone would happily save part of their income at the good time so as to improve their supply at the bad time. Quite evidently, however, this does not allow everyone to reach their goal: it necessarily drives up prices in the bad season, when they go on increasing until the unit of money can buy no one a greater utility in this season than in the bad season. On the other hand, at least in the case of goods carried over from earlier points in time, it would not be worthwhile to bear the higher associated costs and so not even the economically feasible degree of supply balance can be attained. Of course, we are abstracting here – as we shall always do for the time being – from the existence of credit, for otherwise saving would lead neither to a fall in the sums of money spent during the time *in* which the saving takes place, nor to a rise in these sums during the time *for* which it takes place; indeed, because of investment of the saved money, the total sums spent in the economy would not have to change in accordance with individual savings. Besides, to take the phenomenon of credit into account would at this point only needlessly complicate the argument, without changing anything in the essential conclusions.

The conclusions are that a difference in all or at least most prices at different points in time may be necessary, and that in some circumstances, therefore, *the movements of the so-called 'general price level' also serve a function*. It is hardly necessary to dwell here on the naive view of quantity theory from which alone one could deny the necessity of such goods-determined changes in the price level. We shall just add a brief remark on the significance of conceivable seasonal changes in the 'price level' for the theory of money value. The possibility of such regularly recurring price movements – for example, a general rise in prices every winter – is nothing other than an expression of the different supply of most goods, and hence their different value, at different points in time. And this clearly shows how absurd it is always to see movements in the general price level as if they involved avoidable 'changes in money value', caused only by the imperfection of our monetary system and to be steered clear of whenever possible. Quite apart from the impossibility, to be explained elsewhere, of discovering anything like a supra-individual general 'value of money', it would also be nonsensical to speak of a differing value of money, because it is in monetary price differences that the different value of goods finds expression. If one does use the imprecise image of a general value of money, then to be consistent one would have to deny – like Mises disputing the possibility of local differences in money value[13] – that temporal differences in money value are possible within an equilibrium system extending in time.

9. So far, one would think, the account of the connections between prices at different points in time could hardly meet with opposition, although as far as I am aware these connections have never before been explicitly presented. What would at first appear more surprising is the assertion that essentially the same relations persist where changes in the data are not of a periodical nature but involve a well-known and regular development in one direction. In what follows, we shall attempt to show that even with such development only one quite definite level of relative prices at successive points in time permits the achievement of equilibrium,

and that any other price gradation leads to shifts in the structure of production which must in the end cause a disparity between supply and demand and hence further price changes that will usually involve losses. This is the central point of our present analysis – and the key to the thesis on the relationship between 'movements in the value of money' and the natural price gradation, which will be considered in the following sections.

Let us first assume again that it is possible to foresee with certainty that the production costs of one good will continually diminish over a relatively long period of time, perhaps because a drainage programme undertaken for health reasons will each year make available areas of former marshland that are particularly suited to production of a natural product. If, in such a case, the price of the natural product did not constantly fall, it would not be worthwhile – although it would doubtless accord with equilibrium and be in the general interest – to raise output, even before the expected increase in production area, by more intensively cultivating the already available land at the expense of its future fertility. Owners of the existing fields would rather, in the expectation of later securing the same price, arrange their current production in such a way that they could produce the same quantities at the same costs for evermore. But as soon as they have to compete with products from the new and better land, it becomes plain that they would have done better to have raised their output in advance instead of waiting until later. Thus, the assumption that the price obtainable for the good remains unchanged with its increased supply can only hold on one of the following conditions: either all other prices must have climbed accordingly, or demand does not match supply at that price but lags behind it. This will be immediately clear if one considers that, on the stated assumptions, the good in question will be more plentiful on the market at the later time, so that it will only sell if its price is lower in comparison with that of all other goods. Thus, either the producer will be unable to sell part of his later output, or he will only be able to acquire a smaller amount of other goods for the same monetary return; and in any case he will be worse off than if he had increased his output at the earlier time instead of producing part of this product now. If this experience often repeats itself and the circumstances lowering production costs are expected to continue, the producer will eventually have to decide in his own interests to raise his current production by cultivating the land more intensively. But he will incur losses as a result of the whole period in which he trusted in his price expectations and divided his production up accordingly in time.

As in any other case of a gradation of prices that does not accord with equilibrium, so in our case too will this have the result that (a) supply differences minimized at equilibrium will become greater; and (b) until

176

equilibrium has emerged, the producers' actual prices will not represent the highest obtainable profit. The same might be shown for any other case in which a regular change in a good's conditions of production can be foreseen in one direction or another. So as not to prolong the analysis unduly, however, let us pass straight on to the case where the changes do not only affect the production conditions of one good, but foreseeable improvements in production methods are regularly taking place and cheapening the production process throughout the economy. The economy at issue here is of the type which theory describes as the 'steadily advancing economy', where it is the investment of current savings of a fairly constant magnitude which continually leads to increased output in all branches of the economy. In essence we would have to treat the opposite case in the same way – the case where, under the persistent effect of such factors as mine exhaustion, climatic change or falling population and division of labour, the productivity of a national economy is constantly declining. The question that we must consider is whether in this case – as in that of regular increase or decrease in the output of a good – the changes in total output determine certain alterations in all prices and hence in the so-called price level, and whether each price variation deviating at successive times from this quasi-static price structure must have the same consequences that we have been able to identify in the case of a single good.

The practical import of this question will be evident if we bear in mind that essentially the results must also apply to the actually frequent case where each producer, even after cost-saving improvements to production, can count on being able to sell his product at prices which either remain unchanged or have not fallen by the full amount of the reduction in costs, because the organization or regulation of the country's monetary system prevents a general fall in prices. This case will be examined more thoroughly in the next section. For the moment, let us continue to base our analysis on the assumption which has made it possible directly to apply the concept of equilibrium: namely, that production increases are not simply known to individual entrepreneurs, but can be generally foreseen as a result of generally known circumstances.

If, during such a general increase in production, there is a definite expectation that product prices will not fall but remain unchanged or even increase, so that at a more distant time the same or even a higher price can be obtained for what is produced with a lesser outlay, this will necessarily have the effect that production for the later, anyway better-supplied period is further expanded at the expense of the earlier, worse-supplied period. Thus, even someone who does not intend to save will in this case expect to gain most from dividing up his production in this way, because he will

177

thereby boost his total income for the whole period and, according to the state of the market, will think he can count on being compensated by a greater increase in profits for the temporary limitation of his income until his increased output comes onto the market.

Just as in the case of increased output of one good, so in the case of a general production increase does the expectation of unchanged prices cause an excessive expansion of production for the future – an expansion which occurs on the assumption that it will be possible to provide for oneself as usual in the interim and pay for the requirements of that time with the future proceeds of the increased output. Again as in the previous case, however, the quantity of current goods which the producers wish to acquire at the given price will not be available precisely because of the expansion of production for the future. In view of the different production conditions, the exchange ratios between present goods and future goods, which are established by the same money prices at both times, will prove to be too favourable to future goods, and so the supply of present goods will lag behind demand.[14]

The exaggerated incentive to expand production for the later time at the expense of the earlier makes it even more difficult for the (not inherently appropriate) price level to remain the same throughout the period, and over time this will inevitably exert an ever stronger pressure upon prices. The discrepancy between supply and demand at current prices, expressed in demand which is at first too low and later too high, will already at the earlier time force a price rise on the part of those who do not at that time succeed in meeting their requirements at the expected lower prices. Thus, given that a decline in prices is not expected in the future, they will have to rise temporarily very soon, even before the increased production comes onto the market. In this way, however, the assumptions on the basis of which entrepreneurs decided to expand their production for the later time show themselves to be false. Not only must the entrepreneurs discover that they would have obtained better prices by selling their output at a point closer in time; they must also pay more than the expected price for goods required to carry on production for the later time, so that for at least some of them their expected profit turns into a loss – which is to say that they are not able to sell their products at the later time at a price that covers costs.

These consequences, which inevitably follow from the expectation that prices will remain constant as output rises, are therefore in type if not in degree the same as those of inflation. Without an increase in the money supply, stable prices amid rising production are inconceivable, and even if the increase is only just enough to prevent prices from falling, its effect on the structure of production will be essentially the same as that of any other rise in money that is not 'justified' by higher output. Since it obstructs the temporal price gradation caused by the 'goods situation', it gives rise to shifts in production which prevent the necessary balancing of supply over successive points in time and which later, after some of these shifts have gone beyond any possibility of recall, will necessitate much sharper price changes that result in loss of part of the expenditure.

Essentially the same can be said of the case where continually declining output goes together with unchanged or even falling prices, so that there are supply disturbances and obstacles to compensation in the other direction but the consequences are perhaps not as serious. A further shift into the future of goods wrongly produced in too great a quantity for the present would as a rule probably be quite feasible, whereas a backward shift of output assigned to the future would in most cases not be possible, or only at great cost.

A special analysis, which can only be hinted at here, would to some extent be required for the case in which the changed conditions of production refer to the size of the population. Here the possibility of deferred use of the variable productive forces is necessarily absent, nor can a 'false' formation of their price cause them to be used at a false point in time. Neither the new labour-power nor the exchange subject who commands it is present anywhere at the earlier time. It is still the case, for example, that if output rises as a result of more plentiful labour-power, equilibrium will be established only with quite definite price gradations at both of the two times and any deviation from them must have the well-known type of consequences. This can be proved in a manner analogous to the derivation in section 6, but it would take us too far from our present purpose.

Much the same could be said of intertemporal price gradations where single foreseen changes occur in the conditions of production – for instance, the lapsing of a patent – although here it would no longer be correct to use the former concept of equilibrium to describe actually existing tendencies, and the result of such an investigation would at best count as a folly in clear contradiction to the actual course of events.

10. A natural price gradation in time corresponding to the intertemporal exchange ratios that emerge in barter, which alone could assure trouble-free development even in a money economy, is by no means prevented only by monetary policy designed arbitrarily to influence the 'value of money', but also by the mechanism of any monetary system real or conceivable. Above all, it is true of any controlled currency, and not just one which is 'manipulated' from the point of view of a stable price level, that a tendency to price stabilization must work against any tendency to a general price change originating from the 'goods side' and hinder the emergence of a movement in prices that corresponds to the temporal

equilibrium-system. By controlled currency[15] is meant a system in which the money supply is automatically regulated by the possibility of converting a strictly determined quantity of a good into a definite sum of money and vice versa, whether by direct transformation or through exchange. For the sake of simplicity, in what follows we shall only consider the gold standard as the typical manifestation of such a controlled currency, although everything to be said about it also naturally applies to any other controlled currency.

The essential feature of a controlled currency, and of a gold standard in particular, is that any change in prices – provided two such changes do not cancel each other out – leads to changes in the money supply and hence to further price changes. If, for the moment, we abstract from changes in gold production and the industrial demand for gold and consider only the effect of the gold-standard mechanism in the event of a price change for certain goods (ones which are not produced from gold and do not participate in its production) or a fairly general change in prices, then it turns out that this effect will regularly consist in partly obstructing or reversing the price change that has been caused by other factors. So as not to dwell on very minor effects of no practical interest, we shall only take the case of a fairly general price change – more specifically, a fall in prices – which begins to assert itself in the wake of extensive improvements in production. The increased purchasing-power of gold in comparison with a large number of commodities will, as is well known, have the result that production of gold and a fortiori its conversion into money will increase, so that prices will climb back up or a further fall will be wholly or partly blocked. The price differentiation which is made necessary by the relationship between the supply and demand for goods at the two points in time, and which serves to balance the supply situation, is thus here partly prevented by another circumstance, alien to the original impetus behind economic activity, which appears on the scene only with a specific economic form, the system of indirect exchange. When the natural formation of prices is blocked, however, not only is the possibility of supply balance prevented but the equilibrium between supply and demand is also disturbed, in the way outlined in preceding sections.

A tendency to stability of the 'value of money' – preventing, that is, temporal gradation of the exchange ratios expressed in money which must arise in a natural economy – is therefore inherent in controlled currencies though to a lesser degree than in a free currency regulated with the aim of such stability, and it necessarily leads to disturbances in the course of the economy. *In the sharpest contrast to the prevailing view, then, we must assume from what has already been said that one of the most important monetary sources of disturbances to the economy lies not in some instability of the purchasing power of money but, on the contrary, in the tendency peculiar to commodity currencies for the purchasing power of money to be stabilized even when the general state of supply is changing – a tendency which is alien to the fundamental determinants of economic activity.* The same naturally applies a fortiori to any free currency that is regulated in accordance with the greatest possible stability of the price level, since then changes to the general price situation stemming from the goods side are completely blocked, whereas with a controlled currency a balance emerges at half-way, so to speak, between the tendency to price change and the tendency to price stability. To remain with the example of a price drop stemming from the goods side, we can say that it will here bring about an increased flow of gold into monetary circulation, but the new equilibrium will develop before prices return to the old level, both because an increase in gold production is possible only at higher costs and because here too the flow of gold away from industrial uses will raise its price in comparison with that of other commodities.

If the monetary system were such as to preclude any change in the money supply, it would still be possible to conceive of a structure for the price of gold at successive times which corresponded to the intertemporal equilibrium-system. Such a regulation of the monetary system, as we have yet to discuss, is not feasible in practice. But it is worth considering for a moment the significance of an unchanging money supply for the price structure or its relationship to the 'natural' price system. Clearly, in this case there can be no question of using changes in the money supply to offset price variations stemming from the goods side. If we abstract for the time being from certain disturbances that have already been discussed in a different context and will have to be examined later with reference to our basic assumptions – disturbances which in the case of indirect exchange always operate against the achievement of complete equilibrium – then without a change in the money supply prices will evidently fall when output increases and must evidently rise when output declines, in both cases by such an amount that the changed costs which led to a different scale of production are expressed in the price change. If, for example, production methods have improved and costs therefore fallen, then, other things being equal, product prices must fall by such an amount that the greater output which can now be achieved with the same quantity of means of production will be sellable at the same total price as that of the previously smaller output. However, this does away with the incentive (present if prices remain the same) to expand further at the expense of current output the better future supply which is anyway possible as a result of improvements in production, because this promises a higher profit than production for the present. Let us now assume for the sake of simplicity that the increased output occurs evenly and simultaneously in all branches and that afterwards the relative size of the demand for the different products remains unchanged – which means that the movement in prices allows precisely that expansion of output through which equilibrium is restored. By the nature of things, the relationships become qualitatively more complicated when the change in production conditions and hence output occurs only in some branches of industry; displacements then become necessary between relative output and relative prices – although it would take us too far afield to discuss them here. Nevertheless, the fact that the picture obtained from the assumption of a general, even and simultaneous increase in output, as well as the conclusions drawn from it, are not completely impractical, calls for a brief remark upon the frequent case where the production improvements occur in all branches not simultaneously but successively over a short period of time, and yet the organization of the monetary system does not permit a decline in the general level of prices, so that after a temporary reduction in prices all producers can count on eventually being able to sell their increased output at the same unit prices as before. It is clear that this very common expectation, which has a practical foundation, must have the same overall consequences as a foreseeably constant level of prices during a general and equally foreseeable increase in output – that is, an expansion of production which, in relation to equilibrium, is excessive for the time after the more favourable conditions have appeared. The opposite case of a decline in output would lead to essentially the same outcome.

As a rule, then, the disturbances which may arise from the use of a means of exchange in an economic system should not at all be regarded as a consequence of a mere change in the absolute level of money prices, but under certain circumstances as, on the contrary, a result of the failure of such a change to take place. It is just as little part of the nature of equilibrium that the money prices of some or all goods (or the 'general level of prices') should be the same at two different times as it is that the prices of two different goods should be the same at one point in time, although both can obviously happen in a concrete case. A difference in 'money value' at different times within the intertemporal equilibrium system is thus perfectly compatible with the existence of equilibrium. A disturbance to equilibrium would only produce a value structure at the different times which uneconomically shaped the relative level of individual prices at different times – a level which is supposed to serve a quite specific economic function. *The harmful effects that may originate in money should therefore always be accounted for only in terms of economically functionless disturbances to the intertemporal price system, and not of changes in money value.* Only if it realized that prices formed under the influence of money do not correspond to the equilibrium prices of a hypothetical system without a means of exchange, and that their consequences must therefore be the same as those of any other formation of prices that conflicts with equilibrium, will it be possible to grasp their significance theoretically. Except in this context, any concrete change or lack of change in the so-called value of money is completely devoid of interest.

It is not at all a new idea that, to avoid disturbances associated with money, 'money value' should not remain the same amid changes in the market situation, but must be constantly adjusted to the changed conditions. Thus, in the bimetallism controversy in the seventies and eighties of the last century, it was argued on many sides that with rising productivity and therefore falling production costs it is desirable for there to be a corresponding decline in prices.[16] And one also finds among the most diverse authors the idea that changes in the general supply situation must be reflected in corresponding changes in money value. However, a theoretical grounding of this idea – which, in my view, is possible only on the basis of considerations of the above kind – has not been produced. Nor, as far as I am aware, has there been an analysis which looks at the function of the relative level of prices at different times. But this is therefore also a lack of the criterion by which the significance of concrete price structures could alone be assessed.

Just recently *Haberler*[17] has looked at a special problem – the significance of general price movements for an undisturbed flow of the economy – and convincingly shown that a fall in the price level due to constant changes in all branches of production does not have the same ill effects as those of deflation. Theory has scarcely yet gone beyond this difference in the consequences of price changes stemming from the 'commodity side' and the 'money side', and the idea supported here, that 'commodity-side' changes in the price level are not only not harmful but actually necessary to avoid disturbances to equilibrium, must still strike many as rather paradoxical – all the more so because the now-dominant view according to which only an unchanging price level can assure an undisturbed flow of production, so that any general increase in prices necessarily leads to overexpansion and any general fall in prices to an unjustified reduction in output, appears to be confirmed by general experience and the fruits of statistical research. Nevertheless, the result of this enquiry does not seem to me to contradict the facts in any way.

11. With few exceptions, of which the best known will be mentioned shortly, an increasing volume of production and rising prices – or a shrinking volume of production and falling prices – have historically run in parallel. This fact is completely consistent with the recognition that,

other things being equal, a rise in output can occur without a disturbance to equilibrium only if prices are falling and a reduction in output only if they are rising. The limiting phrase 'other things being equal' means here that changes occur only in the conditions of production and not coincidentally in the level of wants, which would have the effect of cancelling them out. On this assumption, however, precisely the circumstance considered above – that the current monetary systems at least partly block the necessary price changes – will always entail that any improvement in the conditions of production first leads to an excessive expansion of output, and any deterioration to an excessive limitation of output in relation to the given demand. However, in the case of a secondary disproportion between supply and demand resulting from such an erroneous movement in prices, the relative movement in prices and output must be the exact opposite of that which occurs in the case of a simple change in output. This can be shown most clearly by means of the supply and demand curves in the well-known schematic representations of the conditions for equilibrium. Thus, whereas a change in the conditions of production with a constant level of demand always causes the point of equilibrium to move along the demand curve – which denotes either falling prices and rising output or rising prices and falling output – the point of equilibrium must always move along the supply curve if output and prices have adjusted *to each other* but do not accord with demand; output and prices will have to fall or rise at the same time especially when 'false' prices have triggered an erroneous volume of production. Where output is temporarily steered by 'false' prices, the path to equilibrium must therefore always pass through a parallel evolution of prices and output. This is not contradicted by the fact that, for equilibrium to be maintained with changes in the conditions of production, output and prices must move in numerically opposite directions. That is why the regular parallel movement of the two phenomena means nothing other than that the economy is not actually moving by the shortest route from one state of equilibrium to another in accordance with a kind of 'moving equilibrium',[18] but is continually fluctuating around equilibrium. Not only is this a well-known fact; it also proves to be necessary for the case where no unforeseen changes occur, precisely because of the circumstance we have discussed, namely, that with changes in the general level of prices counteracted by the prevailing organization of money, the necessary price changes regularly win through only when output has already been pushed in the wrong direction. In particular, it must be assumed that even if production costs are falling, the tendency to price stability inherent in the gold standard provides an excessive stimulus to the expansion of output and regularly makes it impossible to avoid a later price drop with simultaneous cuts in output. Conversely since, on the given assumptions, any deterioration in the conditions of production must have analogous consequences, it is theoretically probable that the actual evolution of the economy will move in constant oscillations around equilibrium, which will be impossible to attain, however, because of monetary influences disturbing the natural formation of prices. The parallel empirical movements of prices and output, themselves explicable by these special circumstances, are evidently no proof that a rise in prices must regularly lead to a rise in output, and a price cut to a reduction in output. Rather, it is thoroughly probable that with undisturbed adjustment of prices the opposite correlation would apply, and the price movements would then be an expression not of regularly recurring disturbances to equilibrium (that is, displacements between supply and demand) but of the necessary difference in supply at different points in time.[19]

There can be no question here of building these ideas up into a theory of crisis, which would be completely unreal without some consideration also of credit phenomena. It will be enough if we have established that certain disturbances to economic equilibrium are not only associated with the appearance of credit but are also, though perhaps to a lesser extent, indissolubly bound up with the use of a means of exchange, and that they can least be overcome through attempts to stabilize the purchasing power of money. There can be no doubt that such disturbances are more pronounced, and therefore easier to observe, in a credit economy. From this point of view it may even be justified to do what *R. G. Hawtrey*[20] and *L. A. Hahn*[21] have attempted: that is, in explaining the significance of monetary phenomena for the course of the economy, to start from the assumption that only credit and no cash whatsoever mediates in the exchange. However, in assessing all attempts to eliminate as far as possible money-side disturbances to economic equilibrium, it is crucially important to recognize that such disturbances are an inevitable feature of any conceivable monetary system. Just to overcome the most important money-side effects discussed above, which block automatic adjustment of the economy to changes in external circumstances, would be possible only if the quantity of the means of exchange could be fixed once and for all.[22] But it is clear that this cannot be done – because it is always possible to use a substitute instead of actual money, whose quantity cannot be precisely tied to that of the real money but whose creation has precisely the same effect as that of any other increase in money. It should not be thought desirable, moreover, to fix the money supply with the aim of preventing any active influence on the part of money. Perhaps it would be fortunate for mankind if the organization of the monetary system – and from what has been said, this applies to the effect of all controlled currencies where the economy is advancing, and not only to the effect of credit relevant here which is nowadays quite generally recognized – had impelled a step forward for which it would not have been prepared to make the necessary sacrifices of its own free will. To investigate this is not what concerns us here. What is certain is that such a step forward is inseparably bound up with the disturbances that people are today endeavouring to overcome, and that it would not be possible to overcome them without hindering the step forward. If these considerations are correct, we must finally clear our mind of all thoughts of completely eliminating monetary influences, of restricting money to its passive role of intermediary, according to which a money economy should proceed as if no money were actually used. We shall have to get used to the idea that money always has a determining influence on the direction of the economy, that theorems derived for a moneyless economy apply to a money economy only with major reservations, and that the goal of monetary policy cannot just be to influence the course of the economy as little as possible; efforts must always be made at the same time to give the most desirable form possible to the effects which cannot be avoided.

Here we must also forgo any further investigation of the tendencies to recurrent equilibrium disturbances inherent in any money economy and, in particular, their significance for the famous 'business cycles'. We can, however, briefly touch upon a few practical applications of the knowledge gained so far. Above all, we must look at one of the already mentioned exceptions to the empirical rule that rising prices mean rising output and falling prices falling output. Much attention has been aroused by the fact that the extraordinary conjunctural upturn of the United States economy in recent years largely took place in the presence of falling prices, and above all that for an uncommonly long time it continued without provoking a crisis in its wake. According to the view indicated above, one would have assumed that the upward movement in output could not last so long – not despite but *because of* the accompanying fall in prices. But exceptionally, for reasons that we cannot not discuss here, the forces which usually prevent a price drop when production costs are declining were not able to win through, and so price formation and price expectations gave no incentive to overexpand production for future times in the way that otherwise regularly leads to sales problems. It would appear, then, that the secret of that persistent high conjuncture in the United States should be sought in the falling prices, and that its further continuation was to be expected only so long as prices continued to fall. Thus, although the widely proposed hindering of a price increase during conjunctural up-swings would not be sufficient to prevent disproportionate development of the various branches of production and a resulting downturn at a later date, a price cut in line with the costs reduction connected to rising output would just as effectively prevent overexpansion, but in an economically more appropriate way than the rise in interest rates which is alone considered necessary by the dominant theory.[23]

In light of these same considerations, there seems to be no basis at all for those concerns about the threat of a gold shortage which have recently been expressed in many quarters – if, that is, the fear is that current gold production will not suffice to 'adjust' the money supply to economic growth, rather than that the shortage will go so far that gold is withdrawn from circulation for industrial purposes. A mere failure of the tendencies stabilizing the 'value of money' – which so far in the gold standard have opposed a fall in prices due to rising output – would be something that could only be desired.

But even a gold standard, in which such stabilizing tendencies are unrestricted, is altogether preferable to a monetary system in which the purchasing power of a unit of currency is kept stable by means of planning. As we have already seen, in a controlled currency as opposed to one that is artificially kept stable, the necessary price changes are only partly blocked and milder disturbances to equilibrium are therefore to be expected from the money side. The reason for this is that with a controlled currency larger quantities of money can be obtained only at greater cost and money flowing out of circulation can be invested in industry only at the falling price, so that after a change in the production conditions determining changes in the general price situation, the new equilibrium will be attained at prices lying somewhere between the old prices and those which would have resulted with an unchanged money supply. Here, then, there is only a partial offsetting of the adverse changes in money value.

The gold standard (and any other material money) has one further merit, however. While a policy of rigidly defining the money supply must break down because the various substitute-moneys are not fully amenable to quantitative regulation, an attempt to offset changes in their quantity by a change in the supply of real money must fail because it is not possible to identify their quantity; there are no other criteria for regulating the money supply so that the natural formation of prices is not disturbed, and the gold standard automatically takes care of offsetting changes in the supply of substitute-moneys within the same limits in which it permits a necessary change in the general price situation. Although the displacement of gold-money by substitutes can never go so far that the aggregate supply of means of exchange remains unchanged, there does occur at least a partial correction, for the planned implementation of which the grounds do not exist in the case of a controlled currency. The great drawback of the gold standard lies in the fact that decisive changes might occur in the production conditions of gold as a result of the discovery of new deposits or

187

improved extraction methods – but precisely that drawback is the one most likely to be overcome. On the whole, however, the gold standard should be seen as relatively best from the point of view of this investigation – that is, as the monetary system which, *relatively speaking*, causes the least disturbance to the natural formation of prices.

12. There is no justification in economic theory for the idea that the money supply must be adjusted to changes in the economy in order to maintain equilibrium or – what comes to the same thing – to prevent monetary disturbances in the economy. Yet this is generally treated as a self-evident proposition. Although the concept of a demand for money can receive a detailed critique only at another place in this research, it seems appropriate to add here already a few remarks on the origin of that idea and the misunderstandings connected with it. Thus, it appears to me that the main reason for this dogmatic weight lies in an uncritical transference of a procedure recognized as necessary for some nations to the whole world economy or to a hypothetically isolated national economy. In my view, however, it is relatively easy to show that such a transference is completely illegitimate, because the change in the money supply which serves a necessary function for one nation in its trade with others is not only useless but positively harmful in the world economy as a whole.

The well-known theory, going back to *North* and *Hume*,[24] that the stock of money is distributed among nations according to their requirements suggests that the world's total money supply must automatically be distributed among the various national economies in such a way that, in an economy with a high turnover or large output, there will always be more money than in one of smaller size existing at the same time. This theory of the relative money supply necessary in two countries at one time then led to the idea that, in each individual country too, the money supply must grow in proportion to the size of turnover. In the first case, however, the changes taking place in the relative money supply of separate countries are a necessary condition for the restoration of equilibrium – that is, for the change which has become necessary in the relative price levels of the different countries – but a change does not ensue in the absolute money supply of the countries joined together within an economic system. In fact, a change in the total money supply would not at all bring restoration of the disturbed equilibrium within the economy, but would mean a temporary disturbance to the goods-output equilibrium so that a new equilibrium could be achieved with the production of gold. If the difference between the two phenomena did not appear more clearly, this was because researchers of interlocal money movements were content to stress that, under certain circumstances, changes must occur in the relative money supply of several countries, but did not take into account that by such means alone equilibrium is not restored among them. Just as, for the individual in a money economy, a rise in his money income is only a necessary link in the chain of processes which put him in a position to obtain an increased share of the social product for an increased share in its production, so for a national economy as a whole, a rise in its money income is only a necessary precondition of an increase in its share of the total world product. But this unique function of a change in the money supply circulating within a group cannot, of course, be served by a change in the whole world's money supply.

This distinction may best be shown with the aid of two examples. Let us first assume that, following a rise in a country's agricultural production due to cheaper costs, gold begins to flow into it. As is well known, the reason for this is that money always flows where its purchasing power is greatest, and so that country's money supply will increase until its prices remain in balance with those of other countries. This conventional explanation, however, deals only with one part of the adjustment process. And in its incompleteness, it gives the quite false impression that, for example, the country whose rising productivity has triggered a movement in gold can definitively accept for at least part of its surplus product a pointless increase in its stock of money, thereby, so to speak, making a sacrifice in the interests of international price equilibrium. In reality, this is just as implausible as the idea of a person's drawing a higher money income as a preliminary to an augmented real income. There seems to be a difference between this and our example: namely, that it involves an increase in the money income received by other economic subjects, whereas a movement of gold to one country can never mean a rise in the money income received by other countries. As we shall see at once, however, this only appears to be a difference.

In discussing our example, we started from the assumption that the prices of agricultural products are falling in one country as a result of production improvements. Such a price drop entails that it will be more advantageous for other countries to buy there the product in question (if transport and other costs generally make this an option), and its exports will rise without necessarily involving an increase in their total value. But since, owing to the fall in prices, gold is imported only if the total value of exports is now higher than before, let us further assume that this is the case. The increased demand abroad, which will cause prices to rise again or at least prevent a further decline, will then make itself felt, other things being equal, in the form of gold imports, for in line with our assumptions lower prices will be obtained here than abroad for increased imports of all other commodities (otherwise the increase would have taken place earlier) and so gold imports constitute the most advantageous method of payment.

This importing will continue so long as the gold itself – or the increased income of the sellers of agricultural products which it represents – causes such a rise in the prices of other goods that it becomes profitable to import those goods instead of gold. It would take us too far afield to follow this process here in all its details. A little reflection shows that the country's share in the value of the total world product will eventually increase to the same degree to which, owing to the flow of gold, the total money income of its inhabitants increases in comparison with that of the other countries.[25] Partly as a result of its changed share of value, the nation will keep for itself an absolutely larger part of its increased agricultural output and an absolutely and relatively larger part of its unchanged output of other export items, and at the same time will be able to import more of other goods. After a period of transition in which the new gold movements have their effect on prices, the country's value share in the world product will thus have grown by precisely the same amount as the total product value of the commodities whose production increased at the beginning, the prerequisite for its higher value share being that the sum of money incomes in the country has grown accordingly.[26]

The movement of money from one country to another, and the resulting increase in the latter's 'stock of money', are thus nothing other than intermediate stages towards a movement of goods – and in a money economy they must precede a change in the market positions of the two countries. The fact that the money incomes of a locally associated group of people thereby increases – and not only the portion derived from foreign sales but also the one stemming from reciprocal trade within the group – necessarily entails that a proportionally greater quantity of money will permanently remain within that group of people. This phenomenon may certainly be described in terms of a rising demand for money, but that does not actually provide an explanation. And it can easily lead one to regard so-called changes in the demand for money as independent causes of monetary movements, and adjustment of the money supply to the changed demand as a prerequisite in any situation for the maintenance of equilibrium.

It is clear, however, that changes in the world money supply (i.e., movements of gold into and out of monetary use and changes in gold output due to price movements) cannot serve the same kind of function as do movements of money from country to country, since the world's share of its own real income cannot change. It was further shown in preceding sections that such changes in the money supply must in some definite way have a disturbing effect. Let us now simply supplement those demonstrations with a somewhat different aspect of the same process derived from the last remarks: it is clear, namely, that changes in the total money supply can never help to maintain equilibrium but must always disturb it.

If, for this purpose, we slightly vary our earlier example and assume that the cheapening of agricultural output has occurred not just in one country but throughout the world, and that the price drop resulting from this increased output triggers a rise in gold production and a subsequent expansion of the money supply, then even in that case a number of people whose products and services are first required with the new inflow of money will initially secure a rise in their money income which also involves a rise in their real income, but no lasting change of the same proportion in their market position will correspond to this rise in nominal income – for similar rises in nominal income will take place successively for all other persons, and in the end there will have been no essential change in the share of the social product falling to each individual.[27] At any event, the temporarily higher profitability in the branches first touched by the gold inflow will have induced an expansion of them which must prove to be unjustified as soon as the gold inflow ceases as a result of the raising of branch prices. At the moment when this additional demand falls off, a part of the surplus production to which it gave rise will only be sellable at a loss rather than at prices which cover costs, and so eventually the branches in question must be reduced to the output level they had before the gold began to flow in. The end result of the gold movements, then, will be that because the economy temporarily handed over part of its total output to the gold producers, equilibrium between supply and demand will only be restored after losses have taken place. Apart from the losses caused by this disturbance to equilibrium, every individual must also regard as a loss the fact that at least part of the increase in his money income is for him not a means to the acquisition of more goods but a final payment per se. Thus, for the part of his product with which he has earned it, he receives no other recompense than a useless increase in the money he owns. Contrary to the case of money movement within an economy, therefore, changes in its total money supply do not provide the basis for a different satisfaction of wants on the part of individual economic subjects. Change in the money supply is here rather the final and concluding event, so that in the case of monetary increase the individual is forced to take as final payment something that he would not have wished to take as such.

Appendix

The preceding analysis has argued that in the event of increased production due to technical improvements and the like, prices must fall if an overexpansion of output is not to result. Now, it might be objected that it is already the function of the interest-rate to maintain equilibrium between output for the

191

future and output for the present, and so further regulation by price movements is not necessary. But this objection, at first sight so obvious, overlooks the fact that – at least if interest is regarded as a static phenomenon, as is most usually the case – two quite different functions are involved: those served by the interest-rate and price movements respectively. There must be an interest-rate because, for reasons that are of no further interest here,[28] it is not possible for the output of goods producible in a more distant future with present means of production to be expanded to such a degree that their price falls to that of the means of their production; the interest-rate thus serves, as it were, to maintain equilibrium by preventing an inappropriate level of production for the future. On the other hand, price changes are necessary if, owing to shifts in production possibilities, differences appear between the price of the means of production and that of the goods they are used to produce – differences which must not persist because of the shortage of capital. Whether the rate of interest remains the same or decidedly changes, there may need to be shifts in the relative price level of present and future goods – that is, price changes – in order to maintain equilibrium.

If, for example, a new technical method is invented which makes it possible to produce, with the given quantity of means of production, a greater output than before in a country's only capital-utilizing branch, this may well lead to a rise in the rate of interest, but it can never prevent temporary overexpansion in the relevant line of production unless the product price falls at the same time. For even if – which can never be the case – cheaper production were to cause a permanent strengthening of demand for means of production and so a rise in interest-rates, this alone would still not offset the special incentive to expand output which consists in the temporary fact that, at the same costs, a greater quantity of the product can be produced and still be sold at the same price. The rate of interest will not be set higher, then, because there must be a lasting difference between the price of the means of production and that of the goods now produced by them. Even if the product prices do not fall, this initially very large difference must fall over time to the level determined by the rate of interest – and actually the product prices do not fall until output has expanded by so much that the stronger demand for means of production has driven their prices up to a corresponding level. It can be seen at once that this is possible only at the price of a reduction in current consumption which, accepted in anticipation of higher money profits, will disappear as soon as this profit is realized and used to purchase items for consumption. The price of current goods will then rise further, while part of the already expanded output will become unprofitable and have to be cancelled. This simply means, however, that the temporary expansion was just as excessive as if it had been caused, say, by inflation.

This exposition must suffice here to show that, in the event of rising physical productivity, 'natural' shifts in the rate of interest are not enough to prevent overexpansion of production for the future unless a corresponding fall in the product prices takes place at the same time. The preceding account can thus make absolutely no claim to completeness. It could only be a question of briefly indicating the direction in which one must try to solve questions that arise when one is dealing with the problems investigated here – although an adequate answer would be possible only in the framework of a complete system of economic theory. All that can be added is that the different, independent nature of interest-rates and intertemporal price gradations already follows from the fact that there is no connection at all between the directions in which they have to move to maintain equilibrium. According to circumstances, it may be necessary for the price of a future good, in comparison with a present good, either to rise or to fall simultaneously with an increase in interest-rates. Thus, for example, whereas an invention which raises physical productivity may necessitate a rise in the rate of interest and a fall in prices, an increase in capital equipment at the same level of technical capacity will cause both a fall in the rate of interest and a fall in prices. In fact, it is well known that with constant physical productivity – i.e., an unchanging quantity producible with the same goods – a fall in the rate of interest must result at least in a relative fall in the product price vis-à-vis the prices of the means of production. It can come as no surprise, then, that if this physical productivity changes as a result of new discoveries and so on, even with the same rate of interest certain shifts in prices at different times would definitely be necessary to restore equilibrium.

Of course, we also cannot consider here the extent to which the two types of temporal value differences – those expressed in interest and in price variations for the same goods at different times – may influence or take the place of each other.[29] The fact that each of them has a specific function makes it a priori unlikely that the one could replace the other without causing disturbances to equilibrium. On the other hand, it may well be assumed that each can properly serve its function only if the other is also in conformity with equilibrium.

NOTES

1. The following essay is intended to form part of a not yet completed work on the goals of monetary policy, which will investigate especially the theoretical bases of the frequently encountered demand for

193

artificial stabilization of the 'price level'. In this context it will be necessary to examine more closely some extremely difficult problems of pure theory which have hardly yet been treated in the literature, and whose first systematic examination will as a rule be insufficient. This made it seem desirable to publish separately for the time being this attempt to provide an account of certain hitherto neglected correlations. I would simply stress that the way of posing the problem in this work seems to me especially important, irrespective of its concrete solution and still more of the deficiencies which undoubtedly remain in the argument. There is no need to emphasize further that the results of such an isolated investigation of a particular problem, however important it may be, cannot claim to provide an adequate solution to practical issues of monetary policy, and that insofar as attempts are made in this article to apply them to concrete phenomena, they can be regarded only as an aid to comprehension and not as a sufficient explanation of those phenomena.

2. Only if even infinitesimal successive economic periods could be assumed to be completely identical with one another would at least one extreme, idealized case of a temporally unfolding economy be adequately explained. But since this possibility is completely excluded by the essentially discontinuous flow of most economic processes, there can be no area of application for theorems derived on the basis of the above assumption.

3. See especially L. Mises, *Theorie des Geldes und der Umlaufsmittel*, 2nd edn (Munich, 1924), pp. 151ff.

4. Unfortunately, as far as I am aware, it is only in the two editions of his textbook that Fetter has dealt with the problem of *time value* in a form corresponding to the present context, but he has never done so in any great depth. In general Fetter's older expression, *time value*, seems to go closer to the core of the problem than the one later used in its place for other reasons: *time preference*. The most valuable remarks, however, are to be found precisely in the second book, where he does limit in this way the more general expression that he originally chose but makes up for it by examining time more thoroughly as one of the factors to be taken into account in economic dispositions. See F. A. Fetter, *The Principles of Economics* (New York, 1904) and later; and *Economic Principles* (New York, 1915) and later, vol. i, pp. 20, 29 and esp. pp. 101ff. and 235–77. See also Fetter's very interesting essay, which only became known to me after I had completed this work: 'Interest Theory and Price Movements', *The American Economic Review*, vol. xvii (1927), no. 1, Supplement, pp. 62ff. Early attempts at such a line of analysis, which naturally only served to

prepare the way for his well-known theory of the undervaluation of future wants, can be found in E. v. Böhm-Bawerk, *Positive Theorie des Kapitals*, 3rd edn (Innsbruck, 1912) – e.g., pp. 439 and 587f.

5. See R. Streller, *Statik und Dynamik in der theoretischen National-ökonomie* (Leipzig, 1926).

6. In addition, of course – and this accounts in general for the mutual dependence of economic activity at different times – there must always be the possibility of using the same goods for the satisfaction of wants at one or the other point in time.

7. This is only apparently contradicted by one result of comparing the utility obtainable at two separate points in time. See my article: 'Zur Problemstellung der Zinstheorie', *Archiv für Sozialwissenschaft und Sozialpolitik*, vol. 58 (1927), pp. 517ff.

8. Contrary to a common assumption, however, it is not necessary that the parties to the exchange should have a precisely opposite valuation of any random unit of the good at both the times in question – for example, that A should today value a quantity of good x more highly than in a year's time, while B sets a lower value on the same quantity of the good now at his disposition than in the prospect of a year later. Rather, the only prerequisite for exchange is that one of the parties considering it should value some quantity of the one good (or, in our case, some quantity of the good at one time) more highly than some quantity of the other good (or of the same good at another time), and that the other party should have an opposite valuation of these randomly selected quantities of goods or – which comes to the same thing – that the difference between the marginal utilities of the goods is different for the two persons in question. The outcome of exchange carried to its economic margin is therefore that for any randomly selected units of the two goods (or of the same good at both times) the gradation of marginal utilities is the same in the two individuals, or – as it may perhaps be most simply expressed – *the marginal differences are equal*.

9. On the relation between this and the problem of interest, see the appendix to this essay.

10. Only as I was correcting the proofs of this essay did I receive a copy of G. P. Watkins, 'Parity in the Exchange of Future Money and Future Commodities', *Quarterly Journal of Economics*, vol. 42 (Cambridge, Mass., 1927/28), pp. 366ff., in which the same question is given a similar answer in a different context.

11. See Mises, pp. 151ff.

12. These considerations are in general completely analogous to those by which it is shown that, wherever commodities are exchanged between

two countries, there must be a definite ratio, an equilibrium, not only between the prices of those commodities in the two countries but also between the prices of all other commodities in the two countries – a ratio which, to be sure, is expressed not in the necessity of the *same* ratio holding between the prices of all commodities in the two countries, but in the fact that each price change for any commodity in one country can essentially trigger a price change for any commodity in the other country.

13. See Mises, pp. 151ff.

14. So as not to overburden the text, the connection between this and the phenomenon of interest will be discussed in the appendix below.

15. The lack of a more accurate term makes it necessary in this context, unlike elsewhere in this essay, to use the concept of currency [*Währung*] which is of legal rather than economic origin. [The German word *Währung* stems from the notion of guaranteeing (*Gewährleistung*) the value of coinage. *Trans. note.*] Mises's term 'material money' (*Sachgeld*), used above in direct apposition, is too narrow because it does not include the various kinds of credit money which also fall under the category of controlled currency. To be absolutely correct, one would have to speak of something like 'materially controlled money'. See Mises, pp. 33ff.

16. See the remarks of C. M. Walsh concerning supporters of a 'cost standard' in his valuable book: *The Fundamental Problem in Monetary Science* (New York, 1903), pp. 235ff.

17. G. Haberler, *Der Sinn der Indexzahlen. Eine Untersuchung über den Begriff des Preisniveaus und die Methoden seiner Messung* (Tübingen, 1927), pp. 112ff.

18. See H. L. Moore, 'A Moving Equilibrium of Demand and Supply', *Quarterly Journal of Economics*, vol. 39 (1924/25), pp. 357ff.

19. The empirically most common but, as we have seen, by no means necessary correlation between rising prices and rising output, or between falling prices and falling output, is a fine example of how dangerous it is to wish to derive theorems from the results of statistical investigations or even to use them as the basis for practical demands. For the highest coefficient of correlation between output and price movements could not prove that rising output is only possible with rising prices or that falling prices must always entail a decline in output. It is precisely from such considerations, however, that the stabilization efforts which ought to appear questionable from the point of view stressed in this essay receive their strongest support. The false link in the argument which led to them was to conclude that, if rising prices cause an increase in output and falling prices a decline

in output, the level of prices must be kept stable in order to eliminate all the effects of money on output. The goal of stabilization efforts, which is to acquire certainty about future prices, can naturally be least achieved when one tries to block the changes required to maintain output equilibrium and so causes disturbances to equilibrium that must eventually result in sharper price moments.

20. See R. G. Hawtrey, *Currency and Credit*, 2nd edn, F. Oppenheimer (ed.) (London, 1923).

21. L. A. Hahn, *Volkswirtschaftliche Theorie des Bankkredits* (Tübingen, 1920 and later).

22. On those who advocate this see Walsh, p. 5.

23. On this see also the appendix below.

24. See J. W. Angell, *The Theory of International Prices. History, Criticism and Restatement* (Cambridge, 1926).

25. It should be noted that this says nothing at all about the extent of price movements for particular goods or all goods together, and especially not for the agricultural products that became cheaper at the start. For the change in national income came about entirely through simultaneous changes in prices and in the quantity of goods consumed. Only of the total product price changed by the initial rise in the output of one branch can it be said with certainty that it has increased by the same amount as total income.

26. As I am here analysing this complex of problems only secondarily for a special purpose, I should like to leave it open whether the rise in the sum of individual incomes stands in a strict numerical relation to the newly expanded money supply. The question is without interest, moreover, because the change in individual prices means that there is no yardstick for the increase in real national income. In principle, at least, the only change in a country's value share capable of numerical expression could not be ascertained except from the relative change in the country's total money income – a change, however, which itself defies measurement.

Let us just mention here that the considerations in the text show that the mercantilists' view of a country's relative money stock as an important index of its welfare was by no means as completely wrong as one usually assumes, although the maxims of political economy stemming from their imperfect grasp of correlations could evidently not serve the desired purpose.

A view kindred in many respects to the one in the text may be found in F. W. Taussig, *Principles of Economics*, 2nd edn, vol. i, ch. 35, sect. 1 (New York, 1925), pp. 502f.

27. See Mises, pp. 116ff.

28. Cf. my previously mentioned article 'Zur Problemstellung der Zinstheorie'.
29. See the well-known work of I. Fisher on these questions: 'Appreciation and Interest', *Publications of the American Economic Association*, vol. xi, no. 4 (New York, 1896); and *The Rate of Interest* (New York, 1906).

E 22

200-233
[1935]

Friedrich Hayek, 'The Maintenance of Capital', *Economica*, New Series vol. 2 (1935), pp. 241–76.

D 24

In this paper Hayek explores fundamental issues in the measurement of capital and income. The paper foreshadows the more extended investigations into capital theory undertaken in Hayek's *Pure Theory of Capital* (1941).

not an Econ t

28

The Maintenance of Capital[1]

FRIEDRICH HAYEK

Contents: I – The Nature and Significance of the Problem. II – Professor Pigou's Treatment. III – The *Rationale* of Maintaining Capital Intact. IV – The Action of the Capitalist with Perfect Foresight. V – Obsolescence and Anticipated Risks. VI – The Reaction of the Capitalist on Unforeseen Changes. VII – The Impossibility of an Objective Standard with Different Degrees of Foresight. VIII – 'Saving' and 'Investing.' IX – Capital Accounting and Monetary Policy.

I. *The Nature and Significance of the Problem*

It is not likely that in the whole field of economics there are many more concepts which are at the same time so generally used and so little analysed as that of a 'constant amount of capital.' But while in the investigation of the effects of nearly any change this is almost without exception treated as a given datum, the question what this assumption exactly means is rarely asked. To most economists the answer to it has apparently seemed so simple and obvious that they have never attempted to state it. In consequence the difficulties involved have hardly ever been realised, still less have they been adequately investigated.

The difficulties of the problem would undoubtedly have been realised if economists had been more generally conscious of its importance. But although, even in the analysis of a stationary equilibrium, the inclusion of the 'quantity of capital' among the determinants of that equilibrium means that something, which is the result of the equilibrating process, is treated as if it were a datum,[2] this confusion was made relatively innocuous by the essential limitations of the static method, which while it describes the conditions of a state of equilibrium, does not explain how such a state is brought about.

It was only with the more modern attempts to make the descriptions of the conditions of equilibrium the basis of the analysis of the dynamic processes, that the exact meaning of this assumption became of serious consequence. But we need not go far beyond the description of one state of equilibrium to see why it matters. Even the very simplest 'problem of variation' as the effect of a shift in demand can only be answered on the basis of a definite assumption as regards the 'supply of capital,' and the usual answer shows immediately how problematic is the assumption on which it rests.

The idea implicit in the discussion of problems of this sort is that there is a quantitatively determined fund of capital, which can be distributed and redistributed in any way between the different lines of production without changing its aggregate value.[3] But has this assumption of a perfectly mobile capital fund any definite meaning? And if so, what determines whether this value remains constant, what are the conditions under which it will remain constant, how is it measured, and by what is this constant magnitude represented? Certainly not by the concrete capital goods. It is the essential difference between them and factors like labour or land that they will not remain physically the same when prices change, but that the physical composition of the aggregate called capital will change in consequence of any change in the data. Any of the problems of variation with which we are concerned will involve what is commonly called a transformation of capital into other forms. It is not the list of the different pieces of individual capital goods which is assumed to remain unchanged, when we speak of a constant supply of capital, in the same way as we assume that the total supply of labour or land is composed of elements of the same kind, when we regard its supply as unchanged.

Even if a definite meaning can be attached to the statement that the value of the capital goods has an existence independent of the capital goods themselves, it does not help us in any way to explain why, or under what conditions, this aggregate value should remain constant, when conditions change. There can be no doubt that the value of at least some of the existing capital goods will be very materially affected by almost any conceivable change. The question then is why should the capitalists, in spite of this change in the value of their concrete capital goods, be able and willing, by an appropriate adjustment of their investment activity, to maintain the total value of their possessions at exactly the same figure as before the change. Is there any justification for considering this in any sense to be the 'normal' behaviour of the entrepreneurs, or is it even conceivable that they can, under all circumstances, behave in such a way?

Must we not rather assume that under some conditions it will be impossible for the capitalist to maintain the value of his capital constant, while under others it could hardly be considered in any sense 'normal' if he did no more than this?

What, then is that neutral state in which the owners of capital are supposed to take a merely passive attitude, performing no new saving or dissaving? This question, already of considerable importance when we try to trace the consequences of any other change, becomes of special importance when we turn to the autonomous changes which can be said to originate on the side of capital. Then already the initial problem, of what can be regarded as such an autonomous change on the side of capital, depends on our definition of that neutral state. In the usual discussions of this sort of problem, it seems to be generally implied that there is a clear line between the normal process of maintaining and replacing the existing capital, and any net addition to it. It is assumed that it is always possible to decide in an unequivocal way whether capital remains constant, increases, or decreases, and that there are typical phenomena connected with each of these processes which, at least conceptually, can be clearly separated. Indeed, so long as all the other data remain constant, no difficulty arises in this connection. But as soon as one tries to apply these categories to a world where things are changing, all these alluringly simple concepts become dependent in more than one way on exactly what is meant by a given stock of capital. It is impossible to define income (or 'earnings') and therefore savings before one has separated from the gross produce those quantities which are required to 'maintain' capital, and it is equally impossible to say what are additions to the stock of real capital before one has shown what capital goods are required to make up for current depreciation.

If it should prove that serious difficulties arise in this connection, this would be a matter of great importance for the theory of the trade cycle. In the course of the last generation theorists in that field have tended more and more to agree that industrial fluctuations consist essentially in alternating periods of accumulation and decumulation of capital with all their typical consequences. More recently there has seemed to be considerable unanimity in seeking for causes of these fluctuations in the accumulation of capital in conditions which make the movement of investment to a certain extent independent of that of saving. But although the quantitative relationship between saving and investing, their correspondence or noncorrespondence, has become the central point of attack, it seems that all the writers who have made use of that approach have failed to make clear exactly what they meant either by saving or investing. This would have required a careful definition of that neutral position in which neither positive nor negative saving were made, because all the income and no more than the income was consumed, and in which capital goods were produced in exactly that quantity and composition that is required to keep the stock of capital intact.

But while it cannot be denied that modern trade cycle theorists (including the present writer) have lamentably failed to provide a concept which is indeed indispensable if their deductions are to have a clear meaning, it seems that they are not the only group of economists who have been deceived by the apparent simplicity of the problem. Even more than this group one should expect the writers on the income concept to have provided a clear answer. And even if the general discussions of the income concept should prove disappointing, one would certainly feel entitled to expect a definite answer in the discussions of business profits, since profits of all things can evidently only be defined as the excess of the total business assets over the equivalent of the capital invested at the beginning of the period. But while we find in general discussions of the income concept, particularly in the writings of Professor Irving Fisher,[4] at least some references to our problem, the standard works on business profits, like Professor F. H. Knight's *Risk, Uncertainty, and Profits*, or Mr Ch. O. Hardy's *Risk and Risk Bearing*, are almost bare of any reference to the problem.

II. *Professor Pigou's Treatment*

In view of these circumstances the solitary attempt first made by Professor Pigou a few years ago in the third edition of his *Economics of Welfare* deserves far greater attention than it has actually received. Although Professor Pigou discusses the problem for a special purpose, the definition of a national dividend, he raises most of the problems that need investigation. And it is only an additional reason for gratitude to that distinguished author that he has apparently not felt satisfied with his first attempt towards an answer and that he has in the fourth edition of the same work given us an entirely new version of his solution.[5] In the third edition he had still considered that the problem could simply and only be answered by 'employing money values in some way as our measuring rod,' but that we cannot employ crude money values but must introduce 'corrections.'[6] Accordingly, he defined as constant quantities of capital collections of capital goods, whose aggregate money value, divided by an appropriate index number of general prices, remained constant. After making some further allowances for changes in this magnitude caused by changes in the rate of interest, which need not concern us here, he proceeded to apply this definition to cases where the value of capital goods 'is destroyed through a failure of demand or through a new discovery which renders existing instruments obsolete,'[7] and suggests, consistently with the criterion adopted, that in such a case it is convenient, although arbitrary, to say that the stock of capital has decreased (or in the reverse case of an expansion of demand that it has increased).

In the fourth edition of the *Economics of Welfare* the entire chapter is rewritten. Although no explicit explanation is given why the former answer has been abandoned, it is fairly evident from the nature of the changes made, and the general shift of emphasis, that the aim has been to make the decision more dependent on the reasons why it is thought desirable to maintain capital intact. Considerations relating to the constancy of the money value of capital which formerly occupied the chief place are now relegated to a subordinate place, and mentioned only to show that if, all other things remaining the same, in consequence of a contraction in the supply of money, money values all round are substantially reduced, and the money value of capital contracts along with the rest, nobody would consider this as a decrease of capital. The second case mentioned is again that of the effects of a change in the rate of interest on the value of capital, and it is decided (apparently on the assumption that such a change will not affect the return from the existing capital goods) that such changes are not to be considered as changes in the quantity of capital, so far as the estimation of the national dividend is concerned. But then the effects of changes in demand and of inventions are taken up, and here the decision is now the reverse from what it was before. In Professor Pigou's opinion 'we may say quite generally that all contractions in the money value of any part of the capital stock that remains physically unaltered are irrelevant to the national dividend; and that their occurrence is perfectly compatible with the maintenance of capital intact.'[8] The same applies to actual destruction of the capital goods by 'acts of God or the King's enemy,' where the distinguishing criterion is that they are not incidental to the use of them, or as I shall suggest instead, because and in so far as they cannot be foreseen.[9] But all other physical deterioration in the capital stock, such as the ordinary wear and tear of machinery and plant, destruction by accidents like fire and storm, in so far as these are, as in the case of ships, incidental to their use, ought to be made good by adding ' to the capital stock something whose value is equal to that which the machine, had it remained physically intact, would have now.'[10] By this are explicitly excluded all the losses in value, which are not due to physical deterioration, but are due to causes like the changes in demand or the new inventions mentioned before, to which Professor Pigou now adds foreign competition. This is expressly confirmed by the concluding sentence of the paragraph, in which, summarising the result, he says, 'Maintenance of capital intact for our purposes means then, not replacement of all value losses (not due to acts of God and the king's enemies), but replacement of such value losses as are caused by physical losses other than the above.'[11]

We shall have to discuss these cases in greater detail in the systematic part of this article. Here only one difficulty arising out of Professor Pigou's answer may be mentioned, since it opens up the vista on a set of problems which he has left untouched. What seems most surprising in his classification is that obsolescence, even where it is foreseen at the time a capital good is produced or acquired, and where accordingly the investment is made in the expectation that the product will cease to have value long before it has physically decayed, should not have to be made good in order to maintain capital intact. This means that gradually all existing capital may be squandered, in the ordinary sense, by erecting durable structures for very transient purposes, and replacing them, when they become obsolete after a short time, only by capital goods of a value equal to that which they still possess after their temporary utility has passed. Surely there must be some cases where obsolescence, a decrease of usefulness of a capital good not connected with any change in its physical condition, has to be taken into account. And, apparently, the distinction must somehow be based on whether that change can be foreseen or not. But if this is so, does it not provide a criterion of much more general use that the casuistic distinctions drawn by Professor Pigou? This is the problem to which we have to turn.[12]

III. *The Rationale of Maintaining Capital Intact*

To 'maintain capital intact' is not an aim in itself. It is only desired because of certain consequences which are known to follow from a failure to do so. And as we shall see, it is not even possible to attach a definite sense to this phrase if we try to apply it to a changing world, independently of why we want to do so. We are not interested in its magnitude because there is any inherent advantage in any particular absolute measurement of capital, but only because, *ceteris paribus*, a change in this magnitude would be a cause of a change in the income to be expected from it, and because in consequence *every* change in its magnitude may be a symptom for such a change in the really relevant magnitude, income. Professor Pigou has abandoned the attempt to define in terms of a value dimension of capital the position, in which the stock of capital undergoes no changes that need to be added to or deducted from the output of consumers' goods for the computation of the national dividend. He has thereby not only acknowledged the inherent difficulties of any value measurement, which in the present case indeed are particularly serious,[13] but he has apparently also recognised the much more fundamental fact that such constancy of the value dimension has no necessary connection with the reasons why we wish to 'maintain capital intact,' and that in consequence there is no reason to assume that people will in fact normally act in such a way as to keep the value of the stock of capital constant.[14]

What, then, are the reasons why we wish capital to behave in a particular way? In the first instance, this reason is evidently that the persons who draw an income from capital, want to avoid using up unintentionally parts of the source of this income, which must be preserved if income is to be kept at the present level. We want to avoid an unintentional temporary 'splashing' or 'stinting' which would have the effect of later reducing income below or raising it above the level at which we aim. Capital accounting in this sense is simply a technical device, an abbreviated method of solving the complicated problems arising out of this task of avoiding involuntary infringements upon future income. Whatever the time shape of the future income stream derived from the capital in his possession at which an individual aims, there still remains the problem of deciding what is the required action with regard to the individual parts of his possessions. And although we have certainly no right to assume that every person will normally aim at a permanent constant stream of income from his capital, there is probably some justification for regarding this case as one of special interest. In any case, even when the capitalist aims at some other shape of the income stream, the problem remains the same, and the case of the constant income stream might simply be regarded as the standard with which the other cases are compared.

So long as we confine ourselves to the effects of the decisions of the capitalist on his own income stream, it may seem arbitrary to treat any one of the different sets of consistent decisions regarding his future income stream as in any way more 'normal' than any other. It may even have a certain theoretical attraction simply to define whatever incomes he wants to have at different periods as equal incomes. We are, however, constrained by other reasons to abstain from such a pure subjectivism and to adopt a more objective standard. These other reasons are that we are interested in the maintenance of capital, not only because of the people who themselves deliberately distribute income over time and by so doing become capitalists, but also because of the effect of their activity on the income of other people. In the case of the workman, whose labour receives a greater remuneration because of the cooperation of capital, but who is not himself an owner of capital, we have no expression of his preference as regards the shape of his income stream, and we have to *assume* that he wants an income stream which does at least not decrease. Such a constant income stream in an objective sense might provisionally be defined as consisting at every successive moment of varying collections of commodities actually bought at an aggregate price, at which the collection of commodities actually bought at the beginning of the period might have been obtained.

IV. *The Action of the Capitalist with Perfect Foresight*

The next task, then, is to find out how the individual owner of capital goods will behave, if he wants to keep the income he derives from his possession constant, and if he has complete foresight of all relevant changes.[15] Complete foresight in this sense need not refer to all the relevant future. It is sufficient for our purpose to assume that at any one moment he foresees all changes that will affect the return of the investment he then makes. His anticipation need only be correct for a period equal to that for which his investment runs, and if he makes investments in different fields, the extent of his foresight need only cover the relevant facts affecting the different investments during such different periods as these investments last. Beyond this, only some more general expectation as regards the rate of interest at which it will be possible to reinvest the capital recovered, will be necessary.

Within these periods, his anticipations must in the first instance cover the relevant price changes. But such fore-knowledge is hardly conceivable without some foresight of the real changes, which bring about the changes in prices. The main types of changes, which he will have to foresee and the effects of which we shall have to discuss, will be changes in the demand for the products and the consequent changes, not only of the prices of the products, but also of the prices of the factors, changes in the quantities of the factors of production, and changes in their prices caused in this way (including, in particular, in both these cases, changes in the rate of interest), and finally, changes of technical knowledge or inventions. With respect to this last case the idea of foresight evidently presents some difficulty, since an invention which has been foreseen in all details would not be an invention. All we can here assume is that people anticipate that the process used now will at some definite date be superseded by some new process not yet known in detail. But this degree of knowledge may be sufficient to limit investments in the kind of equipment, which is bound to be made obsolete by the expected invention, in such a way that the old equipment wears out as the new invention can be introduced.

If we take first the case of an anticipated change in the demand, either away from or towards the product produced by our capitalist, his knowledge of this impending change, a full investment period in advance of its actual occurrence, will evidently put him in a position so to redistribute the earned amortisation quotas of his capital between the different industries, that he will derive the greatest return from them possible under the new conditions. But in what sense will these amortisation quotas represent a constant magnitude, and under what conditions can we assume that the capitalist will invest them and no more and no less, if he merely aims at keeping his income from capital from now onwards constant?

There is no reason to assume that, if he just continues to reinvest, after the change has become known, the amounts he used to invest, in what appears the most profitable way in the light of the new knowledge, this will have that effect. The shift in demand between different products, if the co-efficients of production in the different lines of industry are not exactly the same, is bound to change the relative prices of the factors, and these changes will occur gradually as all the entrepreneurs redirect their resources in anticipation of the impending change. If we take the simplest imaginable case where there is only one uniform scarce factor besides 'capital,' namely labour, it will depend on the relative quantities of labour required in the lines of industry, to and from which demand is expected to shift, whether the product of labour invested for longer periods will fall relatively to that of labour invested for shorter periods, or *vice versa*.

If we assume that the industry, whose product will be in stronger demand, is one where relatively more capital is required, the tendency will be for wages to fall, and prospective returns on capital to rise. The way in which this is brought about is that, out of the amortisation quotas shifted to the industry now more favoured by demand, the capitalist will be willing to pay only wages corresponding to the lower marginal productivity of labour there. And since the withdrawal of these amortisation quotas from the other industry will decrease demand for labour there, wages will gradually fall.

The position of the capitalist will thereby be affected in a double way. The gradual fall of wages will leave in his hands a greater amount of gross profits to be divided between investment and consumption. And the expected returns on the reinvestment of these receipts will be increased. How much of these gross receipts from capital will he have to reinvest, if he wants to obtain a constant income stream from that moment onwards? There are three main types of possible reactions of which only one corresponds to that criterion. Either he may go on, until the change has actually occurred, to consume only as much as before. In that case he will have invested during the period constantly increasing amounts of money, and will consequently find himself at the end of the period in possession of a greater stock of capital, which will probably give him a greater percentage return (on the assumption that all other entrepreneurs act in the same way, but that the consequent increase of capital will not lead to proportionally greater reduction of interest, i.e. that the elasticity of the demand for capital under the new conditions is greater than unity). In this case his net income would at the end of the transition period suddenly increase, a change which does not correspond to the postulate that income should remain constant from the moment when the impending change becomes known.

Or we may assume that during the transition period he continues to reinvest amortisation quotas of the same magnitude as before. In this case his expenditure on consumers' goods will gradually increase during the transition period as the rate of interest increases, his capital will remain the same in money value, and will give him from the moment the anticipated change has actually occurred onwards, a permanently higher income. This

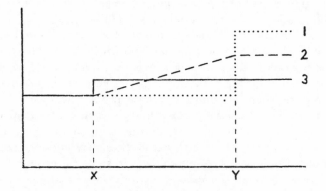

again clearly does not correspond to the assumption that he disposes of his resources in such a way, that in the light of his knowledge he may at every moment expect a constant income stream.

To do so he would have to raise his consumption, at the moment the impending change becomes known, to a level at which it can be permanently maintained. This implies that during the transition period he will increase his consumption and reduce his reinvestment to such a figure that at the end of the period he will be in possession of a quantity of capital which, although in every conceivable dimension it may be smaller than that he owned before, will at the higher rate of interest give him an income equal to that enjoyed during the transition period, and higher than that which he had before the change became known.

These alternative policies of the capitalist can easily be depicted by means of a diagram. The alternative income streams are here represented by the lines marked 1, 2, and 3 respectively. The ordinate for every point of the abscissa, on which time is measured, represents the magnitude of the income stream at that moment. The change is supposed to occur at Y, and to be first foreseen at X (which precedes Y by at least the maximum investment period). The line 1 then represents the income stream of the capitalist who goes on spending during the transition period XY as much as he did before, and thereby increases his capital in money terms, line 2 that of the capitalist who gradually increases his consumption and keeps his capital in money terms constant, and line 3 the income stream of the capitalist who immediately raises his consumptive expenditure to the level at which it can be permanently maintained (i.e. until some further change occurs), and thereby decreases the money value of his capital.

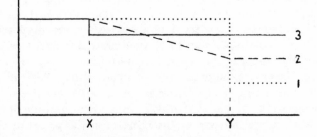

There is no difficulty in applying the same kind of analysis to the reverse case of an expected decrease of the return from capital, or to almost any other type of change that may be foreseen. If the shift of demand, instead of taking place from a less to a more capitalist line of industry, takes the reverse direction and the rate of interest is therefore due to fall, then a similar choice arises. Either the capitalist will anticipate the fall in his income and reduce it immediately in order to avoid, by an increase of his capital in monetary terms, the full force of the later reduction which would otherwise be inevitable (case 3). Or he will only gradually reduce it as his gross receipts from capital fall (case 2). Or he will maintain his expenditure until the change actually takes place, and so reduce even the money value of his capital, from which henceforth he will draw a smaller percentage return (case 1).

Action of the type 3, which I suggest in both cases comes nearest to what is really aimed at by capital accounting, but does not imply the maintenance of any dimension of capital as such, means in other words that the capitalist treats his gross receipts during the transition period as a terminable annuity of which he wants to consume no more than such a constant amount, that the sinking fund accumulated at the end of the period will secure him the same income in perpetuity. It is such action, which in my opinion best fulfils the purpose for which it is commonly desired to keep capital intact, from the point of view of the individual capitalist. It remains now to show what such action implies in the case of other types of changes, and what will be the effect of such action on the part of the capitalists on other incomes.

There is little more to be said about the effects of changes in the supply of factors, or – what is fundamentally the same thing – changes in technology. Since even an initial change in consumers' demand brings about changes in the relative scarcity of the different factors, there is really here no new problem beyond those already discussed. The anticipation of the forthcoming change will require the same kind of decision, and if the capitalist wants to keep his income stream constant after the impending change becomes known, he will have to redivide his changed gross receipts on the same principles as shown before. If, for instance, the supply of a factor of production is expected to decrease, or the production of a commodity in some other way to become more difficult,[16] or if on the other hand the discovery of new natural resources, or the invention of a new process facilitates the production of a commodity, this will again, as soon as the impending change becomes known, affect the decisions of the capital owners in a double way: it will affect the magnitude of the gross receipts from capital by way of the changes in the prices of the other factors that will occur in consequence of the adjustments to the expected change, and it will affect the return to be expected from the reinvestment of capital. The decision of the capitalists will accordingly depend in the same way on the effect of the change on the relative productivity of capital and the other factors, as was true in the former case. If the capitalist acts on the principle we have described as being most in accordance with what is the most obvious purpose of 'maintaining capital intact,' he will tend to let the money value of his capital decrease when in the future it promises to give a greater percentage return, because he will anticipate that greater future return; and he will attempt to increase the money value of his capital by reducing his expenditure immediately when he expects in the future a lower percentage return.

While in this way the capitalist will minimise the fluctuations of his own income, his action will rather tend to accentuate the effect of the change on other incomes. At least, if instead of acting in this way he would try to keep the money value of his capital constant (and still more if he acted according to the third alternative – case 1 – i.e. if he kept his consumption constant until the expected change actually occurred), the incomes of the other factors would have to change to a much smaller degree than in the case where he aims at keeping the income from his capital constant. In the case where the marginal productivity of labour tends to fall and that of capital to rise, wages would have to fall less if the capitalists kept at least the money value of their capital constant and still less if they increased it. And in the reverse case would rise less if instead of maintaining or even raising the money value of their capital, capitalists allowed it to decrease. But there is little reason to assume that they will act in this way. Even where the capitalists do not want to keep their income constant under all circumstances but where, as will probably be the case to some extent, every increase of their expected income will induce them to plan for a gradually increasing consumption, i.e. to save, and perhaps an expected decrease in their income will in the same way induce them to plan for a decreasing consumption, i.e. to dissave, this is not very likely to result in a maintenance of the monetary value of capital (i.e. to make their action similar to case 2 above). One would have to assume a very peculiar shape of the indifference curves expressing the 'willingness to save' of the capitalists in order to obtain such a result.

V. *Obsolescence and Anticipated Risks*

There remain two special cases to be considered before we abandon the assumption of correct foresight on the part of the capitalists. The first is obsolescence as distinguished from wear and tear, as a cause of destruction of existing capital values. Although at first it may appear otherwise, this is a phenomenon which will occur even with perfect foresight. The second case on the other hand is somewhat intermediate between that of correct and incorrect foresight; it is the case where the probability of the occurrence of certain changes is correctly and equally foreseen and estimated by all members of the society. Since this case also raises the problem of obsolescence, it is convenient to treat the two cases together.

The first case would hardly require much discussion if Professor Pigou had not originally excluded obsolescence from the capital losses which have to be made up by new investment if capital is to be maintained intact. Obsolescence in this sense occurs everywhere where the usefulness of any piece of real capital diminishes faster than it decays in a physical sense. There can be no doubt that many investments in actual life are made with complete awareness of the fact that the period, during which the instrument concerned will be useful, will be much shorter than its possible physical duration. In the case of most very durable constructions like the permanent way of a railroad, the prospective 'economic life' ought to be regarded as considerably shorter than the possible 'physical life.' In many cases it lies in the very nature of the product that it must be made almost infinitely durable, although it is only needed for a very transient purpose.

213

It is impossible to adjust the durability of a machine to the short period during which it may be needed, and in many other cases the strength needed from a construction while it is used necessitates it being made in a form which will last much longer than the period during which it is needed.

In all these cases it is known beforehand that the stream of receipts to be obtained from the investment is limited, not only to the period for which the good will last physically, but for the shorter period during which it can be used. The capitalist who aims at a constant income stream will have to take this into account in deciding about the division of his gross receipts between consumption and amortisation. He will again have to treat the gross receipts as a terminable annuity, and to consume no more than such an amount that the sinking fund accumulated at the end of the period will give him in the form of a perpetual income. This means that he will have to put aside amounts proportional, not to the physical wear and tear, but to the decrease in the value of the investment.

If, instead of acting in this way, he would, as Professor Pigou suggests, at the end of every accounting period put aside out of his gross receipts only such a part of the value of the instrument as is proportional to the physical deterioration that has taken place during the period, this would clearly mean that he would consume considerably more than he could expect to derive from the much smaller sinking fund accumulated when the instrument ceases to be useful.

The significance of such a decision on the part of the capitalist becomes particularly clear if we consider the case where the capitalist has to choose between two investments of equal cost, both represented by equally durable instruments, but one of the kind that is expected to remain useful so long as it lasts physically, while the other serves a very transient purpose. Under what conditions will he consider the two investments as equally attractive? The first answer is, of course, if they promise him the same permanent income. But under what conditions do they promise him the same permanent income? If the gross receipts from the investments while they flow were in both cases equal and just sufficient to provide the same income *plus* an allowance for depreciation proportional to the physical deterioration, the effect would clearly be that in the case where the instrument ceases to be useful long before it has worn out physically, only a fraction of the sum originally invested would have been recovered which would bring only a much lower income in the future. To decide for this alternative would mean that an income stream which starts at a given magnitude but decreases later on is treated as equal to an income stream which is permanently kept at the initial magnitude of the former. In order that investment in the instrument of only transitory usefulness may appear equally attractive as that of lasting usefulness, it would be necessary that, while the former remains in use, it would produce gross returns sufficiently large to allow for full amortisation of its original value. In other words, only if the expected returns cover, in addition to the same income, not only depreciation in the narrower sense but also obsolescence, can the two investments be regarded as equally attractive.

Thus, to neglect obsolescence, in deciding about the investments to be chosen, would in the same way frustrate the endeavour to keep the income stream at any definite level, as would a neglect of depreciation proper. In fact, from a purely economic point of view, there is no real difference between depreciation and obsolescence. Whether an instrument ceases to be useful because of physical decay, or for any other reason, makes no difference to the capitalist, when he has to decide whether it is worth while to invest in it or not.

That there could exist any doubt whatever about this point is probably due to the fact that, while the case where it is definitely foreseen that an instrument will become obsolescent at a certain date is by no means rare, it is not the case of which we think in the first instance when we speak of obsolescence. Of much greater practical importance than this case, where an instrument has for technical reasons to be made more durable than is really needed, is the case where it has been given a greater durability than turns out ultimately to have been necessary, because the period during which it would be needed was not known for certain. In so far as the effects of completely unforeseen and unforeseeable changes are here concerned, we shall consider them only in the following section of this paper. But, as has already been mentioned, there is an intermediate class between this case and that of compete foresight, the case where a definite probability exists and is generally known that a change will occur. And this case, as will be shown, is fundamentally similar to that just discussed, in the sense that here, too, the anticipated risk of obsolescence has to be taken into account if capital is to be maintained intact.

The capitalist who considers a number of different investment opportunities will usually find that they promise different returns with different degrees of probability. And while the degree of certainty with which he will be able to predict returns may be fairly high in so far as the immediate future is concerned, uncertainty will generally be much greater as regards the period during which he may hope to receive these or any returns. But while he will be unable to predict with certainty the periods during which he may expect returns in the different cases, he will have fairly definite ideas about the different degrees of probability that they will give returns for longer or shorter periods. In his choice between different investment opportunities, these estimates of the probable periods after which they will

215

cease to give returns will play an important role. He will evidently consider an investment, where the risk, that it will soon cease to give any returns, is greater than in other cases, only if the gross returns are such that he can expect to amortise the capital sunk in it during a correspondingly shorter period. Only when he distributes his capital in such a way between the different investment opportunities, that the gross returns cover the probable rate of obsolescence, can he hope to obtain a constant income stream. If he acts in this way, and if his estimates of the probabilities were correct, even if in none of the individual cases he should have guessed quite correctly, his losses are likely to be balanced, so that on the whole he will succeed in maintaining his income stream constant. This presupposes that his investments are sufficiently numerous and diverse to make such compensation possible, and that in the cases where he makes unexpected profits, i.e. where the investment continues to bring returns after its original value has been fully amortised, he does not treat these profits as net income, but he uses them to offset the losses suffered from other investments. Where the investments of the individual capitalists are not sufficiently numerous and diverse to make such internal compensation possible, the same results will follow for the capitalists as a class, provided again that those who make profit do not consume them but use them, or at least the greater part of them, for new investment. Is there any reason to expect that in this case the capitalist, following the general principle we have regarded as normal, will behave in such a way? This brings us to the general question of how the capitalists will react on an entirely unforeseen change.

VI. *The Reaction of the Capitalist on Unforeseen Changes*

The changes whose effects we have now to study differ from those considered in the earlier parts of this paper by the fact that they are not foreseen but become known only when they actually occur (or at least some time after the investment affected by them has irrevocably been made). That is, we abandon at this point the assumption of more or less complete foresight on the part of the capitalist, and ask how he will have to act when an unexpected change affects the returns from an investment, to which he has already committed himself, if he wants to keep his income stream from that moment onwards constant.

The owner of any piece of real capital, who finds that in consequence of such unforeseen change the gross returns which he may expect during the remaining 'life' of that instrument will be either greater or smaller than he had anticipated, will have to choose between the same main types of action as those discussed in connection with a foreseen change, If we consider only the case where, in consequence of the change his gross receipts have decreased, he may in the first instance consume, during the remaining 'life' of his investment as much as before (if the gross receipts are still as great as the amount he used to consume) and reduce only his depreciation allowance. The effect of this would be that when the returns from the investment cease he will only have accumulated a sinking fund considerably smaller than would be necessary to give him an income equal to that enjoyed up to that moment. Or, in other words, he would have maintained his consumption after the change has occurred at the pre-existing level at the expense of an inevitable later reduction of his consumption, a reduction which would clearly have to be greater than if he had immediately reduced his consumption to a level at which it could be permanently maintained. To act in the latter way, i.e. again to treat the gross receipts to be expected during the remaining life of the investment as a terminable annuity, whose capital value is to be maintained constant, would evidently be the only course of action consistent with the aim of a constant income stream. The third possibility would be to continue, after the change has occurred, so far as possible the same allowances for depreciation and to reduce consumption to what remains beyond this, if anything does remain. In this way it would be possible in many cases to recover the full capital value originally invested. But could this properly be regarded as maintaining the capital constant? It would mean that the owner would have to reduce consumption for a period below the level at which it could be permanently maintained in order to increase it later above that level. It seems that this would have to be regarded in every sense as new saving, saving it is true to make up for a loss, but for a loss which has already occurred. This loss was irrevocably incurred when the investment was made in ignorance of the impending change.

The same applies, *mutatis mutandis*, to the case of profits due to an unexpected change. If, after a change which has increased the gross returns from his investment, the owner wants to keep his income permanently at the same higher level, this means that he must only consume so much of the gain as to leave an amount which, reinvested at the current rate of interest, would give him the same additional income in perpetuity. If, for instance, his additional receipts after the change are £210, and the rate at which he can reinvest is 5 per cent., he must only consume £10, and invest the remaining £200, which at 5 per cent. will give him the same returns in every future year. Such 'windfall profits' are, therefore, not income in the sense that their consumption is compatible with maintaining capital intact. Also consumption need not be reduced by the amount of 'windfall losses' in order to maintain capital intact. In both cases only the current interest on the (positive or negative) capital gain ought to be counted as income.

This principle applies, whether the change in question was completely foreseen, or whether it is a change, the probability of whose occurrence was anticipated, but which does not occur at the moment that was regarded as most probable. The difference between the two cases is that where the probability of the occurrence of the change was correctly anticipated, deviations of the individual cases from what was regarded as most probable are likely to balance in their effect, so that capitalists as a whole will succeed in keeping their income stream constant. But, where the changes were completely unforeseen, there is no reason to expect that gains and losses will balance in this way, so that at least total incomes from capital would remain constant. It is much more likely that in such a case, if the capitalists behave as described, it will have the effect of either permanently decreasing or permanently increasing the income from capital.

Of the different types of changes which would have to be considered in the exhaustive discussion we may confine ourselves here to that of an invention, which is in many ways the most interesting. The application to the case of a shift in demand between different types of consumers' goods, or of changes in the supply of factors, will present no difficulty. In so far as the invention is concerned, two kinds of effects have to be considered; on the one hand the possibility of a loss of capital invested in plant that is made obsolete by the invention, and on the other hand, the possible gains on plants and stock which, at least during a transition period, may bring higher returns than was expected. Although there is some reason to suppose that any unexpected change is much more likely to lead to considerable capital losses than to capital gains, it is not impossible that in the individual case the gains may be greater than the losses.

The conditions, which must be given, in order that it may be advantageous to introduce newly invented machinery for the production of a commodity, which up to the present has been produced by a different still existing plant, are too well known to need more than a short restatement.[17] In order that the invention should lead to the complete abandonment of the old machinery, it would be necessary that it should reduce the total cost of production below the prime cost of running the old plant (or, quite exactly, to such a figure that the difference between it and the prime cost is lower than the return to be expected from the investment of the scrap value of the old plant). In this case the capital value of the old plant would be completely destroyed (or reduced to the scrap value of the plant). Much more frequently will it be the case that, while the new invention does not result in a sufficient lowering of cost to drive the old plant out of business altogether, it will make an increase of sales at the reduced price possible. In this case only the additional output will be produced by the new process, and the value of the old plant will be reduced to a figure corresponding to the capitalised value of the lower surplus over running costs, which is henceforward to be expected. In all these cases capital losses will occur, which may be further increased by a rise in the rate of interest, which may be the general effect of the increased demand for capital caused by the new invention. In so far as such a rise in the rate of interest takes place, the losses in capital values caused thereby are not inconsistent with maintaining capital (i.e. income from capital) constant in our sense.

Capital gains will occur in consequence of an invention – apart from the increases in capital values of natural resources, like mineral deposits and other non-reproduceable factors – mainly during such transition periods until it is possible to increase the supply of particular instruments, which are now also required in the newly invented process. If, e.g. the new machinery required can be produced only in a particular plant, which before was expected to be used up only very slowly over a long period, and if it takes a long time to erect an additional plant of the same sort, the owner of the existing plant will clearly be able to make considerable and unexpected profits during the interval. Since these profits will be of a temporary character, he ought not to regard them as ordinary income, but to reinvest so much of it as will secure him in perpetuity an additional income equal to that which he actually consumes during the transition period.[18]

VII. The Impossibility of an Objective Standard with Different Degrees of Foresight

So far the criterion, for what is to be understood as maintaining capital intact on the part of the individual entrepreneur or capitalist, is purely subjective, because it depends on the extent to which the individual capitalist foresees the future. Entirely different actions by two capitalists who hold different views on the future, but who are otherwise in exactly the same position, may satisfy our criterion. Both may, in the light of their different knowledge, do their best to obtain a constant income stream, and yet both will probably fail, earlier or later, and in different degrees. Are we to say that neither has been maintaining his capital, and ought we to reserve this term to the case of action with perfect foresight? In a world where very imperfect foresight is the rule this would clearly lead to absurd results. We should not only have to say that nobody ever succeeds in maintaining his capital intact – which in a sense of course would be true – but we should also be prevented from using this concept of maintaining capital intact as a description of the actual behaviour of the entrepreneurs, who want neither to decrease or to increase their income from their possessions. Taking into account the fact that human foresight is of necessity very imperfect, and that all economic activity must be based on anticipations, which will partly prove incorrect, it would still seem desirable to find a criterion which would enable us to distinguish between losses – or rather missed opportunities of faster improvement – which are unavoidable in view of the unpredictability of the change, and capital losses due to what appear to be avoidable mistakes.

At first one might feel inclined to base the definition of what is to be regarded as adequate maintenance of capital on such a degree of foresight as the intelligent capitalist can reasonably be expected to possess. But closer examination of the problem soon reveals that any attempt to find an objective test of what can be regarded as maintenance of capital, short of the case of absolute foresight, must necessarily fail. It seems common-sense to say that if an entrepreneur expects a change in taste, e.g. because he hopes to interest the public in a novelty, but is disappointed in his expectations, and loses the capital invested in the venture, this is a loss of capital which must be made up out of new savings, if capital is to be kept intact. If this did not happen, and similar failures were frequently repeated, the capital available for the production of things which people want would be considerably reduced by conversion into equipment for making things which nobody wants. On the other hand, the loss of capital due to an unforeseen change in taste seems merely the incidental and unavoidable concomitant of a process leading to what is now a preferred income. Yet if entrepreneurs had correctly anticipated the change – and some entrepreneurs may have done so – the wants of the public would have been supplied even better. Is, therefore, the loss of the entrepreneurs who did not foresee correctly, to be counted as a capital loss to be deducted from gross output? and does it already mean that they might have foreseen the change if a single happy speculator chanced to do so, who, according to all reasonable expectations should have proved to be a waster of capital?

It is not possible to base the distinction here on the concept of a change, and to say that to invest in anticipation of a change which does not occur is wasting capital, while to invest in the mistaken assumption that things will remain as they are is only a cause of unavoidable loss. In the first instance, it is by no means evident what is to be regarded as a change. If a temporary change is mistakenly considered as permanent, or if the expectation that the seasonal fluctuations of the past will be repeated is disappointed, are these to be regarded as mistaken expectations of a change, or as a mistaken expectation that things will remain constant? Clearly in economic life, and outside of a fictitious stationary state, the concept of a change itself has frequently no meaning except in the sense of a change relative to expectations. In the second place, and even more important, an approximately correct anticipation of the majority of 'changes' in the usual sense is an indispensable condition of that degree of progress which is observed in actual life. One need only consider for a moment what would happen if entrepreneurs always acted as if things would remain forever as they are at present, and changed their plans only after a change in demand (or some other change) had actually occurred, in order to see what would necessarily be the effect on general productivity. Every change would mean an enormous loss, or rather, the adaptation of production to the change would become so expensive (not because the loss on existing investment would have to be counted as cost, but because the 'free capital' required for the new production would be so scarce) as to make it in many cases impossible. How rich, on the other hand, should we now be if all past changes had been correctly foreseen from the beginning of things!

All this means simply that the mobility of capital, the degree to which it can be maintained in a changing world, will depend on the foresight of the entrepreneurs and capitalists. If this is a commonplace, it is at least a commonplace to which far too little regard is paid in usual reasoning. It means nothing less than that the amount of capital available at any moment in a dynamic society depends much more on the degree of foresight of the entrepreneurs than on current saving or on 'time preference.' This is simply a corollary to the equally obvious and neglected fact that 'capital' is not a factor, the quantity of which is given independently of human action even in the comparatively short run. How great a contribution to the possibility of satisfying human wants a given stock of capital goods will still represent some time later, will depend largely on how correctly the entrepreneurs foresee the situation at this moment. Their anticipations in this respect are quite as important a 'datum' for the explanation of the dynamic process as the 'stock of capital,' and the latter concept has in fact little meaning without the former. As an enumeration of individual capital goods existing at the beginning, the 'stock of capital' is of course an important datum, but the form in which this capital will still exist some time afterwards, and how much of it will still exist, depends mainly on the foresight of the entrepreneurs and capitalists. It would probably be no exaggeration to say that to maintain his capital so as to receive the greatest lasting return, is the main function of the capitalist-entrepreneur.[19] But not only is in this sense the size of the productive equipment of society dependent on the success of the entrepreneur, it is also dependent in a world of uncertainty on his capitalising capital gains ('windfall profits'). It

221

should be recognised that much of the new formation of capital equipment (which need not represent net additions to capital in the traditional terminology) does not arise out of savings proper, but out of those gains of individual capitalists which are part of the process of capital maintenance. This process will, as shown above, always involve unforeseen profits on the part of some and unforeseen losses on the part of other entrepreneurs, changes on capital account, which are part of an ever-proceeding process of redistribution of wealth, not to be confused with the distribution of income. The entrepreneur who finds that a risky undertaking succeeds, and who for a time makes extraordinary profits because he has restricted the amount of investment so as to give him in case of success a margin of profit over cost which is proportionate to the risk, will not be justified if he regards the whole profit as income. If he aims at a constant income stream from his investment, he will have to reinvest such part of his profits as will be sufficient to give him an income equal to the part he has consumed, when the rate of profit in what has now proved to be a successful line of business falls to normal.[20] It is in such a way that, in case of changes in demand or technical progress, etc., capital is newly formed without new saving in place of that which is lost elsewhere. There is, of course, no reason to assume that the capital lost and that which is newly formed will correspond in any quantitative sense; and it is exactly for this reason that the usual concept of a net change in capital, which is supposed to correspond in some way to saving, is of little value. There has in this case been no abstention from consumption which could have been maintained at that level. If anybody can be said to have refrained from consumption which would be compatible with enjoying the same income permanently, it is not the entrepreneurs, but rather the consumers who for a time had to pay a price in excess of the cost which the production of the commodity entails after it has proved an assured success. But this 'saving' is of course neither voluntary nor does it represent an abstention from consumption, which would have been regarded as permanently possible so long as the outcome of the venture was uncertain. It can hardly be questioned that in the actual world a great deal of the equipment which is made necessary by some change is financed out of these temporary differences between cost and price. But it may appear somewhat paradoxical that where it can be provided in this way this ought not to be classed as saving but as a capital gain, a kind of transfer of capital which means that not only new capital is formed in place of that lost elsewhere, but that it is formed exactly where it is most needed, and in the hands of those most qualified to use it; this follows, however, necessarily from the consistent use of the definition of maintaining capital and saving, which we have adopted. It will be shown in the next section that this use of the terms proves convenient in other directions also.

VIII. 'Saving' and 'Investing'

The upshot of the discussions of the last sections is that if changes in the data occur (such as new inventions, shifts in consumers' demand or changes in the supply of factors), the amount of capital (conceived as a multiple of the income of a given period, or – what amounts to the same thing – the result of a certain 'average' waiting period, or in any other conceivable quantitative sense), which is available and required to maintain income from then onwards at a constant level, will change also, and that in consequence there is no reason to expect that any of the conceivable dimensions of capital will remain constant. It remains true, of course, that *ceteris paribus* it is necessary to maintain or replenish a reservoir of goods of a constant size, in order to maintain a given output. But when conditions change so as to make a smaller or larger reservoir necessary for the same purpose, its contents will tend to change automatically in such a way as to preserve income constant from the moment when the change becomes known. The fact that an impending change is likely to become known to different people at different times will lead to capital gains and capital losses of individuals, with the effect that persons who have shown the greatest foresight will command the greatest amount of resources. But in a world of imperfect foresight not only the size of the capital stock, but also the income derived from it will inevitably be subject to unintended and unpredictable changes which depend on the extent and distribution of foresight, and there will be no possibility of distinguishing any particular movement of these magnitudes as normal.

These conclusions have rather far-reaching consequences with respect to the much used, or much abused, concepts of saving and investing. If the stock of capital required to keep income from any moment onwards constant cannot in any sense be defined as a constant magnitude, it becomes also impossible to state that any sacrifices of present income in order to increase future income (or the reverse) must lead to any net changes in the amount of capital. Saving and investment in the ordinary meaning of the terms are, of course, one of the causes, but by no means the only cause, which affect the magnitude of capital (in any conceivable quantitative sense), and the changes in the size of the capital stock cannot therefore be regarded as indications of what sacrifices of present income have been or are being made in the interest of future income. This idea, appropriately enough for the analysis of the effects of a change under otherwise stationary conditions, must be completely abandoned in the analysis of a dynamic process. If we want to retain the connection between the ideas of saving and investment, and that of a sacrifice of potential present income in the interest of future income (and it will be shown that it is this concept which is of importance in the connection in which those terms are commonly used), we cannot determine the size of either saving or investment by any references to changes in the quantity of capital. And with the abandonment of this basis of the distinction, there will, of course, have to fall the habitual practice of economists of separating out such part of general investment activity as happens to leave the capital stock in some sense constant, as something different from activities which add to it, a distinction which has no relationship to anything in the real world.[21]

To deny that the usual distinctions between new and merely renewed investment, and between new savings out of net income and merely maintained savings, as distinctions based on the idea of quantitative increases or decreases of capital, have any definite meaning, is not to deny that they aim at a distinction of real importance. There can be no doubt that the decision of the consumers as to the distribution of consumption over time are something separate from the decisions of the entrepreneur-capitalist as regards what quantities of consumers' goods to provide for different moments of time, and that the two sets of decisions may or may not coincide. What I do want to deny is only that the correspondence or non-correspondence between these two sets of conditions can be adequately expressed in terms of a quantitative correspondence between (net) saving and (net) investment. But if this distinction is not to be formulated in this particular way, what are we to put in its place? In general terms the answer is not difficult. If we must no longer speak in terms of absolute increases and decreases of capital we must attempt a more direct comparison of the time distribution of income. Capital accounting, as has been mentioned before, is itself only an abbreviated method of effecting this comparison in an indirect way, and when this indirect method fails it is only natural to go back to its *rationale*, and to carry out the comparison explicitly. Instead of comparing them each with the supposed standard case of capital remaining 'constant,' and so arriving at the concepts of net saving (net income *minus* consumption) and net investment, and then to juxtapose these derived concepts, we shall have to compare directly the intentions of the consumers and the intentions of the producers with regard to the income stream they want to consume and produce respectively.

The question, then, is essentially whether the demand for consumers' goods tends to keep ahead of, to coincide with, or to fall behind the output of consumers' goods irrespective of whether either of the two magnitudes is increasing, remaining constant or decreasing in an absolute sense. But in order to give this question a clear meaning we have yet to settle in terms of what are the demand for and the supply of consumers' goods to be measured, in order to establish whether they coincide or whether the one exceeds the other. In a sense of course demand and supply are always equal, or made equal by the pricing process, and to speak of their relative magnitudes presupposes some unit in terms of which their magnitude is measured independently of the prices formed on the market.

Consider first the decision of the 'savers' or the body of consumers as a whole. What we can assume of them is, not that they will under all conditions aim at an income stream of a particular shape, but that if they are offered a present income of a given magnitude, *plus* the sources of a future income of a certain magnitude they will attach certain relative values to these incomes. For every such combination of a given present income and the sources of a certain future income we must assume these valuations to be determined.

If the relative value consumers attach to the sources of future income, compared with present values, should be higher (or lower) than the cost (in terms of present income) of reproducing new sources of future income of the same magnitude, more (or less) such sources will be produced. And assuming that the relative valuations of the consumers do not change abruptly – which is least to be expected when in each successive period the available income is equal to that for which they have planned – then production will tend to provide in each successive period such amounts of present income and sources of future income, that their relative cost (in terms of each other) will approximately correspond to the relative values attached to them by the consumers. But if for some reason – say because additional money has become available for investment purposes – the price of the sources of future income have been raised out of correspondence with the valuation of consumers, more sources of future income and less current income will be provided for the next period than consumers will be then willing to take at prices corresponding to their relative cost. Consumers will find that they get less current real income, and in consequence will attach a greater value to it compared with the sources of future income – investment will have exceeded saving in the usual terminology.

Under the assumption of otherwise constant conditions (i.e. unchanged knowledge, taste, etc.) this process can be described in the familiar way in terms of changes of the investment period, to which correspond changes in the quantity of capital (in terms of income of a period). We would say that, by increasing the waiting period and thereby accumulating more capital, producers have caused a temporary gap in the income stream which leads to a relative rise in the prices of consumers' goods. But as soon as we drop this *ceteris paribus* assumption this is no longer true. The correspondence between the value attached to the sources of future income and their cost is then no longer dependent on the cost of reproducing the same amount of capital, which under changed conditions will make it possible to produce the same future income.

Additional investment, in the sense that total output is reduced for a time in order to increase it at a later date, may take place, although at the same time the quantity of capital is reduced (and the 'period of production' shortened).[22] Breaks in the even flow of consumers' goods, which make corresponding changes in the attitude of the consumers necessary if disturbances are to be avoided will only occur when that quantity of capital is not maintained which under the conditions prevailing at any moment is required to provide such a constant flow.

The correspondence between the supply of current consumers' goods and the demand for them, which is what has been aimed at by the saving-investment equations, can only be stated adequately if we measure both supply and demand in terms of the alternatives open to consumers and producers under the circumstances existing at the moment.[23] To do this it seems necessary to abandon entirely the concepts of saving and investment as referred to something beyond and outside the normal process of maintaining capital quantitatively intact, and to substitute an analysis on the lines suggested, which does not try to separate 'old' and 'new' investment, and 'new' and 'maintained' saving as distinguishable phenomena. Or, if we want to retain the familiar terms and to use them without any reference to changes in the quantity of capital, we might say that 'savings' correspond to 'investment' when the value of the existing capital goods (in terms of consumers' goods) is such that it becomes profitable to replace them by the capital goods that are required to produce the income in the expectation of which people have decided currently to consume as much as they actually do. I believe that some theories, which used to be stated in terms of net saving and net investment, can be restated in terms of these concepts, and I have tried to sketch such a reformulation of my own views in another place.[24] But I am rather doubtful whether the same is possible with some other theories which seem more dependent on the concepts of saving and investing as absolute magnitudes.

All this is, of course, no reason for not using the concepts of absolute increases or decreases of capital under any circumstances. In the discussion of comparatively long-term changes it may sometimes be quite innocuous. And in the discussion of short-run changes it would be equally legitimate to speak of causes, which *ceteris paribus* would lead to increases or decreases of capital. But we must be very careful not to assume that they actually do, and not to base any distinctions on supposed net changes in the quantity of capital which do not actually take place. Particularly the phenomenon of the trade cycle is probably largely concerned with changes within that region of indeterminateness between clear increases and clear decreases of capital, inside which the concept of an absolute change has no meaning. But it remains probably true that net accumulations and decumulations of capital in the usual sense will present similar phenomena as booms and depressions – at least when real accumulation proceeds faster and real decumulation proceeds slower than saving and dissaving.[25]

IX. *Capital Accounting and Monetary Policy*

This discussion of the problems connected with the concept of the maintenance of capital has by no means been exhaustive. We have touched on many points which have not been cleared up, and there are many others equally important which have not even been mentioned. This is, however, unavoidable in an article which treats what is in many respects one of the central problems of economic dynamics. But there is one further problem of great importance on which some remarks must be added in this concluding section.

Up to this point we have been largely concerned with an attempt to derive the appropriate action from the *rationale* of 'maintaining capital intact,' but we have said little about the effects of the actual practice of the entrepreneur, that 'abbreviated method' which consists in regarding capital as a money fund of definite magnitude, and on which actual capital accounting is based. This practice is, of course, largely due, and partly justified, by the fact that the capital of the individual enterprise is to a great extent furnished in the form of money loans, and that in consequence the entrepreneur has in the first instance to provide for a repayment of the money loans.

It was also this practice of treating capital as a money fund which has given rise to the theoretical concept of capital as a quantitatively determined fund. But while the actual use of this concept in real life does not mean that we have to accept it as the basis of theoretical analysis, and does not relieve us from the duty of going back to the *rationale* of its use, the results of this theoretical investigation are little more than a starting point for a study of the effects of the actual practice.

A more exhaustive investigation would, therefore, have to proceed after this preliminary clearing up of the fundamental concepts to the main task of explaining what the effects are of the actual accounting methods used by capitalists, to what extent, and under what conditions, they fulfil their purpose, and when they fail. That there are cases where the rigid application of the money fund concept fails is, of course, generally recognised and to some extent taken account of in the distinction made between changes on income account and changes on capital account. It is also obvious that the results achieved by this method will be largely dependent on monetary policy. Of course, no monetary policy can make the money value of capital behave in such a way that a constant value will always correspond to a quantity of capital which will give the same real income, and that all attempts to increase the future output of consumers' goods at the expense of the present and *vice versa* will lead to corresponding changes in the money value of capital; and in consequence a policy of the capitalist-entrepreneur which aims at nothing but this, will always err to a considerable extent, i.e. will lead to positions where their distribution of resources between current consumption and the provision of future consumption is not in accord with consumers' preferences. But the degree to which capital accounting in terms of money will prove deceptive will depend on the particular monetary policy followed.

To realise these effects in different situations would require a fairly detailed analysis of a number of representative instances. It is only possible to discuss here in the most general way one case, probably the most important and the one which has received the greatest attention in recent discussion; that of a continued increase in output due to 'technical progress.' Now, in spite of all the complications discussed before, it still remains true that *in any given situation* the value of capital required to provide an income stream at a certain constant or increasing rate will have to stand in a definite proportion to the value of current income. This proportion will change with any change in the relevant data, but where we have to deal with a development from moment to moment it is still approximately true to say that in order that the replacement of capital be sufficient to maintain the income stream at least at a constant rate its value should maintain a constant proportion to that of income. With the money value of capital being kept constant this will evidently only be true if the money value of aggregate income be kept constant also. Any policy which increases the money value of current income and particularly a policy which stabilises the average prices of consumers' goods and therefore raises the aggregate value of income in proportion as real income rises would mean that the money value of capital has to be raised in the same proportion and to be maintained at this increased value if sufficient provision for the replacement of this income is to be made. Any use of the nominal profits of the money value of capital so made for consumption purposes, as would follow from a policy of maintaining money values constant, would lead to insufficient replacement or a consumption of capital in the usual sense.

There can be no doubt that this sort of 'paper profits' has played an enormous role not only during the great inflations, but also during all major booms – even if no rise in the absolute level of the prices of the consumers' goods has taken place. And even more important than the pseudo-profits computed by enterprises under such conditions are the gains on capital appreciation made on the Stock Exchange. Stock Exchange profits made during such periods of capital appreciation in terms of money, which do not correspond to any proportional increase of capital beyond the amount which is required to reproduce the equivalent of current income, are not income, and their use for consumption purposes must lead to a destruction of capital.[26] So long as the expansion of credit, which has caused this movement, continues at a sufficient rate, this tendency may be overcompensated and the money value of capital continue to grow. But the monetary demand for consumers' goods fed out of such pseudo-profits will prove too large to permit of a maintenance of capital at a proportional value without constant further expansion of credit. That the increasing money values of capital cannot be maintained without further inflation if the amount of appreciation is generally used for consumption purposes, is, of course, only another form of expressing the truism that capital values, which people in general try to convert into income, cannot be maintained beyond the time during which some outside cause operates in the direction of a further rise. But as soon as the cause of a further rise disappears the inherent tendency to 'realise' the nominal profits, i.e. to convert part of the capital into income, will assert itself and lead to a fall even in the money value of capital.

But at this point we must stop. This final sketch of some of the conclusions that seem to arise was only meant to suggest some of the problems out of the wide field which opens up at the point where we left the main investigations. It seems that the approach to which it leads may ultimately help much to judge the significance of actual business practices, particularly the practices of joint stock companies, the different methods of financing and the Stock Exchange. The students of these fields have in the past had little enough help from the theory of capital. The ultimate clearing up of the issues raised in this article should go far to provide them with better tools.

NOTES

1. This article was sketched and most of it actually written a considerable time ago. I have delayed publication because I felt that a satisfactory treatment of the subject would require further investigation of some of the more general aspects of the theory of capital. But although I have since come to the conclusion that such a treatment, on the basis

of re-examination of the whole complex of questions raised by capitalistic methods of production, would make some reformulation of the argument of this article necessary, I do still feel that a discussion, which starts from the more conventional approach, and which is, therefore, intelligible apart from the setting that a more complete treatment would require, may not be quite useless.

2. Cf. K. Wicksell, *Lectures on Political Economy*, vol. i (London, 1934), p. 202.

3. This common assumption has recently been stated with particular emphasis by Professor Pigou in his latest article on the subject to be quoted later. He finds the basis of his deductions 'in the concept of capital as an entity capable of maintaining its quantity while altering its form and by its nature always drawn to those forms on which, so to speak, the sun of profit is at the time shining.' *Economic Journal*, June 1935, p. 239.

4. By his definition of income, which identifies it with actual consumption, I. Fisher seems to avoid the problem altogether. But it recurs in connection with his concept of earnings, which corresponds to the ordinary income concept. And although he does not provide an explicit answer, the solution of the problem which seems to be implied in his discussion, or at least the only solution which seems to be consistent with it, appears to be very much the same as that attempted in this paper.

5. Since this paper has been completed a further study of this problem has been published by Professor Pigou under the title 'Net Income and Capital Depletion' (*Economic Journal*, June 1935). Some references to this paper will be made in further footnotes.

6. *Economics of Welfare*, 3rd edn (1929), p. 45.

7. *Economics of Welfare*, 3rd edn, p. 47.

8. Ibid., 4th edn (1932), p. 45. In his latest article on the subject Professor Pigou goes even further and suggests that also physical changes which, while leaving a capital good as productive as ever, bring nearer the day of sudden and final breakdown, should be disregarded in the same way as the nearer approach of the day that will make it obsolete (*Economic Journal*, p. 238).

9. In his recent article (p. 240), Professor Pigou now suggests the same distinction.

10. *Economics of Welfare*, 4th edn, p. 47.

11. Ibid. In the latest version of his views, to which reference has been made in the preceding footnotes, Professor Pigou now regards it as necessary in order to make good the depletion of capital implied in the discarding of a capital good, that a quantity of resources be engaged in

the production of a new capital good which would suffice in actual current conditions of technique to reproduce the discarded element (loc. cit.,p. 239). Professor Pigou seems to overlook here the fact that 'in actual current conditions of technique' it may be much more expensive to reproduce the identical capital good than it either was when it was first produced or than it would be to replace it by a much more up-to-date instrument. It would certainly be much more expensive to reproduce a new 1926 model of a car to replace one that is worn out, than to replace it by a 1935 model.

12. Professor Pigou's views on the subject have recently been discussed in some detail in two Italian articles by A. M. Neuman (Osservazioni sul concetto di 'capitale inalterato' e sulla recente formulazione del prof. Pigou) and F. Vito (La nozione di lunghezza media del processo produttivo) in the *Revista Internazionale di Scienze Sociale e Discipline Ausiliare*, anno xli, serie iii, September 1933 (vol. iv, fasc. v) and by R. F. Fowler, *The Depreciation of Capital* (London 1934), pp. 14–21.

13. In the case of the comparison of different money incomes of a person or a group of persons, the result of a computation of an index number can be given a definite meaning, if the index number is constructed in such a way as to show that the one income would buy all that could be bought with the other income *plus* something else, or that it will not buy all that can be obtained with the other income. (On all this cf. G. Haberler, *Der Sinn der Indexzahlen, passim,* and J. M. Keynes, *A Treatise on Money*, book ii.) But it must appear very doubtful whether there are any assumptions on which price levels, not only of consumers' goods, but of all goods composing the stock of capital, i.e. of all goods of any description, can be given a similar meaning.

14. Professor Pigou's treatment of the problem in his recent article seems, however, to some extent rather a return to a much earlier materialist conception which sees in capital some physical substance whose magnitude is independent not only of its money value, but also of its serviceability.

15. It is, of course, not assumed that the capitalist under consideration has always possessed complete foresight, since in this case the problem of adaptation of his plans to an anticipated change would not arise. All that is assumed is that at a given moment all future changes relevant to his investments become known to him. The difficulties which any such assumption of foresight of all relevant changes involves are well known. The only way in which such foresight, not only of the real changes, but of all prices during the relevant period, is conceivable is that all these prices are actually fixed simultaneously in

advance on some single market, where not only present but also all future commodities that will become available during the relevant period are traded. This introduces the further difficulty that to fulfil the condition it would be necessary that the periods for which people foresee are the same for all individuals, and that the changes that will happen in the more distant future are disclosed periodically and simultaneously to all people. However, it is not necessary here to go further into all the difficulties raised by this assumption, which will be dropped later, difficulties which are by no means exhausted by those mentioned. Attention had to be drawn to them only in order to make us realise how unreal the assumption of perfect foresight is (even for the limited periods relevant to our problem).

16. Negative inventions, although apparently an absurd idea, are unfortunately by no means impossible. Losses of knowledge already possessed do occur, particularly in the field of economics, and the most glaring instance of this sort is, of course, the recrudescence of protectionism with its erection of negative railroads, to use Bastiat's very appropriate phrase.

17. Cf. Pigou, *Economics of Welfare*, 4th edn, p. 188, Robbins, *An Essay on the Nature and Significance of Economic Science* (1932), pp. 50 *et seq.,* and my inaugural address 'On the Trend of Economic Thinking,' *Economica*, May, 1933.

18. It is not possible to enter into a discussion of the distinction between capital-saving and labour-saving inventions. But it should be clear that at least the older concept of capital-saving inventions which was based on the idea that capital which in the past was used in the industry affected by the invention will in consequence become available for use elsewhere, assumed a kind of capital maintenance which will not occur in the real world. The part of the capital embodied in the now antiquated machinery will be lost at the same time as it becomes 'superfluous.'

19. In this connection it is hardly possible to draw a sharp distinction between the entrepreneur and capitalist.

20. It is of course possible that he regards himself as so much more clever than his competitors that he will count on being able to make permanently supernormal profits of this sort. To this extent he would be quite justified in regarding them as income.

21. The same applies, of course, in an even stronger degree to the assumption implied in this distinction that the activities which lead to such net increases of capital are in any way subject to a different set of determining influences from those which lead to a mere quantitative maintenance. This should always have been obvious from the mere

fact that when additions in this sense are being made (i.e. if capital increases in the usual terminology) this will always affect the concrete form of the new capital goods by which the old ones are replaced.

22. This does not, of course, affect the fundamental proposition that the additional saving is required to make an extension of the process of production possible compared with the time dimension that would be possible without this saving.

23. All this might apparently have been explained in simpler fashion by comparing the cost of the output of consumers' goods coming on the market during a given period with the expenditure on this output (or by comparing the share of all factors of production which have contributed to the output of a given period with the share of their income which is spent on the output), if it were not for the fact that the concept of cost (and, of course, income) is itself dependent on the concept of maintaining capital intact. This way of stating the relation would be adequate only if we count the cost (in terms of present consumption) which is required, *not* to keep capital intact in some quantitative sense, but to provide sources of so much future income as consumers want to buy at prices covering cost.

24. 'Preiserwartungen, monetäre Störungen und Fehlinvestitionen', *Nationalökonomisk Tidsskrift*, vol. 34 (1935).

25. Ricardo seems to have seen clearly the difficulties which exist in this connection when he wrote: 'The distress which proceeds from a revulsion of trade is often mistaken for that which accompanies a diminution of the national capital and a retrograde state of society; and it would perhaps be difficult to point out any marks by which they may be accurately distinguished.' *Principles*, ch. xix, *Works*, edn McCulloch, p. 160.

26. It is in this way, and in this way only, that during a boom the Stock Exchange is likely to 'absorb savings.'

234 - 57

920

[1940]

Friedrich Hayek, 'Socialist Calculation: The Competitive "Solution"', *Economica*, New Series, vol. 7 (1940), pp. 125–49.

In this paper Hayek responds definitively to an array of attempted solutions, advanced by socialist and other economists during the 1930s, to the problem of rational economic calculation under central planning. The paper first appeared in *Economica*, May 1940. It was reprinted as chapter nine in F. A. Hayek, *Individualism and Economic Order* (Routledge and Kegan Paul, 1949), pp. 181–208.

not in
Econ

29

Socialist Calculation III:
The Competitive 'Solution'[*]

FRIEDRICH HAYEK

1

Two chapters in the discussion of the economics of socialism may now be regarded as closed. The first deals with the belief that socialism will dispense entirely with calculation in terms of value and will replace it with some sort of calculation *in natura* based on units of energy or of some other physical magnitude. Although this view is not yet extinct and is still held by some scientists and engineers, it has been definitely abandoned by economists. The second closed chapter deals with the proposal that values, instead of being left to be determined by competition, should be found by a process of calculations carried out by the planning authority, which would use the technique of mathematical economics. With regard to this suggestion, Pareto (who, curiously enough, is sometimes quoted as holding this view) has already said what probably will remain the final word. After showing how a system of simultaneous equations can be used to explain what determines prices on a market, he adds:

'It may be mentioned here that this determination has by no means the purpose to arrive at a numerical calculation of prices. Let us make the most favourable assumption for such a calculation, let us assume that we have triumphed over all the difficulties of finding the data of the problem and that we know the *ophélimités* of all the different commodities for each individual, and all the conditions of production of all the commodities, etc. This is already an absurd hypothesis to make. Yet it is not sufficient to make the solution of the problem possible. We have seen that in the case of 100 persons and 700 commodities there will be 70,699 conditions (actually a great number of circumstances which we have so far neglected will

235

further increase that number); we shall therefore have to solve a system of 70,699 equations. This exceeds practically the power of algebraic analysis, and this is even more true if one contemplates the fabulous number of equations which one obtains for a population of forty millions and several thousand commodities. In this case the rôles would be changed: it would not be mathematics which would assist political economy, but political economy would assist mathematics. In other words, if one really could know all these equations, the only means to solve them which is available to human powers is to observe the practical solution given by the market.'[1]

In the present article we shall be concerned mainly with a third stage in this discussion, for which the issue has now been clearly defined by the elaboration of proposals for a competitive socialism by Professor Lange and Dr Dickinson. Since, however, the significance of the result of the past discussions is not infrequently represented in a way which comes very near to an inversion of the truth, and as at least one of the two books to be discussed is not quite free from this tendency, a few further remarks on the real significance of the past development seem not unnecessary.

The first point is connected with the nature of the original criticism directed against the more primitive conceptions of the working of a socialist economy which were current up to about 1920. The idea then current (and still advocated, e.g., by Otto Neurath) is well expressed by Engels in his *Anti-Dühring,* when he says that the social plan of production 'will be settled very simply, without the intervention of the famous "value".' It was against this generally held belief that N. G. Pierson, Ludwig von Mises, and others pointed out that, if the socialist community wanted to act rationally, its calculation would have to be guided by the same *formal* laws which applied to a capitalist society. It seems necessary especially to underline the fact that this was a point made by the critics of the socialist plans, since Professor Lange and particularly his editor[2] now seem inclined to suggest that the demonstration that the formal principles of economic theory apply to a socialist economy provides an answer to these critics. The fact is that it has never been denied by anybody, except socialists, that these formal principles *ought* to apply to a socialist society, and the question raised by Mises and others was not whether they ought to apply but whether they could in practice be applied in the absence of a market. It is therefore entirely beside the point when Lange and others quote Pareto and Barone as having shown that values in a socialist society would depend on essentially the same factors as in a competitive society. This, of course, had been shown long before, particularly by von Wieser. But none of these authors has made an attempt to show how these values, which a socialist society ought to use if it wants to act rationally, could be found, and Pareto, as we have seen, expressly denied that they could be determined by calculation.

It seems then that, on this point, the criticisms of the earlier socialist schemes have been so successful that the defenders, with few exceptions,[3] have felt compelled to appropriate the argument of their critics and have been forced to construct entirely new schemes of which nobody thought before. While against the older idea that it was possible to plan rationally without calculation in terms of value, it could be justly argued that they were logically impossible; the newer proposals designed to determine values by some process other than competition based on private property raise a problem of a different sort. But it is surely unfair to say, as Lange does, that the critics, because they deal in a new way with the new schemes evolved to meet the original criticism, 'have given up the essential point' and 'retreated to a second line of defense.'[4] Is this not rather a case of covering up their own retreat by creating confusion about the issue?

There is a second point on which Lange's presentation of the present state of the debate is seriously misleading. The reader of his study can hardly avoid the impression that the idea that values should and could be determined by using the technique of mathematical economics, i.e., by solving millions of equations, is a malicious invention of the critics, intended to throw ridicule on the efforts of modern socialist writers. The fact, which cannot be unknown to Lange, is, of course, that this procedure has more than once been seriously suggested by socialist writers as a solution of the difficulty – among others, by Dr Dickinson, who now, however, expressly withdraws this earlier suggestion.[5]

2

The third stage in the debate has now been reached with the proposal to solve the problems of determining values by the reintroduction of competition. When five years ago the present author tried to appraise the significance of these attempts,[6] it was necessary to rely on what could be gathered from oral discussion among socialist economists, since no systematic exposition of the theoretical bases of competitive socialism was then available. This gap has now been filled by the two books here to be discussed. The first contains a reprint of an essay by Lange, originally published in 1936 and 1937, together with an older article by the late Professor Taylor (dating from 1928), an introduction by the editor, B. E. Lippincott, which, in addition to a quite unnecessary restatement of Lange's argument in cruder terms, does much, by the unmeasured praise he bestows on this argument and the extravagant claims he advances for

237

it,[7] to prejudice the reader against the essentially scholarly piece of work that follows. Although written in a lively style and confining itself to the outlines of the subject, it does seriously grapple with some of the main difficulties in the field.

H. D. Dickinson's more recent book is a far more comprehensive survey of the field, proposing essentially the same solution.[8] It is unquestionably a book of great distinction, well organized, lucid, and concise, and should rapidly establish itself as the standard work on its subject. To the economist, the reading of the book provides indeed the rare pleasure of feeling that recent advances of economic theory have not been in vain and have even helped to reduce political differences to points which can be rationally discussed. Dr Dickinson himself would probably agree that he shares all his economics with – and indeed has learned most of it from – nonsocialist economists and that in his essential conclusion on the desirable economic policy of a socialist community he differs much more from most of his socialist colleagues than from 'orthodox' economists. This, together with the open-mindedness with which the author takes up and considers the arguments advanced by his opponents, makes discussion of his views a real pleasure. If the socialists, like the economists, are ready to accept his book as the most up-to-date general treatment of the economics of socialism from the socialist point of view, it should provide the basis for much fruitful further discussion.

As has already been mentioned, the main outlines of the solution offered by the two authors are essentially the same. They both rely to some extent on the competitive mechanism for the determination of relative prices. But they both refuse to let prices be determined directly in the market and propose instead a system of price-fixing by a central authority, where the state of the market of a particular commodity, i.e., the relation of demand to supply, merely serves as an indication to the authority whether the prescribed prices ought to be raised or lowered. Neither of the two authors explains why he refuses to go the whole hog and to restore the price mechanism in full. But as I happen to agree (although probably for different reasons) that this would be impracticable in a socialist community, we can leave this question aside for the moment and shall take it for granted that in such a society competition cannot play quite the same role as it does in a society based on private property and that, in particular, the rates at which commodities will be exchanged by the parties in the market will have to be decreed by the authority.

We shall leave the details of the proposed organization for later consideration and first consider the general significance of this solution under three aspects. We shall ask, first, how far this kind of socialist system still conforms to the hopes that were placed on the substitution of a planned socialist system for the chaos of competition; second, how far the proposed procedure is an answer to the main difficulty, and, finally, how far it is applicable.

The first and most general point can be dealt with fairly briefly, although it is not unimportant if one wants to see these new proposals in their proper light. It is merely a reminder of how much of the original claim for the superiority of planning over competition is abandoned if the planned society is now to rely for the direction of its industries to a large extent on competition. Until quite recently, at least, planning and competition used to be regarded as opposites, and this is unquestionably still true of nearly all planners except a few economists among them. I fear that the schemes of Lange and Dickinson will bitterly disappoint all those scientific planners who, in the recent words of B. M. S. Blackett, believe that 'the object of planning is largely to overcome the results of competition.'[9] This would be even more true if it were really possible to reduce the arbitrary elements in a competitive socialist system as much as is believed by Dickinson, who hopes that his 'libertarian socialism' 'may establish, for the first time in human history, an effective individualism.'[10] Unfortunately, as we shall see, this is not likely to be the case.

3

The second general question we must consider is how far the proposed method of central price-fixing, while leaving it to individual firms and consumers to adjust demand and supply to the given prices, is likely to solve the problem which admittedly cannot be solved by mathematical calculation. Here, I am afraid, I find it exceedingly difficult to understand the grounds on which such a claim is made. Lange as well as Dickinson asserts that even if the initial system of prices were chosen entirely at random, it would be possible by such a process of trial and error gradually to approach the appropriate system.[11] This seems to be much the same thing as if it were suggested that a system of equations, which was too complex to be solved by calculation within reasonable time and whose values were constantly changing, could be effectively tackled by arbitrarily inserting tentative values and then trying about until the proper solution was found. Or, to change the metaphor, the difference between such a system of regimented prices and a system of prices determined by the market seems to be about the same as that between an attacking army in which every unit and every man could move only by special command and by the exact distance ordered by headquarters and an army in which every unit and every man can take advantage of every opportunity offered to

239

them. There is, of course, no *logical* impossibility of conceiving a directing organ of the collective economy which is not only 'omnipresent and omniscient,' as Dickinson conceives it,[12] but also omnipotent, and which therefore would be in a position to change without delay every price by just the amount that is required. When, however, one proceeds to consider the actual apparatus by which this sort of adjustment is to be brought about, one begins to wonder whether anyone should really be prepared to suggest that, within the domain of practical possibility, such a system will ever even distantly approach the efficiency of a system where the required changes are brought about by the spontaneous action of the persons immediately concerned,.

We shall later, when we consider the proposed institutional setting, come back to the question of how this sort of mechanism is likely to function in practice. In so far as the general question is concerned, however, it is difficult to suppress the suspicion that this particular proposal has been born out of an excessive preoccupation with problems of the pure theory of stationary equilibrium. If in the real world we had to deal with approximately constant data, that is, if the problem were to find a price system which then could be left more or less unchanged for long periods, then the proposal under consideration would not be so entirely unreasonable. With given and constant data such a state of equilibrium could indeed be approached by the method of trial and error. But this is far from being the situation in the real world, where constant change is the rule. Whether and how far anything approaching the desirable equilibrium is ever reached depends entirely on the speed with which the adjustments can be made. The practical problem is not whether a particular method would eventually lead to a hypothetical equilibrium, but which method will secure the more rapid and complete adjustment to the daily changing conditions in different places and different industries. How great the difference in this respect would be between a method where prices are currently agreed upon by the parties of the market, and a method where these prices are decreed from above, is, of course, a matter of practical judgment. But I find it difficult to believe that anybody would doubt that in this respect the inferiority of the second method would be very great indeed.

The third general point is also one where I believe that preoccupation with concepts of pure economic theory has seriously misled both our authors. In this case it is the concept of perfect competition which apparently has made them overlook a very important field to which their method appears to be simply inapplicable. Wherever we have a market for a fairly standardized commodity, it is at least conceivable that all prices should be decreed in advance from above for a certain period. The situation is, however, very different with respect to commodities which cannot be standardized, and particularly for those which today are produced on individual orders, perhaps after invitation for tenders. A large part of the product of the 'heavy industries,' which, of course, would be the first to be socialized, belongs to this category. Much machinery, most buildings and ships, and many parts of other products are hardly ever produced for a market, but only on special contract. This does not mean that there may not be intense competition in the market for the products of these industries, although it may not be 'perfect competition' in the sense of pure theory; the fact is simply that in those industries identical products are rarely produced twice in short intervals; and the circle of producers who will compete as alternative suppliers in each instance will be different in almost every individual case, just as the circle of potential customers who will compete for the services of a particular plant will differ from week to week. What basis is there in all these cases for fixing prices of the product so as 'to equalize demand and supply'? If prices are here to be fixed by the central authority, they will have to be fixed in every individual case and on the basis on an examination by that authority of the calculations of all potential suppliers and all potential purchasers. It is hardly necessary to point out the various complications that will arise according as the prices are fixed before or after the prospective buyer has decided on the particular piece of machinery or building which he wants. Presumably it will be the estimates of the producer, which, before they are submitted to the prospective customer, will have to be approved by the authority. Is it not clear that in all these cases, unless the authority in effect takes all the functions of the entrepreneur on itself (i.e., unless the proposed system is abandoned and one of complete central direction substituted), the process of price-fixing would become either exceedingly cumbersome and the cause of infinite delay or a pure formality?

4

All these considerations appear to be relevant whatever particular form of organization is chosen. Before we go further, however, it becomes necessary to consider somewhat more in detail the concrete apparatus of industrial control which the two authors propose. The sketches they provide of the organization are fairly similar, although in this respect Lange gives us somewhat more information than Dickinson, who, for most of the problems of economic organization, refers us to the works of the Webbs and G. D. H. Cole.[13]

Both authors contemplate a socialist system in which the choice of occupation would be free and regulated mainly by the price mechanism (i.e., by the wage system) and in which the consumers also would be free to spend their incomes as they chose. Apparently both authors also want prices of consumers' goods to be fixed by the ordinary market processes (although Dickinson does not seem to be quite decided on this point)[14] and also to leave the determination of wages to the bargaining between the parties concerned.[15] Both also agree that for various reasons not the whole of industry should be socialized but that besides the socialized there should also remain a private sector, consisting of small enterprises run on essentially capitalistic lines. I find it difficult to agree with their belief that the existence of such a private sector parallel with the socialized sector creates no special difficulties. But as it would be difficult within the space of this article to deal adequately with this problem, we shall, for the purposes of this discussion, disregard the existence of the private sector and assume that the whole of industry is socialized.

The determination of all prices, other than those of consumers' goods and of wages, is the main task of the central economic authority – Lange's Central Planning Board or Dickinson's Supreme Economic Council. (We shall following Dickinson, henceforth refer to this body as the 'S.E.C.') As regards the technique of how particular prices are announced and changed, we get more information, although by no means enough, from Lange, while Dickinson goes more fully into the question of the considerations by which the S.E.C. should be guided in the fixing of prices. Both questions have a special importance, and they must be considered separately.

According to Lange, the S.E.C. would, from time to time, issue what, following Professor Taylor, he calls 'factor valuation tables,' that is, comprehensive lists of prices of all means of production (except labour).[16] These prices would have to serve as the sole basis for all transactions between different enterprises and the whole calculation of all the industries and plants during the period of their validity, and the managers must treat these prices as constant.[17] What we are not told, however, either by Lange or by Dickinson, is for what period these prices are to be fixed. This is one of the more serious obscurities in the exposition of both authors, a gap in their exposition which makes one almost doubt whether they have made a real effort to visualize their system at work. Are prices to be fixed for a definite period in advance, or are they to be changed whenever it seems desirable? F. M. Taylor seemed to suggest the former alternative when he wrote that the appropriateness of particular prices would show itself at the end of the 'productive period,'[18] and Lange, on at least one occasion, gives the same impression when he says that 'any price different from the equilibrium price would show at the end of the accounting period a surplus or shortage of the commodity in question.'[19] But on another occasion he says that 'adjustments of those prices would be constantly made,'[20] while Dickinson confines himself to stating that after, 'by a process of successive approximation,' 'a set of prices can ultimately be established in consonance with the principles of scarcity and substitution,' 'small adjustments will be sufficient to keep the system in equilibrium except in the case of major technical innovations or of big changes in consumers' tastes.'[21] Could the failure to understand the true function of the price mechanism, caused by the modern preoccupation with stationary equilibrium, be better illustrated?

While Dickinson is very uninformative on the mechanism of bringing price changes into effect, he goes much more fully than Lange into the considerations on which the S.E.C. would have to base their decisions. Unlike Lange, Dickinson is not satisfied with the S.E.C. merely watching the market and adjusting prices when an excess of demand or supply appears and then trying to find by experimentation a new equilibrium level. He rather wants the S.E.C. to use statistically established demand-and-supply schedules as a guide to determine the equilibrium prices. This is evidently a residue of his earlier belief in the possibility of solving the whole problem by a method of simultaneous equations. But, although he has now abandoned this idea (not because he regards it as impossible, since he still believes it could be done by solving merely 'two or three thousand simultaneous equations,'[22] but because he realizes that 'the data themselves, which would have to be fed into the equation-machine, are continually changing'), he still believes that the statistical determination of demand schedules would be useful as an aid to, if not as a substitute for, the method of trial and error and that it would be well worth while to try to establish the numerical values of the constants (*sic*) in the Walrasian system of equilibrium.

5

Whatever the method by which the S.E.C. fixes prices, and particularly whatever the periods at which and for which prices are announced, there are two points about which there can be little question: the changes will occur later than they would if prices were determined by the market parties, and there will be less differentiation between prices of commodities according to differences of quality and the circumstances of time and place. While with real competition price changes occur when the parties immediately concerned know that conditions have changed, the S.E.C. will be able to act only after the parties have reported, the reports have been verified, contradictions cleared up, etc.; and the new prices will become effective only after all the parties concerned have been notified, that is, either a date will have to be fixed in advance at which the new prices will become effective or the accounting will have to include an elaborate system by which every manager of production is constantly notified of the new prices upon which he has to base his calculations. Since in fact every manager would have to be informed constantly on many more prices than those of the commodities which he is actually using (at least of those of all possible substitutes), some sort of periodic publication of complete lists of all prices would be necessary. It is clear that, while economic efficiency demands that prices should be changed as promptly as possible, practicability would confine actual changes to intervals of fair length.

That the price-fixing process will be confined to establishing uniform prices for classes of goods and that therefore distinctions based on the special circumstances of time, place, and quality will find no expression in prices is probably obvious. Without some such simplification, the number of different commodities for which separate prices would have to be fixed would be practically infinite. This means, however, that the managers of production will have no inducement, and even no real possibility, to make use of special opportunities, special bargains, and all the little advantages offered by their special local conditions, since all these things could not enter into their calculations. It would also mean, to give only one other illustration of the consequences, that it would never be practicable to incur extra costs to remedy a sudden scarcity quickly, since a local or temporary scarcity could not affect prices until the official machinery had acted.

For both these reasons, because prices would have to be fixed for definite periods and because they would have to be fixed generically for categories of goods, a great many prices would be at most times in such a system substantially different from what they would be in a free system. This is very important for the functioning of the system. Lange makes great play with the fact that prices act merely as 'indices of terms on which alternatives are offered'[23] and that this 'parametric function of prices,'[24] by which prices are guiding the action of individual managers without being directly determined by them, will be fully preserved under such a system of fixing prices. As he himself points out, 'the determinateness of the accounting price holds, however, only if all discrepancies between demand and supply of a commodity are met by an appropriate change of price,' and for this reason 'rationing has to be excluded,' and 'the rule to produce at the minimum average cost has no significance unless prices represent the relative scarcity of the factors of production.'[25] In other words, prices will provide a basis for rational accounting only if they are such that at the ruling prices anyone can always sell as much or buy as much as he wishes or that anyone should be free to buy as cheaply or to sell as dearly as is made possible by the existence of a willing partner. If I cannot buy more of a factor so long as it is worth more to me than the price, and if I cannot sell a thing as soon as it is worth less to me than the price which somebody else would be willing to pay for it, prices are no longer indices of alternative opportunities.

We shall see the significance of this more clearly when we consider the action of the managers of the socialist industries. But, before we can consider their action, we must see who these people are and with what functions they are invested.

6

The nature of the industrial unit under separate management and of the factors which determine its size and the selection of its management is another point on which both our authors are deplorably vague. Lange seems to contemplate the organization of the different industries in the form of national trusts, although this important point is merely touched upon once when the National Coal Trust is mentioned as an example.[26] The very important and relevant question of what is *one* industry is nowhere discussed, but he apparently assumes that the various 'managers of production' will have monopolistic control of the particular commodities with which they are concerned. In general, Lange uses the term 'managers of production' exceedingly vaguely,[27] leaving it obscure whether the directors of a whole 'industry' or of a single unit are meant; but at critical points[28] a distinction between the managers of plant and the managers of a whole industry appears without any clear limitation of their functions. Dickinson is even more vague when he speaks of economic activities being 'decentralized and carried on by a large number of separate organs of collective economy' which will have 'their own nominal capital and their own profit and loss account and will be managed very much as separate enterprises under capitalism.'[29]

Whoever these managers of production are, their main function would appear to be the decision how much and how to produce on the basis of the prices fixed by the S.E.C. (and the prices of consumers' goods and wages determined by the market). They would be instructed by the S.E.C. to produce at the lowest possible average costs[30] and to expand production of the individual plants until marginal costs are equal to price.[31] According to Lange, the directors of the industries (as distinguished from the managers of individual plants) would have also the further task of seeing that the amount of equipment in the industry as a whole is so adjusted that 'the marginal cost incurred by the industry' in producing an output which 'can be sold or "accounted for" at a price which equals marginal cost' is the lowest possible.[32]

In this connection a special problem arises which unfortunately cannot be discussed here, since it raises questions of such difficulty and complexity that a separate article would be required. It concerns the case of decreasing marginal costs where, according to both our authors, the socialist industries would act differently from capitalist industry by expanding production until prices are equal, not to average, but to marginal costs. Although the argument employed possesses a certain specious plausibility, it can hardly be said even that the problem is adequately stated in either of the two books, still less that the conclusions drawn are convincing. Within the space available on this occasion, however, we can do no more than seriously question Dr Dickinson's assertion that 'under modern technical conditions, diminishing costs are far commoner than increasing costs' – a statement which in the context in which it occurs clearly refers to marginal costs.[33]

Here we shall confine ourselves to considering one question arising out of this part of the proposal – the question of how the S.E.C. will insure the actual carrying-out of the principle that prices are equalized to the lowest marginal cost at which the quantity concerned can be produced. The question which arises here is not 'merely' one of the loyalty or capacity of the socialist managers. For the purpose of this argument it may be granted that they will be as capable and as anxious to produce cheaply as the average capitalist entrepreneur. The problem arises because one of the most important forces which in a truly competitive economy brings about the reduction of costs to the minimum discoverable will be absent, namely, price competition. In the discussion of this sort of problem, as in the discussion of so much of economic theory at the present time, the question is frequently treated as if the cost curves were objectively given facts. What is forgotten is that the method which under given conditions is the cheapest is a thing which has to be discovered, and to be discovered anew, sometimes almost from day to day, by the entrepreneur, and that, in spite of the strong inducement, it is by no means regularly the established entrepreneur, the man in charge of the existing plant, who will discover what is the best method. The force which in a competititve society brings about the reduction of price to the lowest cost at which the quantity salable at that cost can be produced is the opportunity for anybody who knows a cheaper method to come in at his own risk and to attract customers by underbidding the other producers. But, if prices are fixed by the authority, this method is excluded. Any improvement, any adjustment, of the technique of production to changed conditions will be dependent on somebody's capacity of convincing the S.E.C. that the commodity in question can be produced cheaper and that therefore the price ought to be lowered. Since the man with the new idea will have no possibility of establishing himself by undercutting, the new idea cannot be proved by experiment until he has convinced the S.E.C. that his way of producing the thing is cheaper. Or, in other words, every calculation by an outsider who believes that he can do better will have to be examined and approved by the authority, which in this connection will have to take over all the functions of the entrepreneur.

7

Let us briefly consider a few of the problems arising out of the relations between the 'socialist managers of production' (whether of a plant or an industry) and the S.E.C. The manager's task is, as we have seen, to order production in such a way that his marginal costs are as low as possible and equal to price. How is he to do this and how is the fact of his success to be established? He has to take prices as given. This turns him into what has recently been called a pure 'quantity adjuster,' i.e., his decision is confined to the quantities of factors of production and the combination in which he uses them. But, as he has no means of inducing his suppliers to offer more (or to induce his purchasers to buy more) than they want to at the prescribed price, he will frequently be simply unable to carry out his instructions; or at least, if he cannot get more of a material required at the prescribed price, the only way for him, for example, to expand production so as to make his cost equal to price, would be to use inferior substitutes or to employ other uneconomic methods; and, when he cannot sell at the prescribed price and until the price is lowered by decree, he will have to stop production where under true competition he would have lowered his prices.

Another great difficulty arising out of the periodic price changes by decree is the problem of anticipations of future price movements. Lange, somewhat too bravely, cuts this Gordian knot by prescribing that 'for purposes of accounting, prices must be treated as constant, as they are treated by entrepreneurs on a competitive market' (!). Does that mean that the managers, although they know for certain that a particular price will have to be raised or lowered, must act as if they did not know? Clearly this will not do. But if they are free to meet expected price movements by anticipatory action, are they to be allowed to take advantage of the administrative delays in making price changes effective? Who is to be responsible for losses caused by wrongly timed or wrongly directed price changes?

247

Closely connected with this problem is another question to which we also get no answer. Both our authors speak about 'marginal costs' as if they were independent of the period for which the manager can plan. Clearly, actual costs depend in many instances, as much as on anything, on buying at the right time. In no sense can costs during any period be said to depend solely on prices during that period. They depend as much on whether these prices have been correctly foreseen as on the views that are held about future prices. Even in the very short run costs will depend on the effects which current decisions will have on future productivity. Whether it is economical to run a machine hard and to neglect maintenance, whether to make major adjustments to a given change in demand or to carry on as well as possible with the existing organization – in fact, almost every decision on how to produce – now depends at least in part on the views held about the future. But, while the manager clearly must hold some views on these questions, he can hardly be held responsible for anticipating future changes correctly if these changes depend entirely on the decision of the authority.

The success of the individual manager will, however, to a large extent not only depend on the action of the planning authority; he will also have to satisfy the same authority that he has done as well as was possible. Either beforehand, or more likely retrospectively, all his calculations will have to be examined and approved by the authority. This will not be a perfunctory auditing, directed to find out whether his costs have actually been what he says they have been. It will have to ascertain whether they have been the lowest possible ones. This means that the control will have to consider not only what he actually did but also what he might have done and ought to have done. From the point of view of the manager it will be much more important that he should always be able to prove that in the light of the knowledge which he possessed the decision actually taken was the right one than that he should prove to be right in the end. If this will not lead to the worst forms of bureaucracy, I do not know what will.

This brings us to the general question of the responsibility of the managers. Dickinson clearly sees that 'responsibility means in practice financial responsibility' and that unless the manager 'bears responsibility for losses as well as for profits he will be tempted to embark upon all sorts of risky experiments on the bare chance that one of them will turn out successful.'[34] This is a difficult problem with managers who have no property of their own. Dickinson hopes to solve it by a system of bonuses. This may indeed be sufficient to prevent managers from taking too great risks. But is not the real problem the opposite one – that managers will be afraid of taking risks if, when the venture does not come off, it will be somebody else who will afterward decide whether they have been justified in embarking on it? As Dickinson himself points out, the principle would be that, 'although the making of profits is not necessarily a sign of success, the making of losses is a sign of failure.'[35] Need one say more about the effects of such a system on all activities involving risk? It is difficult to conceive how under these circumstances any of the necessary speculative activities involving risk-bearing could be left to managerial initiative. But the alternative is to fall back for them on that system of strict central planning to avoid which the whole system has been evolved.

8

All this is even more true when we turn to the whole problem of new investments, that is, to all the questions which involve changes in the size (i.e., the capital) of the managerial units, whether they involve net changes in the total supply of capital or not. Up to a point it is possible to divide this problem into two parts – the decisions about the distribution of the available capital supply and the decisions about the rate at which capital is to be accumulated – although it is dangerous to carry this division too far, since the decision about how much is to be saved is necessarily also a decision about which needs for capital are to be satisfied and which are not. Both our authors agree that, as regards the problem of the distribution of capital between industries and plants, the interest mechanism should as far as possible be retained but that the decision of how much to save and invest would necessarily have to be arbitrary.[36]

Now, however strong may be the desire to rely on the interest mechanism for the distribution of capital, it is fairly obvious that the market for capital can in no sense be a free market. While for Lange the rate of interest is also 'simply determined by the condition that the demand for capital is equal to the amount available,'[37] Dr Dickinson takes great pains to show how the S.E.C. will, on the basis of the alternative plans of activity drawn up by the different undertakings, construct an aggregate demand schedule for capital which will enable it to determine that rate of interest at which the demand for capital will equal supply. The ingenuity and the astounding trust in the practicability of even the most complicated constructions which Dickinson displays in this connection may be illustrated by his statement that in a certain case 'it will be necessary to establish a provisional rate of interest, then to allow the different organs of collective economy to re-contract with each other on the basis of this provisional rate, and so to draw up their final demand schedule for capital.'[38]

All this, however, does not meet the main difficulty. If, indeed, it were

249

possible to accept at their face value the statements of all the individual managers and would-be managers about how much capital they could with advantage use at various rates of interest, some such scheme as this might appear feasible. It cannot be repeated too often, however, that the planning authority cannot be conceived 'simply as a kind of superbank which lends the available funds to the highest bidder. It would lend to persons who have no property of their own. It would therefore bear all the risk and would have no claim for a definite amount of money as a bank has. It would simply have rights of ownership over all real resources. Nor can its decisions be confined to the redistribution of free capital in the form of money and perhaps of land. It would have to decide whether a particular plant or piece of machinery should be left further to the entrepreneur who has used it in the past, at his valuation, or whether it should be transferred to another who promises a higher return for it.'

These sentences are taken from the essay in which the present author discussed five years ago the 'possibility of real competition under socialism.'[39] At that time such systems had been only vaguely discussed, and one could hope to find an answer when systematic expositions of the new ideas became available. But it is most disappointing to find no answer whatever to these problems in the two books now under discussion. While throughout the two works claims are made about how beneficial the control of investment activity would be in many respects, no indication is given of how this control is to be exercised and of how the responsibilities are to be divided between the planning authorities and the managers of the 'competing' industrial units. Such statements as we find, as, for instance, that 'because the managers of socialist industry will be governed in some choices by the direction laid down by the planning authority, it does not follow that they will have no choice at all,'[40] are singularly unhelpful. All that seems to be fairly clear is that the planning authority will be able to exercise its function of controlling and directing investment only if it is in a position to check and repeat all the calculations of the entrepreneur.

It seems that here the two writers are unconsciously led to fall back on the earlier beliefs in the superiority of a centrally directed system over a competitive system and to console themselves with the hope that the 'omnipresent, omniscient organ of the collective economy'[41] will possess at least as much knowledge as the individual entrepreneurs and will therefore be in a position to make the decisions at least as good if not better than that in which the entrepreneurs are now. As I have tried to show on another occasion, it is the main merit of real competition that through it use is made of knowledge divided between many persons which, if it were to be used in a centrally directed economy, would all have to enter the single plan.[42] To assume that all this knowledge would be automatically in the possession of the planning authority seems to me to miss the main point. It is not quite clear whether Lange means to assert that the planning authority will have all this information when he says that 'the administrators of a socialist economy will have exactly the same knowledge, or lack of knowledge, of the production functions as the capitalist entrepreneurs have.[43] If the 'administrators of a socialist economy' here means merely all the managers of the units as well as of the central organization taken together, the statement can, of course, be readily accepted but does in no way solve the problem. But, if it is intended to convey that all this knowledge can be effectively used by the planning authority in drawing up the plan, it is merely begging the whole question and seems to be based on the 'fallacy of composition.'[44]

On the whole of this all-important question of the direction of new investment and all that it involves, the two studies do not really give any new information. The problem remains where it was five years ago, and I can confine myself on this point to repeating what I said then: 'The decision about the amount of capital to be given to an individual entrepreneur and the decisions thereby involved concerning the size of the individual firm under a single control are in effect decisions about the most appropriate combination of resources. It will rest with the central authority to decide whether one plant located at one place should expand rather than another plant situated elsewhere. All this involves planning on the part of the central authority on much the same scale as if it were actually running the enterprise. While the individual entrepreneur would in all probability be given some definite contractual tenure for managing the plant intrusted to him, all new investments will be necessarily centrally directed. This division in the disposition over the resources would then simply have the effect that neither the entrepreneur nor the central authority would be really in a position to plan and that it would be impossible to assess the responsibility for mistakes. To assume that it is possible to create conditions of full competition without making those who are responsible for the decisions pay for their mistakes seems to be pure illusion. It will be at best a system of quasi-competition where the persons really responsible will not be the entrepreneur but the official who approves his decisions and where in consequence all the difficulties will arise in connection with freedom of initiative and the assessment of responsibility which are usually associated with bureaucracy.'[45]

9

The question of how far a socialist system can avoid extensive central direction of economic activity is of great importance quite apart from its

251

relation to economic efficiency; it is crucial for the question of how much personal and political freedom can be preserved in such a system. Both authors show a reassuring awareness of the dangers to personal freedom which a centrally planned system would involve and seem to have evolved their competitive socialism partly in order to meet this danger. Dr Dickinson even goes so far as to say that 'capitalist planning can exist only on the basis of fascism' and that in the hands of an irresponsible controler even socialist planning '*could* be made the greatest tyranny the world has ever seen.'[46] But he and Lange believe that their competitive socialism will avoid this danger.

Now, if competitive socialism could really rely for the direction of production largely on the effects of consumers' choice as reflected in the price system, and if the cases where the authority will have to decide what is to be produced and how were made the exception rather than the rule, this claim would be to a large extent substantiated. How far is this really the case? We have already seen that, with the retention of the control over investment, the central authority wields most extensive powers over the direction of production – much more extensive, indeed, than is easily possible to show without making this discussion unduly long. To this have yet to be added, however, a further number of arbitrary elements of which Dickinson himself gives a quite substantial although by no means complete list.[47] There is, in the first instance, the 'allocation of resources between present and future consumption,' which, as we have already seen, always involves a decision about what particular needs will be satisfied. There is, second, the need for arbitrary decision in respect to the 'allocation of resources between communal and individual consumption,' which, in view of the great extension of the 'division of communal consumption' which he envisages, means that another very large part of the resources of the society is put outside the control of the price mechanism and made subject to purely authoritarian decision. Dickinson expressly adds to this only 'the choice between work and leisure' and the 'geographical planning and the pricing of land'; but at other points of his exposition further questions emerge on which he wants effective planning in order to correct the results of the market. But, although he (and still more so Lange) frequently hints at the possibilities of 'correcting' the results of the price mechanism by judicious interference, this part of the program is nowhere clearly worked out.

What our authors here have in mind perhaps comes out clearest in Dickinson's attitude toward the problem of wage changes: 'If wages are too low in any one industry, it is the duty of the planning organ to adjust prices and quantities produced, so as to yield equal wages to work of equal skill, responsibility, and difficulty in every industry.'[48] Apparently here the price mechanism and the free choice of occupation are not to be relied upon. Later we learn that, although 'unemployment in any particular job affords a prima facie case for lowering the standard wage,'[49] a lowering of wages is objectionable 'on social grounds, because a lowering in wages ... causes discontent; on economic grounds, because it perpetuates an uneconomic allocation of labor to different occupations.' (How?) Therefore, 'as invention and improved organization makes less labor necessary to satisfy human wants, society should set itself to discover new wants to satisfy.'[50] 'The powerful engine of propaganda and advertisement, employed by public organs of education and enlightenment instead of by the hucksters and panders of private profit-making industry, could divert demand into socially desirable directions while preserving the subjective impression [sic] of free choice.'[51]

When we add to this, and many other similar points where Dickinson wants his S.E.C. to exercise a paternalistic control,'[52] the fact that it will be necessary to co-ordinate national production 'with a general plan of exports and imports,'[53] since free trade 'is inconsistent with the principles of collectivism,'[54] it becomes fairly evident that there will be precious little economic activity which will not be more or less immediately guided by arbitrary decisions. In fact, Dickinson expressly contemplates a situation where 'the state, through a definite planning organ, makes itself responsible for the consideration of economic activity as a whole' and even adds that this destroys the 'illusion' maintained in a capitalist society that 'the division of the product is governed by forces as impersonal and inevitable as those which govern the weather.'[55] This can mean only that, with most other planners, he himself thinks of production in his system as one which is largely directed by conscious and arbitrary decisions. Yet, in spite of this extensive role which arbitrary decisions are to play in his system, he is confident (and the same applies to Lange) that his system will not degenerate into an authoritarian despotism.

Dickinson merely mentions the argument that 'even if a socialist planner wished to realize freedom he could not do so and remain a planner,' yet the answer he gives makes one doubt whether he has quite seen on what considerations this argument is based. His answer is merely that 'a plan can always be changed.'[56] But this is not the point. The difficulty is that, in order to plan at all on an extensive scale, a much more extensive agreement among the members of the society about the relative importance of the various needs is required than will normally exist and that, in consquence, this agreement will have to be brought about and a common scale of values will have to be imposed by force and propaganda. I have developed this argument at length elsewhere, and I have not space here to restate it.[57] The thesis I have developed there – that socialism is bound to become totalitarian – now seems to receive support from the most unexpected quarters. This at least appears to be the meaning when Max Eastman, in a recent book on Russia, states that 'Stalinism *is* socialism, in the sense of being an inevitable, although unforeseen, political and cultural accompaniment.'[58]

In fact, although he does not seem to see it, Dickinson himself, in the concluding passages of his book, makes a statement which comes very much to the same thing. 'In a socialist society,' he says, 'the distinction, always artificial, between economics and politics will break down; the economic and the political machinery of society will fuse into one.'[59] This is, of course, precisely the authoritarian doctrine preached by Nazis and Fascists. The distinction breaks down because in a planned system all economic questions become political questions, because it is no longer a question of reconciling as far as possible individual views and desires but one of imposing a single scale of values, the 'social goal' of which socialists ever since the time of Saint-Simon have been dreaming. In this respect it seems that the schemes of an authoritarian socialist, from those of Professor Hogben and Lewis Mumford, whom Dickinson mentions as an example,[60] to those of Stalin and Hitler, are much more realistic and consistent than the beautiful and idyllic picture of the 'libertarian socialism' in which Dickinson believes.

10

There can be no better testimony of the intellectual quality of the two books under discussion than that, after having written about them at such length, one is conscious of having merely scratched the surface of the problems raised by them. But an examination in greater detail would clearly exceed the scope of an article; and, since many of the doubts which are left with the reader concern points which are not answered in the two books, an adequate treatment of the subject would require another book even longer than those discussed. There are, however, also important problems which are discussed at some length, particularly in Dickinson's book, which we have scarcely been able to mention. This applies not only to the difficult problem of the combination of a private sector with the socialized sector, which both authors propose, but also to such important problems as the international relations of a socialist community and to the problems of monetary policy, to which Dickinson devotes a very brief, and on the whole least satisfactory, section.

A fuller discussion would also have to point out various passages in the argument of both authors where apparently residues of earlier beliefs or views which are purely matters of political creed creep in and which strike one as curiously inconsistent with the plane of the rest of the discussion. This applies, for instance, to Dickinson's repeated references to class conflict and exploitation or to his gibes at the wastes of competition,[61] and to much of Lange's interesting section on the 'economist's case for socialism,' where he employs arguments that seem to be of somewhat questionable validity.

These, however, are minor points. On the whole, the books are so thoroughly unorthodox from a socialist point of view that one rather wonders whether their authors have not retained too little of the traditional trappings of socialist argument to make their proposals acceptable to socialists who are not economists. As courageous attempts to face some of the real difficulties and completely to remold socialist doctrine in order to meet them they deserve our gratitude and respect. Whether the solution offered will appear particularly practicable, even to socialists, may perhaps be doubted. To those who, with Dickinson, wish to create 'for the first time in human history, an effective individualism,'[62] a different path will probably appear more promising.

NOTES

* The two books with which this chapter is mainly concerned, Oskar Lange and Fred M. Taylor, *On the Economic Theory of Socialism*, ed. B. E. Lippincott (Minneapolis, 1938), and H. D. Dickinson, *Economics of Socialism* (Oxford, 1939), will be referred to throughout this chapter as 'LT' (Lange-Taylor) and 'D' (Dickinson), respectively.

1. V. Pareto, *Manuel d'economie politique*, 2nd edn (1927), pp. 233–4.
2. See B. E. Lippincott in LT, p. 7.
3. The most notable exception is Dr M. Dobb. See his *Political Economy and Capitalism* (1937), ch. viii, and his review of Professor Lange's book in the *Modern Quarterly* (1939).
4. LT, p. 63.
5. D, p. 104, and K. Tisch, *Wirtschaftsrechnung und Verteilung im zentralistisch organisierten sozialistischen Gemeinwesen* (1932).
6. In *Collectivist Economic Planning* (London, 1935), essay on 'The Present State of the Debate,' reprinted above, ch. ix.
7. Dr Lange's essay is described as the 'first writing to mark an advance on Barone's contribution' and to show by 'irrefutable' argument the 'evident feasibility and superiority' of a socialist system (LT, pp. 13, 24, 37).

8. It is a curious fact that Dr Dickinson nowhere in his book (except in the Bibliography) refers to Professor Lange's work.
9. See Sir Daniel Hall and others, *The Frustration of Science* (London, 1935), p. 142.
10. D, p. 26.
11. LT, pp. 70 and 86; D, pp. 103 and 113.
12. D, p. 191.
13. D, p. 30.
14. LT, p. 78; D, p. 60.
15. LT, p. 78; D, p. 126.
16. LT, pp. 46 and 52.
17. LT, p. 81.
18. LT, p. 53.
19. LT, p. 82.
20. LT, p. 86.
21. D, pp. 100, 102–3.
22. D, p. 104.
23. LT, p. 78.
24. LT, pp. 70 and 86.
25. LT, pp. 93–4.
26. LT, p. 78.
27. LT, pp. 75, 79, and 86.
28. LT, pp. 76 and 82 n.
29. D, p. 213.
30. LT, p. 75.
31. LT, p. 76; D, p. 107.
32. LT, p. 77.
33. D, p. 108.
34. D, p. 214.
35. D, p. 219.
36. LT, p. 85; D, pp. 80 and 205.
37. LT, p. 84.
38. D, p. 83 n.
39. *Collectivist Economic Planning* (1935), pp. 232–7; see above pp. 172–6. [This reference is to Hayek's *Individualism and Economic Order* (1949) in which the present paper was reprinted. – Ed.]
40. D, p. 217.
41. D, p. 191.
42. See the article on 'Economics and Knowledge,' reprinted above as ch. ii. [This reference is to Hayek's *Individualism and Economic Order* (1949) in which the present paper was reprinted. – Ed.]
43. LT, p. 61.

44. Another and even worse instance of this fallacy occurs in Professor Lippincott's introduction to the essays of Professor Lange and Taylor, when he argues that 'there can be no doubt that the Central Planning Board would exercise great power, but would it be any greater than that exercised collectively by private boards of directors? Because the decisions of private boards are made here and there, this does not mean that the consumer does not feel their collective impact, even though it may take a depression to make him aware of it.'

45. *Collectivist Economic Planning*, p. 237; see above pp. 175–6. [This reference is to Hayek's *Individualism and Economic Order* (1949) in which the present paper was reprinted. – Ed.]

46. D, pp. 22 and 227.

47. D, p. 205.

48. D, p. 21.

49. D, p. 127.

50. D, p. 131.

51. D, p. 32.

52. Cf., e.g., the passage (D, p. 52) where Dickinson speaks about the 'people who will not pay voluntarily beforehand for what they are only too glad to have once they have it.'

53. D, p. 169.

54. D, p. 176.

55. D, p. 21.

56. D, pp. 227–8.

57. See *Freedom and the Economic System*, 'Public Policy Pamphlet' no. 29 (Chicago: University of Chicago Press, 1939), and, since this article first appeared, in *The Road to Serfdom* (Chicago, 1944).

58. *Stalin's Russia and the Crisis in Socialism* (New York, 1940).

59. D, p. 235.

60. D, p. 25.

61. D, pp. 22 and 94.

62. D, p. 26.

Friedrich Hayek, 'The Use of Knowledge in Society', *American Economic Review* vol. 35 (1945), pp. 519–30.

This Hayekian classic was first published in *American Economic Review* in September 1945. It was reprinted in *Individualism and Economic Order*, chapter four, pp. 77–91. It marked a decisive advance in Hayek's understanding of the economic process, and implied almost complete rejection of standard approaches to welfare economics. This paper has had an important influence on the contemporary resurgence of interest in the Austrian tradition, especially since Hayek was awarded the Nobel Prize in 1974.

0112
0200

30

The Use of Knowledge in Society

FRIEDRICH HAYEK

1

What is the problem we wish to solve when we try to construct a rational economic order? On certain familiar assumptions the answer is simple enough. *If* we possess all the relevant information, *if* we can start out from a given system of preferences, and *if* we command complete knowledge of available means, the problem which remains is purely one of logic. That is, the answer to the question of what is the best use of the available means is implicit in our assumptions. The conditions which the solution of this optimum problem must satisfy have been fully worked out and can be stated best in mathematical form: put at their briefest, they are that the marginal rates of substitution between any two commodities or factors must be the same in all their different uses.

This, however, is emphatically *not* the economic problem which society faces. And the economic calculus which we have developed to solve this logical problem, though an important step toward the solution of the economic problem of society, does not yet provide an answer to it. The reason for this is that the 'data' from which the economic calculus starts are never for the whole society 'given' to a single mind which could work out the implications and can never be so given.

The peculiar character of the problem of a rational economic order is determined precisely by the fact that the knowledge of the circumstances of which we must make use never exists in concentrated or integrated form but solely as the dispersed bits of incomplete and frequently contradictory knowledge which all the separate individuals possess. The economic problem of society is thus not merely a problem of how to allocate 'given' resources – if 'given' is taken to mean given to a single mind which deliberately solves the problem set by these 'data.' It is rather a problem of

259

how to secure the best use of resources known to any of the members of society, for ends whose relative importance only these individuals know. Or, to put it briefly, it is a problem of the utilization of knowledge which is not given to anyone in its totality.

This character of the fundamental problem has, I am afraid, been obscured rather than illuminated by many of the recent refinements of economic theory, particularly by many of the uses made of mathematics. Though the problem with which I want primarily to deal in this paper is the problem of a rational economic organization, I shall in its course be led again and again to point to its close connections with certain methodological questions. Many of the points I wish to make are indeed conclusions toward which diverse paths of reasoning have unexpectedly converged. But, as I now see these problems, this is no accident. It seems to me that many of the current disputes with regard to both economic theory and economic policy have their common origin in a misconception about the nature of the economic problem of society. This misconception in turn is due to an erroneous transfer to social phenomena of the habits of thought we have developed in dealing with the phenomena of nature.

2

In ordinary language we describe by the word 'planning' the complex of interrelated decisions about the allocation of our available resources. All economic activity is in this sense planning; and in any society in which many people collaborate, this planning, whoever does it, will in some measure have to be based on the knowledge which, in the first instance, is not given to the planner but to somebody else, which somehow will have to be conveyed to the planner. The various ways in which the knowledge on which people base their plans is communicated to them is the crucial problem for any theory explaining the economic process, and the problem of what is the best way of utilizing knowledge initially dispersed among all the people is at least one of the main problems of economic policy – or of designing an efficient economic system.

The answer to this question is closely connected with that other question which arises here, that of *who* is to do the planning. It is about this questions that all the dispute about 'economic planning' centres. This is not a dispute about whether planning is to be done or not. It is a dispute as to whether planning is to be done centrally, by one authority for the whole economic system, or is to be divided among many individuals. Planning in the specific sense in which the term is used in contemporary controversy necessarily means central planning – direction of the whole economic system according to one unified pan. Competition, on the other hand, means decentralized planning by many separate persons. The half-way house between the two, about which many people talk but which few like when they see it, is the delegation of planning to organized industries, or, in other words, monopolies.

Which of these systems is likely to be more efficient depends mainly on the question under which of them we can expect that fuller use will be made of the existing knowledge. This, in turn, depends on whether we are more likely to succeed in putting at the disposal of a single central authority all the knowledge which ought to be used but which is initially dispersed among many different individuals, or in conveying to the individuals such additional knowledge as they need in order to enable them to dovetail their plans with those of others.

3

It will at once be evident that on this point the question will be different with respect to different kinds of knowledge. The answer to our question will therefore largely turn on the relative importance of the different kinds of knowledge: those more likely to be at the disposal of particular indi-viduals and those which we should with greater confidence expect to find in the possession of an authority made up of suitably chosen experts. If it is today so widely assumed that the latter will be in a better position, this is because one kind of knowledge, namely, scientific knowledge, occupies now so prominent a place in the public imagination that we tend to forget that it is not the only kind that is relevant. It may be admitted that, as far as scientific knowledge is concerned, a body of suitably chosen experts may be in the best position to command all the best knowledge available – though this is of course merely shifting the difficulty to the problem of selecting the experts. What I wish to point out is that, even assuming that this problem can be readily solved, it is only a small part of the wider problem.

Today it is almost heresy to suggest that scientific knowledge is not the sum of all knowledge. But a little reflection will show that there is beyond question a body of very important but unorganized knowledge which cannot possibly be called scientific in the sense of knowledge of general rules: the knowledge of the particular circumstances of time and place. It is with respect to this that practically every individual has some advantage over all others because he possesses unique information of which beneficial use might be made, but of which use can be made only if the decisions depending on it are left to him or are made with his active co-operation.

We need to remember only how much we have to learn in any occupation after we have completed our theoretical training, how big a part of our working life we spend learning particular jobs, and how valuable an asset in all walks of life is knowledge of people, of local conditions, and of special circumstances. To know of and put to use a machine not fully employed, or somebody's skill which could be better utilized, or to be aware of a surplus stock which can be drawn upon during an interruption of supplies, is socially quite as useful as the knowledge of better alternative techniques. The shipper who earns his living from using otherwise empty or half-filled journeys of tramp-steamers, or the estate agent whose whole knowledge is almost exclusively one of temporary opportunities, or the *arbitrageur* who gains from local differences of commodity prices – are all performing eminently useful functions based on special knowledge of circumstances of the fleeting moment not known to others.

It is a curious fact that this sort of knowledge should today be generally regarded with a kind of contempt and that anyone who by such knowledge gains an advantage over somebody better equipped with theoretical or technical knowledge is thought to have acted almost disreputably. To gain an advantage from better knowledge of facilities of communication or transport is sometimes regarded as almost dishonest, although it is quite as important that society make use of the best opportunities in this respect as in using the latest scientific discoveries. This prejudice has in a consider-able measure affected the attitude toward commerce in general compared with that toward production. Even economists who regard themselves as definitely immune to the crude materialist fallacies of the past constantly commit the same mistake where activities directed toward the acquisition of such practical knowledge are concerned – apparently because in their scheme of things all such knowledge is supposed to be 'given.' The common idea now seems to be that all such knowledge should as a matter of course be readily at the command of everybody, and the reproach of irrationality leveled against the existing economic order is frequently based on the fact that it is not so available. This view disregards the fact that the method by which such knowledge can be made as widely available as possible is precisely the problem to which we have to find an answer.

4

If it is fashionable today to minimize the importance of the knowledge of the particular circumstances of time and place, this is closely connected with the smaller importance which is now attached to change as such. Indeed, there are few points on which the assumptions made (usually only implicitly) by the 'planners' differ from those of their opponents as much as with regard to the significance and frequency of changes which will make substantial alterations of production plans necessary. Of course, if detailed economic plans could be laid down for fairly long periods in advance and then closely adhered to, so that no further economic decisions of importance would be required, the task of drawing up a comprehensive plan governing all economic activity would be much less formidable.

It is, perhaps, worth stressing that economic problems arise always and only in consequence of change. As long as things continue as before, or at least as they were expected to, there arise no new problems requiring a decision, no need to form a new plan. The belief that changes, or at least day-to-day adjustments, have become less important in modern times implies the contention that economic problems also have become less important. This belief in the decreasing importance of change is, for that reason, usually held by the same people who argue that the importance of economic considerations has been driven into the background by the growing importance of technological knowledge.

Is it true that, with the elaborate apparatus of modern production, economic decisions are required only at long intervals, as when a new factory is to be erected or a new process to be introduced? Is it true that, once a plant has been built, the rest is all more or less mechanical, determined by the character of the plant, and leaving little to be changed in adapting to the ever changing circumstances of the moment?

The fairly widespread belief in the affirmative is not, as far as I can ascertain, borne out by the practical experience of the businessman. In a competitive industry at any rate – and such an industry alone can serve as a test – the task of keeping cost from rising requires constant struggle, absorbing a great part of the energy of the manager. How easy it is for an inefficient manager to dissipate the differentials on which profitability rests and that it is possible, with the same technical facilities, to produce with a great variety of costs are among the commonplaces of business experience which do not seem to be equally familiar in the study of the economist. The very strength of the desire, constantly voiced by producers and engineers, to be allowed to proceed untrammeled by considerations of money costs, is eloquent testimony to the extent to which these factors enter into their daily work.

One reason why economists are increasingly apt to forget about the constant small changes which make up the whole economic picture is probably their growing preoccupation with statistical aggregates, which show a very much greater stability than the movements of the detail. The comparative stability of the aggregates cannot, however, be accounted for – as the statisticians occasionally seem to be inclined to do – by the 'law of large numbers' or the mutual compensation of random changes. The number of elements with which we have to deal is not large enough for such accidental forces to produce stability. The continuous flow of goods and services is maintained by constant deliberate adjustments, by new dispositions made every day in the light of circumstances not known the day before, by B stepping in at once when A fails to deliver. Even the large and highly mechanized plant keeps going largely because of an environment upon which it can draw for all sorts of unexpected needs: tiles for its roof, stationery for its forms, and all the thousand and one kinds of equipment in which it cannot be self-contained and which the plans for the operation of the plant require to be readily available in the market.

This is, perhaps, also the point where I should briefly mention the fact that the sort of knowledge with which I have been concerned is knowledge of the kind which by its nature cannot enter into statistics and therefore cannot be conveyed to any central authority in statistical form. The statistics which such a central authority would have to use would have to be arrived at precisely by abstracting from minor differences between the things, by lumping together, as resources of one kind, items which differ as regards location, quality, and other particulars, in a way which may be very significant for the specific decision. It follows from this that central planning based on statistical information by its nature cannot take direct account of these circumstances of time and place and that the central planner will have to find some way or other in which the decisions depending on them can be left to the 'man on the spot.'

5

If we can agree that the economic problem of society is mainly one of rapid adaptation to changes in the particular circumstances of time and place, it would seem to follow that the ultimate decisions must be left to the people who are familiar with these circumstances, who know directly of the relevant changes and of the resources immediately available to meet them. We cannot expect that this problem will be solved by first communicating all this knowledge to a central board which, after integrating all knowledge, issues its orders. We must solve it by some form of decentralization. But this answers only part of our problem. We need decentralization because only thus can we insure that the knowledge of the particular circumstances of time and place will be promptly used. But the 'man on the spot' cannot decide solely on the basis of his limited but intimate knowledge of the facts of his immediate surroundings. There still remains the problem of communicating to him such further information as he needs to fit his decisions into the whole pattern of changes of the larger economic system.

How much knowledge does he need to do so successfully? Which of the events which happen beyond the horizon of his immediate knowledge are of relevance to his immediate decision, and how much of them need he know?

There is hardly anything that happens anywhere in the world that *might* not have an effect on the decision he ought to make. But he need not know of these events as such, nor of *all* their effects. It does not matter for him *why* at the particular moment more screws of one size than of another are wanted, *why* paper bags are more readily available than canvas bags, or *why* skilled labour, or particular machine tools, have for the moment become more difficult to obtain. All that is significant for him is *how much more or less* difficult to procure they have become compared with other things with which he is also concerned, or how much more or less urgently wanted are the alternative things he produces or uses. It is always a question of the relative importance of the particular things with which he is concerned, and the causes which alter their relative importance are of no interest to him beyond the effect on those concrete things of his own environment.

It is in this connection that what I have called the 'economic calculus' (or the Pure Logic of Choice) helps us, at least by analogy, to see how this problem can be solved, and in fact is being solved, by the price system. Even the single controlling mind, in possession of all the data for some small, self-contained economic system, would not – every time some small adjustment in the allocation of resources had to be made – go explicitly through all the relations between ends and means which might possibly be affected. It is indeed the great contribution of the Pure Logic of Choice that it has demonstrated conclusively that even such a single mind could solve this kind of problem only by constructing and constantly using rates of equivalence (or 'values,' or 'marginal rates of substitution'), that is, by attaching to each kind of scarce resource a numerical index which cannot be derived from any property possessed by that particular thing, but which reflects, or in which is condensed, its significance in view of the whole means-end structure. In any small change he will have to consider only these quantitative indices (or 'values') in which all the relevant information is concentrated; and, by adjusting the quantities one by one, he can appropriately rearrange his dispositions without having to solve the whole puzzle *ab initio* or without needing at any stage to survey it at once in all its ramifications.

Fundamentally, in a system in which the knowledge of the relevant facts is dispersed among many people, prices can act to co-ordinate the separate actions of different people in the same way as subjective values help the individual to co-ordinate the parts of his plan. It is worth contemplating for a moment a very simple and commonplace instance of the action of the price system to see what precisely it accomplishes. Assume that somewhere in the world a new opportunity for the use of some raw material, say, tin, has arisen, or that one of the sources of supply of tin has been eliminated. It does not matter for our purpose – and it is significant that it does not matter – which of these two causes has made tin more scarce. All that the users of tin need to know is that some of the tin they used to consume is now more profitably employed elsewhere and that, in consequence, they must economize tin. There is no need for the great majority of them even to know where the more urgent need has arisen, or in favour of what other needs they ought to husband the supply. If only some of them know directly of the new demand, and switch resources over to it, and if the people who are aware of the new gap thus created in turn fill it from still other sources, the effect will rapidly spread throughout the whole economic system and influence not only all the uses of tin but also those of its substitutes and the substitutes of these substitutes, the supply of all the things made of tin, and their substitutes, and so on; and all this without the great majority of those instrumental in bringing about these substitutions knowing anything at all about the original cause of these changes. The whole acts as one market, not because any of its members survey the whole field, but because their limited individual fields of vision sufficiently overlap so that through many intermediaries the relevant information is communicated to all. The mere fact that there is one price for any commodity – or rather that local prices are connected in a manner determined by the cost of transport, etc. – brings about the solution which (it is just conceptually possible) might have been arrived at by one single mind possessing all the information which is in fact dispersed among all the people involved in the process.

6

We must look at the price system as such a mechanism for communicating information if we want to understand its real function – a function which, of course, it fulfils less perfectly as prices grow more rigid. (Even when quoted prices have become quite rigid, however, the forces which would operate through changes in price still operate to a considerable extent through changes in the other terms of the contract.) The most significant fact about this system is the economy of knowledge with which it operates, or how little the individual participants need to know in order to be able to take the right action. In abbreviated form, by a kind of symbol, only the most essential information is passed on and passed on only to those concerned. It is more than a metaphor to describe the price system as a kind of machinery for registering change, or a system of telecommunications which enables individual producers to watch merely the movement of a few pointers, as an engineer might watch the hands of a few dials, in order to adjust their activities to changes of which they may never know more than is reflected in the price movement.

Of course, these adjustments are probably never 'perfect' in the sense in which the economist conceives of them in his equilibrium analysis. But I fear that our theoretical habits of approaching the problem with the assumption of more or less perfect knowledge on the part of almost everyone has made us somewhat blind to the true function of the price mechanism and led us to apply rather misleading standards in judging its efficiency. The marvel is that in a case like that of a scarcity of one raw material, without an order being issued, without more than perhaps a handful of people knowing the cause, tens of thousands of people whose identity could not be ascertained by months of investigation, are made to use the material or its products more sparingly; that is, they move in the right direction. This is enough of a marvel even if, in a constantly changing world, not all will hit it off so perfectly that their profit rates will always be maintained at the same even or 'normal' level.

I have deliberately used the word 'marvel' to shock the reader out of the complacency with which we often take the working of this mechanism for granted. I am convinced that if it were the result of deliberate human design, and if the people guided by the price changes understood that their decisions have significance far beyond their immediate aim, this mechanism would have to be acclaimed as one of the greatest triumphs of the human mind. Its misfortune is the double one that it is not the product of human design and that the people guided by it usually do not know why they are made to do what they do. But those who clamour for 'conscious direction' – and who cannot believe that anything which has evolved without design (and even without our understanding it) should solve problems which we should not be able to solve consciously – should remember this: The problem is precisely how to extend the span of our utilization of resources beyond the span of the control of any one mind; and, therefore, how to dispense with the need of conscious control and how to provide inducements which will make the individuals do the desirable things without anyone having to tell them what to do.

The problem which we meet here is by no means peculiar to economics but arises in connection with nearly all truly social phenomena, with language and with most of our cultural inheritance, and constitutes really the central theoretical problem of all social science. As Alfred Whitehead has said in another connection, 'It is a profoundly erroneous truism, repeated by all copy-books and by eminent people when they are making speeches, that we should cutlivate the habit of thinking what we are doing. The precise opponent is the case. Civilization advances by extending the number of important operations which we can perform without thinking about them.' This is of profound significance in the social field. We make constant use of formulas, symbols, and rules whose meaning we do not understand and through the use of which we avail ourselves of the assistance of knowledge which individually we do not possess. We have developed these practices and institutions by building upon habits and institutions which have proved successful in their own sphere and which have in turn become the foundation of the civilization we have built up.

The price system is just one of those formations which man has learned to use (though he is still very far from having learned to make the best use of it) after he had stumbled upon it without understanding it. Through it not only a division of labour but also a co-ordinated utilization of resources based on an equally divided knowledge has become possible. The people who like to deride any suggestion that this may be so usually distort the argument by insinuating that it asserts that by some miracle just that sort of system has spontaneously grown up which is best suited to modern civilization. It is the other way round: man has been able to develop that division of labour on which our civilization is based because he happened to stumble upon a method which made it possible. Had he not done so, he might still have developed some other, altogether different, type of civilization, something like the 'state' of the termite ants, or some other, altogether unimaginable, type. All that we can say is that nobody has yet succeeded in designing an alternative system in which certain features of the existing one can be preserved which are dear even to those who most violently assail it – such as particularly the extent to which the individual can choose his pursuits and consequently freely use his own knowledge and skill.

7

It is in many ways fortunate that the dispute about the indispensability of the price system for any rational calculation in a complex society is now no longer conducted entirely between camps holding different political views. The thesis that without the price system we could not preserve a society based on such extensive division of labour as ours was greeted with a howl of derision when it was first advanced by Von Mises twenty-five years ago.

Today the difficulties which some still find in accepting it are no longer mainly political, and this makes for an atmosphere much more conductive to reasonable discussion. When we find Leon Trotsky arguing that 'economic accounting is unthinkable without market relations'; when Professor Oskar Lange promises Professor von Mises a statue in the marble halls of the future Central Planning Board; and when Professor Abba P. Lerner rediscovers Adam Smith and emphasizes that the essential utility of the price system consists in inducing the individual, while seeking his own interest, to do what is in the general interest, the differences can indeed no longer be ascribed to political prejudice. The remaining dissent seems clearly to be due to purely intellectual, and more particularly methodological, differences.

A recent statement by Joseph Schumpeter in his *Capitalism, Socialism, and Democracy* provides a clear illustration of one of the methodological differences which I have in mind. Its author is pre-eminent among those economists who approach economic phenomena in the light of a certain branch of positivism. To him these phenomena accordingly appear as objectively given quantities of commodities impinging directly upon each other, almost, it would seem, without any intervention of human minds. Only against this background can I account for the following (to me startling) pronouncement. Professor Schumpeter argues that the possibility of a rational calculation in the absence of markets for the factors of production follows for the theorist 'from the elementary proposition that consumers in evaluating ("demanding") consumers' goods *ipso facto* also evaluate the means of production which enter into the production of these goods.'[1]

Taken literally, this statement is simply untrue. The consumers do nothing of the kind. What Professor Schumpeter's '*ipso facto*' presumably means is that the valuation of the factors of production is implied in, or follows necessarily from, the valuation of consumers' goods. But this, too, is not correct. Implication is a logical relationship which can be meaningfully asserted only of propositions simultaneously present to one and the same mind. It is evident, however, that the values of the factors of production do not depend solely on the valuation of the consumers' goods but also on the conditions of supply of the various factors of production. Only to a mind to which all these facts were simultaneously known would the answer necessarily follow from the facts given to it. The practical problem, however, arises precisely because these facts are never so given to a single mind, and because, in consequence, it is necessary that in the solution of the problem knowledge should be used that is dispersed among many people.

The problem is thus in no way solved if we can show that all the facts, *if* they were known to a single mind (as we hypothetically assume them to be given to the observing economist), would uniquely determine the solution; instead we must show how a solution is produced by the interactions of people each of whom possesses only partial knowledge. To assume all the knowledge to be given to a single mind in the same manner in which we assume it to be given to us as the explaining economists is to assume the problem away and to disregard everything that is important and significant in the real world.

That an economist of Professor Schumpeter's standing should thus have fallen into a trap which the ambiguity of the term 'datum' sets to the unwary can hardly be explained as a simple error. It suggests rather that there is something fundamentally wrong with an approach which habitually disregards an essential part of the phenomena with which we have to deal: the unavoidable imperfection of man's knowledge and the consequent need for a process by which knowledge is constantly communicated and acquired. Any approach, such as that of much of mathematical economics with its simultaneous equations, which in effect starts from the assumption that people's *knowledge* corresponds with the objective *facts* of the situation, systematically leaves out what is our main task to explain. I am far from denying that in our system equilibrium analysis has a useful function to perform. But when it comes to the point where it misleads some of our leading thinkers into believing that the situation which it describes has direct relevance to the solution of practical problems, it is high time that we remember that it does not deal with the social process at all and that it is no more than a useful preliminary to the study of the main problem.

NOTE

* Reprinted from the *American Economic Review*, vol. xxxv, no. 4, September 1945, pp. 519–30.

1. *Capitalism, Socialism, and Democracy* (New York: Harper & Bros., 1942), p. 175. Professor Schumpeter is, I believe, also the original author of the myth that Pareto and Barone have 'solved' the problem of socialist calculation. What they, and many others, did was merely to state the conditions which a rational allocation of resources would have to satisfy and to point out that these were essentially the same as the conditions of equilibrium of a competitive market. This is something altogether different from showing how the allocation of resources satisfying these conditions can be found in practice. Pareto himself (from

whom Barone has taken practically everything he has to say), far from claiming to have solved the practical problem, in fact explicitly denies that it can be solved without the help of the market. See his *Manuel d'economie pure*, 2nd edn (1927), pp. 233–4. The relevant passage is quoted in an English translation at the beginning of my article on 'Socialist Calculation: The Competitive "Solution"', *Economica*, viii, no. 26, New Series (1940), p. 125; reprinted below as ch. viii. [This reference is to Hayek's *Individualism and Economic Order* (1949). That chapter is reprinted in the present volume as paper 29. – Ed.]

Friedrich Hayek, 'Competition as a Discovery Procedure', *New Studies in Philosophy, Politics, Economics and the History of Ideas* (Chicago: University of Chicago Press, 1978), pp. 179–90.

This paper was first given as a lecture to a meeting of the Philadelphia Society in Chicago in 1968. It was first published in German in *Kieler Vorträge* in 1968, and was included in Hayek's *Freiburger Studien* (Tübingen, 1969). It first appeared in English as chapter twelve in F. A. Hayek, *New Studies in Philosophy, Politics, Economics and the History of Ideas*. The paper carries forward Hayek's critique of the economists' preoccupation with the model of perfect competition (a critique he began with his 'The Meaning of Competition' in *Individualism and Economic Order* (op. cit.)).

0 2 0 0
0 3 6 0

31

Competition as a Discovery Procedure*

FRIEDRICH HAYEK

1

It is difficult to defend economists against the charge that for some 40 to 50 years they have been discussing competition on assumptions that, *if* they were true of the real world, would make it wholly uninteresting and useless. If anyone really knew all about what economic theory calls the *data*, competition would indeed be a very wasteful method of securing adjustment to these facts. It is thus not surprising that some people have been led to the conclusion that we can either wholly dispense with the market, or that its results should be used only as a first step towards securing an output of goods and services which we can then manipulate, correct, or redistribute in any manner we wish. Others, who seem to derive their conception of competition solely from modern textbooks, have not unnaturally concluded that competition does not exist.

Against this, it is salutary to remember that, *wherever* the use of competition can be rationally justified, it is on the ground that we do *not* know in advance the facts that determine the actions of competitors. In sports or in examinations, no less than in the award of government contracts or of prizes for poetry, it would clearly be pointless to arrange for competition, if we were certain beforehand who would do best. As indicated in the title of this lecture, I propose to consider competition as a procedure for the discovery of such facts as, without resort to it, would not be known to anyone, or at least would not be utilised.[1]

This may at first appear so obvious and incontestable as hardly to deserve attention. Yet, some interesting consequences that are not so obvious immediately follow from the explicit formulation of the above apparent truism. One is that the competition is valuable *only* because, and so far as, its results are unpredictable and on the whole different from those which

273

anyone has, or could have, deliberately aimed at. Further, that the generally beneficial effects of competition must include disappointing or defeating some particular expectations or intentions.

Closely connected with this is an interesting methodological consequence. It goes far to account for the discredit into which the microeconomic approach to theory has fallen. Although this theory seems to me to be the only one capable of explaining the role of competition, it is no longer understood, even by some professing economists. It is therefore worthwhile to say at the outset a few words about the methodological peculiarity of any theory of competition, because it has made its conclusions suspect to many of those who habitually apply an over-simplified test to decide what they are willing to accept as scientific. The necessary consequence of the reason why we use competition is that, *in those cases in which it is interesting*, the validity of the theory can never be tested empirically. We can test it on conceptual models, and we might conceivably test it in artificially created real situations, where the facts which competition is intended to discover are already known to the observer. But in such cases it is of no practical value, so that to carry out the experiment would hardly be worth the expense. If we do not know the facts we hope to discover by means of competition, we can never ascertain how effective it has been in discovering those facts that might be discovered. All we can hope to find out is that, on the whole, societies which rely for this purpose on competition have achieved their aims more successfully than others. This is a conclusion which the history of civilisation seems eminently to have confirmed.

The peculiarity of competition – which it has in common with scientific method – is that its performance cannot be tested in particular instances where it is significant, but is shown only by the fact that the market will prevail in comparison with any alternative arrangements. The advantages of accepted scientific procedures can never be proved scientifically, but only demonstrated by the common experience that, on the whole, they are better adapted to delivering the goods than alternative approaches.[2]

The difference between economic competition and the successful procedures of science consists in the fact that the former is a method of discovering particular facts relevant to the achievement of specific, temporary purposes, while science aims at the discovery of what are sometimes called 'general facts', which are regularities of events. Science concerns itself with unique, particular facts only to the extent that they help to confirm or refute theories. Because these refer to general, permanent features of the world, the discoveries of science have ample time to prove their value. In contrast, the benefits of particular facts, whose usefulness competition in the market discovers, are in a great measure transitory. So far as the theory of scientific method is concerned, it would be as easy to discredit it on the ground that it does not lead to testable predictions about what science will discover, as it is to discredit the theory of the market on the ground that it fails to predict particular results the market will achieve. This, in the nature of the case, the theory of competition cannot do in any situation in which it is sensible to employ it. As we shall see, its capacity to predict is necessarily limited to predicting the kind of pattern, or the abstract character of the order that will form itself, but does not extend to the prediction of particular facts.[3]

2

Having relieved myself of this pet concern, I shall return to the central subject of this lecture, by pointing out that economic theory sometimes appears at the outset to bar its way to a true appreciation of the character of the process of competition, because it starts from the assumption of a 'given' supply of scarce goods. But which goods are scarce goods, or which things are goods, and how scarce or valuable they are – these are precisely the things which competition has to discover. Provisional results from the market process at each stage alone tell individuals what to look for. Utilisation of knowledge widely dispersed in a society with extensive division of labour cannot rest on individuals knowing all the particular uses to which well-known things in their individual environment might be put. Prices direct their attention to what is worth finding out about market offers for various things and services. This means that the, in some respects always unique, combinations of individual knowledge and skills, which the market enables them to use, will not merely, or even in the first instance, be such knowledge of facts as they could list and communicate if some authority asked them to do so. The knowledge of which I speak consists rather of a capacity to find out particular circumstances, which becomes effective only if possessors of this knowledge are informed by the market which kinds of things or services are wanted, and how urgently they are wanted.[4]

This must suffice to indicate what kind of knowledge I am referring to when I call competition a discovery procedure. Much would have to be added to clothe the bare bones of this abstract statement with concrete flesh, so as to show its full practical importance. But I must be content with thus briefly indicating the absurdity of the usual procedure of starting the analysis with a situation in which all the facts are supposed to be known. This is a *state* of affairs which economic theory curiously calls 'perfect competition'. It leaves no room whatever for the *activity* called

275

competition, which is presumed to have already done its task. However, I must hurry on to examine a question, on which there exists even more confusion – namely, the meaning of the contention that the market adjusts activities spontaneously to the facts it discovers – or the question of the purpose for which it uses this information.

The prevailing confusion here is largely due to mistakenly treating the order which the market produces as an 'economy' in the strict sense of the word, and judging results of the market process by criteria which are appropriate only to such a single organised community serving a given hierarchy of ends. But such a hierarchy of ends is not relevant to the complex structure composed of countless individual economic arrangements. The latter, unfortunately, we also describe by the same word 'economy', although it is something fundamentally different, and must be judged by different standards. An economy, in the strict sense of the word, is an organisation or arrangement in which someone deliberately allocates resources to a unitary order of ends. Spontaneous order produced by the market is nothing of the kind; and in important respects it does not behave like an economy proper. In particular, such spontaneous order differs because it does *not* ensure that what general opinion regards as more important needs are always satisfied before the less important ones. This is the chief reason why people object to it. Indeed, the whole of socialism is nothing but a demand that the market order (or catallaxy, as I like to call it, to prevent confusion with an economy proper)[5] should be turned into an economy in the strict sense, in which a common scale of importance determines which of the various needs are to be satisfied, and which are not to be satisfied.

The trouble with this socialist aim is a double one. As is true of every deliberate organisation, only the knowledge of the organiser can enter into the design of the economy proper, and all the members of such an economy, conceived as a deliberate organisation, must be guided in their actions by the unitary hierarchy of ends which it serves. On the other hand, advantages of the spontaneous order of the market, or the catallaxy, are correspondingly two. Knowledge that is used in it is that of all its members. Ends that it serves are the separate ends of those individuals, in all their variety and contrariness.

Out of this fact arise certain intellectual difficulties which worry not only socialists, but all economists who want to assess the accomplishments of the market order; because, if the market order does not serve a definite order of ends, indeed if, like any spontaneously formed order, it cannot legitimately be said to *have* particular ends, it is also not possible to express the value of the results as a sum of its particular individual products. What, then, do we mean when we claim that the market order produces in some sense a maximum or optimum?

The fact is, that, though the existence of a spontaneous order not made for a particular purpose cannot be properly said to have a purpose, it may yet be highly conducive to the achievement of many different individual purposes not known as a whole to any single person, or relatively small group of persons. Indeed, rational action is possible only in a fairly orderly world. Therefore it clearly makes sense to try to produce conditions under which the chances for any individual taken at random to achieve his ends as effectively as possible will be very high – even if it cannot be predicted which particular aims will be favoured, and which not.

As we have seen, the results of a discovery procedure are in their nature unpredictable; and all we can expect from the adoption of an effective discovery procedure is to improve the chances for unknown people. The only common aim which we can pursue by the choice of this technique of ordering social affairs is the general kind of pattern, or the abstract character, of the order that will form itself.

3

Economists usually ascribe the order which competition produces as an equilibrium – a somewhat unfortunate term, because such an equilibrium presupposes that the facts have already all been discovered and competition therefore had ceased. The concept of an 'order' which, at least for the discussion of problems of economic policy, I prefer to that of equilibrium, has the advantage that we can meaningfully speak about an order being approached to various degrees, and that order can be preserved throughout a process of change. While an economic eqilibrium never really exists, there is some justification for asserting that the kind of order of which our theory describes an ideal type, is approached in a high degree.

This order manifests itself in the first instance in the circumstance that the expectations of transactions to be effected with other members of society, on which the plans of all the several economic subjects are based, can be mostly realised. This mutual adjustment of individual plans is brought about by what, since the physical sciences have also begun to concern themselves with spontaneous orders, or 'self-organising systems', we have learnt to call 'negative feedback'. Indeed, as intelligent biologists acknowledge, 'long before Claude Bernard, Clerk Maxwell, Walter B. Cannon, or Norbert Wiener developed cybernetics, Adam Smith has just as clearly used the idea in The Wealth of Nations. The 'invisible hand' that regulated prices to a nicety is clearly this idea. In a free market, says Smith in effect, prices are regulated by negative feedback.'[6]

We shall see that the fact that a high degree of coincidence of expectations is brought about by the systematic disappointment of some kind of expectations is of crucial importance for an understanding of the functioning of the market order. But to bring about a mutual adjustment of individual plans is not all that the market achieves. It also secures that whatever is being produced will be produced by people who can do so more cheaply than (or at least as cheaply as) anybody who does not produce it (and cannot devote his energies to produce something else comparatively even more cheaply), and that each product is sold at a price lower than that at which anybody who in fact does not produce it could supply it. This, of course, does not exclude that some may make considerable profits over their costs if these costs are much lower than those of the next efficient potential producer. But it does mean that of the combination of commodities that is in fact produced, as much will be produced as we know to bring about by any known method. It will of course not be as much as we might produce if all the knowledge anybody possessed or can acquire were commanded by some one agency, and fed into a computer (the cost of finding out would, however, be considerable). Yet we do injustice to the achievement of the market if we judge it, as it were, from above, by comparing it with an ideal standard which we have no known way of achieving. If we judge it, as we ought to, from below, that is, if the comparison in this case is made against what we could achieve by any other method – especially against what would be produced if competition were prevented, so that only those to whom some authority had conferred the right to produce or sell particular things were allowed to do so. All we need to consider is how difficult it is in a competitive system to discover ways of supplying to consumers better or cheaper goods than they already get. Where such unused opportunities seem to exist we usually find that they remain undeveloped because their use is either prevented by the power of authority (including the enforcement of patent privileges), or by some private misuse of power which the law ought to prohibit.

It must not be forgotten that in this respect the market only brings about an approach towards some point on that n-dimensional surface, by which pure economic theory represents the horizon of all possibilities to which the production of any one proportional combination of commodities and services could conceivably be carried. The market leaves the particular combination of goods, and its distribution among individuals, largely to unforeseeable circumstances – and, in this sense, to accident. It is, as Adam Smith already understood,[7] as if we had agreed to play a game, partly of skill and partly of chance. This competitive game, at the price of leaving the share of each individual in some measure to accident, ensures that the real equivalent of whatever his share turns out to be, is as large as we know how to make it. The game is, to use up-to-date language, not a zero-sum game, but one through which, by playing it according to the rules, the pool to be shared is enlarged, leaving individual shares in the pool in a great measure to chance. A mind knowing all the facts could select any point he liked on the surface and distribute this product in the manner he thought right. But the only point on, or tolerably near, the horizon of possibilities which we know how to reach is the one at which we shall arrive if we leave its determination to the market. The so-called 'maximum' which we thus reach naturally cannot be defined as a sum of particular things, but only in terms of the chances it offers to unknown people to get as large a real equivalent as possible for their relative shares, which will be determined partly by accident. Simply because its results cannot be assessed in terms of a single scale of values, as is the case in an economy proper, it is very misleading to assess the results of a catallaxy as if it were an economy.

4

Misinterpretation of the market order as an economy that can and ought to satisfy different needs in a certain order of priority, shows itself particularly in the efforts of policy to correct prices and incomes in the interest of what is called 'social justice'. Whatever meaning social philosophers have attached to this concept, in the practice of economic policy it has almost always meant one thing, and one thing only: the protection of certain groups against the necessity to descend from the absolute or relative material position which they have for some time enjoyed. Yet this is not a principle on which it is possible to act generally without destroying the foundations of the market order. Not only continuous increase, but in certain circumstances even mere maintenance of the existing level of incomes, depends on adaptation to unforeseen changes. This necessarily involves the relative, and perhaps even the absolute, share of some having to be reduced, although they are in no way responsible for the reduction.

The point to keep constantly in mind is that *all* economic adjustment is made necessary by unforeseen changes; and the whole reason for employing the price mechanism is to tell individuals that what they are doing, or can do, has for some reason for which they are not responsible becomes less or more demanded. Adaptation of the whole order of activities to changed circumstances rests on the remuneration derived from different activities being changed, without regard to the merits or faults of those affected.

The term 'incentives' is often used in this connection with somewhat misleading connotations, as if the main problem were to induce people to exert themselves sufficiently. However, the chief guidance which prices offer is not so much how to act, but *what to do*. In a continuously changing world even mere maintenance of a given level of wealth requires incessant changes in the direction of the efforts of some, which will be brought about only if the remuneration of some activities is increased and that of others decreased. With these adjustments, which under relatively stable conditions are needed merely to maintain the income stream, no 'surplus' is available which can be used to compensate those against whom prices turn. Only in a rapidly growing system can we hope to avoid absolute declines in the position of some groups.

Modern economists seem in this connection often to overlook that even the relative stability shown by many of those aggregates which macro-economics treat as data, is itself the result of a micro-economic process, of which changes in relative prices are an essential part. It is only thanks to the market mechanism that someone else is induced to step in and fill the gap caused by the failure of anyone to fulfil the expectations of his partners. Indeed, all those aggregate demand and supply curves with which we like to operate are not really objectively given facts, but results of the process of competition going on all the time. Not can we hope to learn from statistical information what changes in prices or incomes are necessary in order to bring about adjustments to the inevitable changes.

The chief point, however, is that in a democratic society it would be wholly impossible by commands to bring about changes which are not felt to be just, and the necessity of which could never be clearly demonstrated. Deliberate regulation in such a political system must always aim at securing prices which appear to be just. This means in practice preservation of the traditional structure of incomes and prices. An economic system in which each gets what others think he deserves would necessarily be a highly inefficient system – quite apart from its being also an intolerably oppressive system. Every 'incomes policy' is therefore more likely to prevent than to facilitate those changes in the price and income structures that are required to adapt the system to new circumstances.

It is one of the paradoxes of the present world that the communist countries are probably freer from the incubus of 'social justice', and more willing to let those bear the burden against whom developments turn, than are the 'capitalist' countries. For some Western countries at least the position seems hopeless, precisely because the ideology dominating their politics makes changes impossible that are necessary for the position of the working class to rise sufficiently fast to lead to the disappearance of this ideology.

5

If even in highly developed economic systems competition is important as a process of exploration in which prospectors search for unused opportunities that, when discovered, can also be used by others, this is to an even greater extent true of underdeveloped societies. My first attention has been deliberately given to problems of preserving an efficient order for conditions in which most resources and techniques are generally known, and constant adaptations of activities are made necessary only by inevitably minor changes, in order to maintain a given level of incomes. I will not consider here the undoubted role competition plays in the advance of technological knowledge. But I do want to point out how much more important it must be in countries where the chief task is to discover yet unknown opportunities of a society in which in the past competition has not been active. It may not be altogether absurd, although largely erroneous, to believe that we can foresee and control the structure of society which further technological advance will produce in already highly developed countries. But it is simply fantastic to believe that we can determine in advance the social structure in a country where the chief problem still is to discover what material and human resources are available, or that for such a country we can predict the particular consequences of any measures we may take.

Apart from the fact that there is in such countries so much more to be discovered, there is still another reason why the greatest freedom of competition seems to be even more important there than in more advanced countries. This is that required changes in habits and customs will be brought about only if the few willing and able to experiment with new methods can make it necessary for the many to follow them, and at the same time to show them the way. The required discovery process will be impeded or prevented, if the many are able to keep the few to the traditional ways. Of course, it is one of the chief reasons for the dislike of competition that it not only shows how things can be done more effectively, but also confronts those who depend for their incomes on the market with the alternative of imitating the more successful or losing some or all of their income. Competition produces in this way a kind of impersonal compulsion which makes it necessary for numerous individuals to adjust their way of life in a manner that no deliberate instructions or commands could bring about. Central direction in the service of so-called 'social justice' may be a luxury rich nations can afford, perhaps for a long time, without too great an impairment of their incomes. But it is certainly not a method by which poor countries can accelerate their adaptation to rapidly changing circumstances, on which their growth depends.

Perhaps it deserves mention in this connection that possibilities of growth are likely to be greater the more extensive are a country's yet unused opprtunities. Strange though this may seem at first sight, a high rate of growth is more often than not evidence that opportunities have been neglected in the past. Thus, a high rate of growth can sometimes testify to bad policies of the past rather than good policies of the present. Consequently it is unreasonable to expect in already highly developed countries as high a rate of growth as can for some time be achieved in countries where effective utilisation of resources was previously long prevented by legal and institutional obstacles.

From all I have seen of the world the proportion of private persons who are prepared to try new possibilities, if they appear to them to promise better conditions, and if they are not prevented by the pressure of their fellows, is much the same everywhere. The much lamented absence of a spirit of enterprise in many of the new countries is not an unalterable characteristic of the individual inhabitants, but the consequence of restraints which existing customs and institutions place upon them. This is why it would be fatal in such societies for the collective will to be allowed to direct the efforts of individuals, instead of governmental power being confined to protecting individuals against the pressures of society. Such protection for private initiatives and enterprise can only ever be achieved through the institution of private property and the whole aggregate of libertarian institutions of law.

NOTES

* This lecture was originally delivered, without the present section 2, to a meeting of the Philadelphia Society at Chicago on 29 March 1968 and later, on 5 July 1968, in German, without the present final section, to the Institut für Weltwirtschaft of the University of Kiel. Only the German version has been published before, first in the series of 'Kieler Vorträge', New Series 56 (Kiel, 1968), and then reprinted in my collected essays entitled *Freiburger Studien* (Tübingen, 1969).

1. Since I wrote this my attention has been drawn to a paper by Leopold von Wiese on 'Die Konkurrenz, vorwiegend in soziologisch-systematischer Betrachtung', *Verhandlungen des 6. Deutschen Soziologentages* (1929), where, on p. 27, he discusses the 'experimental' nature of competition.

2. Cf. the interesting studies of the late Michael Polanyi in *The Logic of Liberty* (London, 1951), which show how he has been led from the study of scientific method to the study of competition in economic

affairs; and see also K. R. Popper, *The Logic of Scientific Discovery* (London, 1959).

3. On the nature of 'pattern prediction' see my essay on 'The theory of complex phenomena' in *Studies in Philosophy, Politics and Economics* (London and Chicago, 1967).

4. Cf. Samuel Johnson in J. Boswell, *Life of Samuel Johnson*, L. F. Powell's revision of G. B. Hill's edition (Oxford, 1934), vol. ii, p. 365 (18 April 1775): 'Knowledge is of two kinds. We know a subject ourselves, or we know where we can find information about it.'

5. For a fuller discussion see now my *Law, Legislation and Liberty*, vol. ii, *The Mirage of Social Justice* (London and Chicago, 1976), pp. 107–20.

6. G. Hardin, *Nature and Man's Fate* (1951), Mentor ed. (1961), p. 54.

7. Adam Smith, *The Theory of Moral Sentiments* (London, 1759), pt vi, ch. 2, penultimate paragraph, and pt vii, sect. ii, ch. 1.

SELECT BIBLIOGRAPHY

PRIMARY WORKS

Böhm-Bawerk, Eugen von, *Kapital und Kapitalzins*, vol. i (1884); vol. ii (1889), translated as *Capital and Interest* (South Holland, IL: Libertarian Press, 1959).

——, 'The Historical vs the Deductive Method in Political Economy', *Annals of the American Academy of Political and Social Science*, vol. 1 (1891), pp. 244–71.

Hayek, Friedrich A., *Prices and Production* (London: Routledge, 1931).

——, *The Pure Theory of Capital* (Chicago, IL: University of Chicago Press, 1941).

——, *Individualism and Economic Order* (London: Routledge and Kegan Paul, 1940).

——, 'Competition as a Discovery Procedure', *New Studies in Philosophy, Politics, Economics and the History of Ideas* (Chicago: University of Chicago Press, 1978).

Kirzner, Israel M., *Competition and Entrepreneurship* (Chicago: University of Chicago Press, 1973).

Lachmann, Ludwig, *Capital, Expectations, and the Market Process* (Kansas City: Sheed, Andrews & McMeel, 1977).

——, *The Market as an Economic Process* (Oxford: Basil Blackwell, 1986).

Mayer, Hans, 'Zurechnung', *Handwörterbuch der Staatswissenschaften*, 4th edn, vol. 8 (Jena: Gustav Fischer, 1928), pp. 1206–28.

——, 'Der Erkenntniswert der Funktionellen Preistheorien', Mayer (ed.), *Die Wirtschaftstheorie der Gegenwart* (Vienna, 1932), vol. 2, pp. 147–239b.

Menger, Carl, *Grundsätze der Volkswirthschaftslehre* (1871), translated and edited by J. Dingwall and B. F. Hoselitz, under the title, *Principles of Economics* (Glencoe, IL: Free Press, 1950); republished by New York University Press (1981).

——, *Untersuchungen über der Methode der Socialwissenschaften und der Politischen Oekonomie insbesondere* (1883), translated by F. J. Nock under the title *Problems of Economics and Sociology* (Urbana, IL:

University of Illinois Press, 1963), republished by New York University Press under the title *Investigations into the Method of the Social Science with Special Reference to Economics* (1985).

——, 'On the Origin of Money', *Economic Journal*, June 1892, pp. 239–55.

Mises, Ludwig von, *Theorie des Geldes und der Umlaufsmittel* (1912), 2nd edn (1924) translated as *Theory of Money and Credit* (London: Jonathan Cape, 1934, trans. H. E. Batson), republished by Yale University Press (1953), and by Liberty*Classics* (1981).

——, *Die Gemeinwirtschaft* (1922), translated by J. Kahane from the 2nd edn (1932) as *Socialism* (London: Jonathan Cape, 1936), republished by Yale University Press (1951), and by Liberty*Classics* (1981).

——, *Grundprobleme der Nationalökonomie* (1933), translated by R. Raico, as *Epistemological Problems of Economics* (Princeton, NJ: Van Nostrand, 1960).

——, *Human Action, a Treatise on Economics* [1949], 3rd edn (Chicago, IL: Henry Regnery, 1966); based on *Nationalökonomie, Theorie des Handelns und Wirtschaftens* (1940).

Morgenstern, Oskar, *The Limits of Economics* [1934] translated by Vera Smith (London: W. Hodge, 1937).

O'Driscoll, Gerald P. Jr, and Rizzo, Mario J., *The Economics of Time and Ignorance* (Oxford: Basil Blackwell, 1985).

Rosenstein-Rodan, Paul, 'Grenznutzen', *Handwörterbuch der Staatswissenschaften*, 4th edn, vol. 4 (Jena: Gustav Fischer, 1927), pp. 1190–213; translated in *International Economic Papers*, no. 10, (1960).

Rothbard, Murray N., 'Toward a Reconstruction of Utility and Welfare Economics', M. Sennholz (ed.), *On Freedom and Free Enterprise* (Princeton, NJ: Van Nostrand, 1956).

——, *Man, Economy and State: A Treatise on Economic Principles* (Princeton, NJ: Van Nostrand, 1962).

Schoenfeld-Illy, Leo, *Grenznutzen und Wirtschaftsrechnung* (1924).

Spadaro, Louis M. (ed.), *New Directions in Austrian Economics* (Kansas City: Sheed, Andrews & McMeel, 1978).

Strigl, Richard von, *Die ökonomischen Kategorien und die Organisation der Wirtschaft* (1923).

Wieser, Friedrich von, *Der Naturliche Werth* (1889), translated as *Natural Value*, W. Smart (ed.) (London: Macmillan, 1893), republished (New York: Kelly, 1956).

——, *Theorie der Gesellschaftlichen Wirtschaft* (1914), translated as *Social Economics* (London: Allen & Unwin), 1927), republished (New York: Kelley, 1967).

SECONDARY WORKS

Addleson, M., 'Robbins's Essay in Retrospect: On Subjectivism and an "Economics of Choice"', *Rivista Internazionale Di Scienze Economiche e Commerciali* 31 (6).

Boehm, Stephan, 'Austrian Economics Between the Wars: Some Historiographical Problems', Caldwell, Bruce J., and Boehm, Stephan (eds), *Austrian Economics: Tensions and New Directions* (Boston/Dordrecht/London: Kluwer, 1992).

Caldwell, Bruce J. (ed.), *Carl Menger and his Legacy in Economics* (annual supplement to vol. 22, *History of Political Economy*) (Durham and London: Duke University Press, 1990).

Garrison, Roger, 'Austrian Economics as the Middle Ground: Comment on Loasby', Israel M. Kirzner (ed.), *Method, Process, and Austrian Economics: Essays in Honor of Ludwig von Mises* (Lexington, MA: Lexington Books, 1982).

Grassl, Wolfgang, and Smith, Barry (eds), *Austrian Economics: Historical and Philosophical Background* (London: Croom Helm, 1986).

Hicks, J. R. and Weber, Wilhelm (eds), *Carl Menger and the Austrian School of Economics* (Oxford: Clarendon Press, 1973).

Kauder, Emil, *A History of Marginal Utility Theory* (Princeton, NJ: Princeton University Press, 1965).

Kirzner, Israel M., 'The Austrian School of Economics', *The New Palgrave*, John Eatwell, Murray Milgate and Peter Newman (eds) (London: Macmillan, 1987) reprinted in Israel M. Kirzner, *The Meaning of Market Process* (London: Routledge, 1992).

Mises, Ludwig von, *The Historical Setting of the Austrian School of Economics* (New Rochelle, NY: Arlington House, 1969).

Moss, L. (ed.), *The Economics of Ludwig von Mises, Toward a Critical Reappraisal* (Kansas City: Sheed and Ward, 1976).

O'Driscoll, Gerald P. Jr, *Economics as a Coordination Problem: The Contributions of Friedrich A. Hayek* (Kansas City: Sheed, Andrews & McMeel, 1977).

Robbins, Lionel, *The Nature and Significance of Economic Science* [1932], 2nd edn (London: Macmillan, 1935).

Sennholz, Hans F., 'The Monetary Writings of Carl Menger', Llewellyn H. Rockwell, Jr (ed.), *The Gold Standard: An Austrian Perspective* (Lexington, MA: Lexington Books, 1985).

Wiseman, Jack, 'Lionel Robbins, the Austrian School, and the LSE Tradition', *Research in the History of Economic Thought and Methodology*, W. Samuels (ed.), vol. 3, pp. 147–59.

CONSOLIDATED INDEX

VOLUMES I–III

The bold figures indicate the volume; the page numbers refer to the folios at the foot of the page.